THIS HAPPENED TO ME

OUTDOOR LIFE

THIS HAPP

ENED TO ME

Edited by
Andrew McKean

weldon**owen**

CONTENTS

1   *ONE STEP FROM TOTAL DISASTER*

2 WHEN ANIMALS ATTACK

3 DANGER AFLOAT

4 THE HUNTER BECOMES THE HUNTED

When Suddenly...

Those of us who spend our lives outdoors, with a rifle or a fishing rod in our hands or a thin tent over our heads, are never more than a step or two away from calamity, whether from a hissing snake, a charging moose, a slip on an icy slope, or a gash of lightning.

Most of us understand that danger is as much a part of our field sports as woodsmoke and gun oil. Maybe that's why *Outdoor Life*'s distillation of the most harrowing true-life disaster tales is traditionally the first feature that readers turn to.

"This Happened To Me," a fixture of *Outdoor Life* since 1940, is real enough that we can recognize ourselves in each illustration. It is dramatic enough that we read it with silent thanks that it *didn't* happen to us—and sober acknowledgement that it could have. And it is accessible enough—rendered in an adrenaline-pumping style and bold colors conveying a simple, first person narrative—that it appeals to anyone who ever cracked a comic book. Or fought off a hungry gator with a boat paddle.

I was reminded of the timeless appeal of "THTM" earlier this year. For once, I was in the right place at the right time as a flock of big Canada geese flew off the Missouri River. A honker flew right over me, and with a single well-placed shot, I folded that bird, then swung to complete a rare double. The next thing I knew, I was on my back in the snow, bleeding hard from my head, a dead goose in my lap. I had been cold-cocked by the first goose, which slammed into my skull with a combination of dead weight and gravity's pull.

My first thought, as I collected my wits—and my birds—wasn't that I might have a concussion. It was that my experience would make a great "THTM" installment!

—Andrew McKean, Editor
Outdoor Life

March 1941

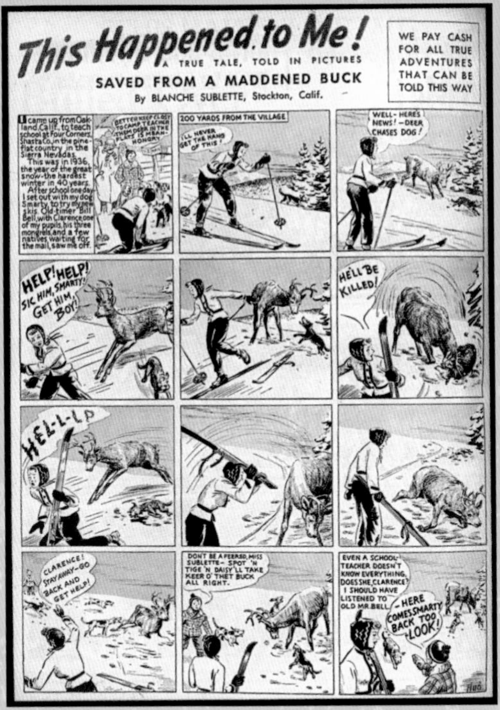
This Happened to Me!
A TRUE TALE, TOLD IN PICTURES
SAVED FROM A MADDENED BUCK
By BLANCHE SUBLETTE, Stockton, Calif.
WE PAY CASH FOR ALL TRUE ADVENTURES THAT CAN BE TOLD THIS WAY
I came up from Oakland, Calif., to teach school at Four Corners, Shasta Co., in the pine-flat country in the Sierra Nevadas. This was in 1936, the year of the great snow–the hardest winter in 40 years. After school one day I set out with my dog Smarty to try my new skis. Old-timer Bill Bell, with Clarence one of my pupils, his three mongrels and a few natives waiting for the mail, saw me off.
200 YARDS FROM THE VILLAGE
I'LL NEVER GET THE HANG OF THIS!
WELL- HERE'S NEWS! –DEER CHASES DOG!
HELP! HELP! SIC HIM, SMARTY! GET HIM, BOY!
HE'LL BE KILLED!
HEL-L-LP
CLARENCE! STAY AWAY–GO BACK AND GET HELP!
DON'T BE AFEERED, MISS SUBLETTE– SPOT 'N TIGE 'N DAISY'LL TAKE KEER O' THET BUCK ALL RIGHT.
EVEN A SCHOOL-TEACHER DOESN'T KNOW EVERYTHING, DOES SHE, CLARENCE? I SHOULD HAVE LISTENED TO OLD MR. BELL.
–HERE COMES SMARTY BACK TOO –LOOK!

March 1950

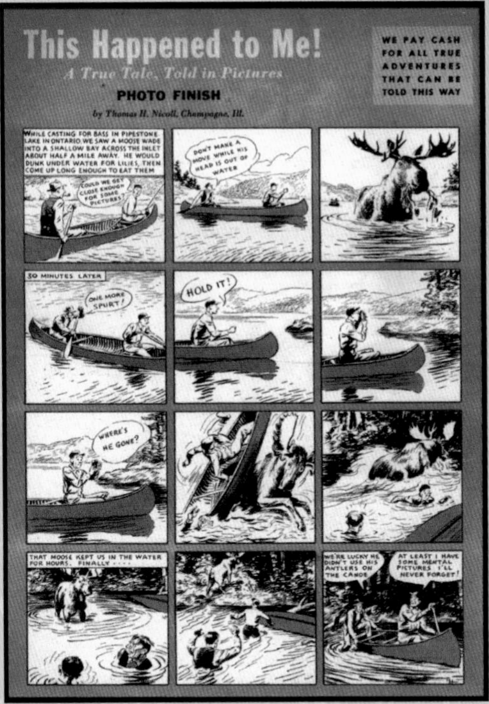
This Happened to Me!
A True Tale, Told in Pictures
PHOTO FINISH
by Thomas H. Nicoll, Champagne, Ill.
WE PAY CASH FOR ALL TRUE ADVENTURES THAT CAN BE TOLD THIS WAY
WHILE CASTING FOR BASS IN PIPESTONE LAKE IN ONTARIO WE SAW A MOOSE WADE INTO A SHALLOW BAY ACROSS THE INLET ABOUT HALF A MILE AWAY. HE WOULD DUNK UNDER WATER FOR LILIES, THEN COME UP LONG ENOUGH TO EAT THEM
COULD WE GET CLOSE ENOUGH FOR SOME PICTURES?
DON'T MAKE A MOVE WHILE HIS HEAD IS OUT OF WATER
30 MINUTES LATER
ONE MORE SPURT!
HOLD IT!
WHERE'S HE GONE?
THAT MOOSE KEPT US IN THE WATER FOR HOURS. FINALLY . . . .
WE'RE LUCKY HE DIDN'T USE HIS ANTLERS ON THE CANOE
AT LEAST I HAVE SOME MENTAL PICTURES I'LL NEVER FORGET!

November 1951

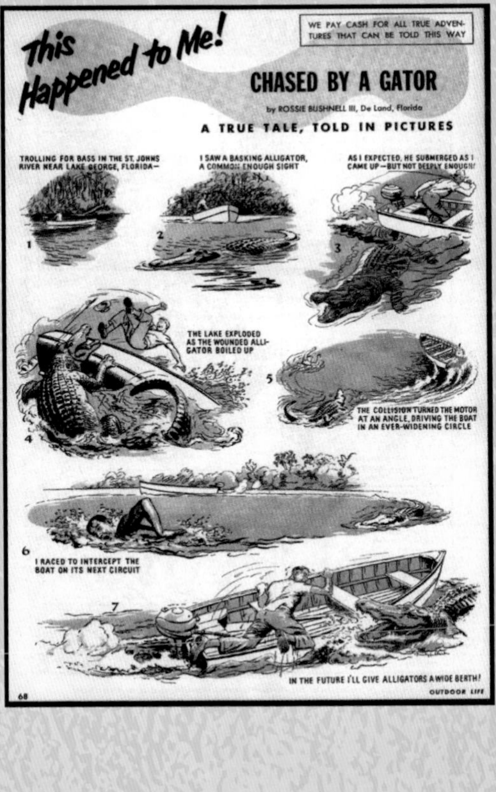
This Happened to Me!
WE PAY CASH FOR ALL TRUE ADVENTURES THAT CAN BE TOLD THIS WAY
CHASED BY A GATOR
by ROSSIE BUSHNELL III, De Land, Florida
A TRUE TALE, TOLD IN PICTURES
TROLLING FOR BASS IN THE ST. JOHNS RIVER NEAR LAKE GEORGE, FLORIDA–
I SAW A BASKING ALLIGATOR, A COMMON ENOUGH SIGHT
AS I EXPECTED, HE SUBMERGED AS I CAME UP–BUT NOT DEEPLY ENOUGH!
1
2
3
THE LAKE EXPLODED AS THE WOUNDED ALLIGATOR BOILED UP
4
5
THE COLLISION TURNED THE MOTOR AT AN ANGLE, DRIVING THE BOAT IN AN EVER-WIDENING CIRCLE
6
I RACED TO INTERCEPT THE BOAT ON ITS NEXT CIRCUIT
7
IN THE FUTURE I'LL GIVE ALLIGATORS A WIDE BERTH!
68
OUTDOOR LIFE

September 1965

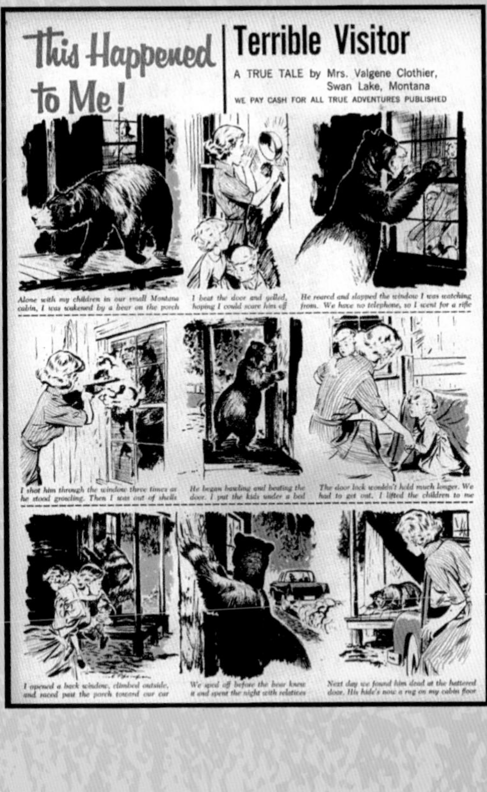
This Happened to Me!
Terrible Visitor
A TRUE TALE by Mrs. Valgene Clothier, Swan Lake, Montana
WE PAY CASH FOR ALL TRUE ADVENTURES PUBLISHED
Alone with my children in our small Montana cabin, I was wakened by a bear on the porch
I beat the door and yelled, hoping I could scare him off
He reared and slapped the window I was watching from. We have no telephone, so I went for a rifle
I shot him through the window three times as he stood growling. Then I was out of shells
He began bawling and beating the door. I put the kids under a bed
The door lock wouldn't hold much longer. We had to get out. I lifted the children to me
I opened a back window, climbed outside, and raced past the porch toward our car
We sped off before the bear knew it and spent the night with relatives
Next day we found him dead at the battered door. His hide's now a rug on my cabin floor

CHAPTER ONE

ONE STEP FROM

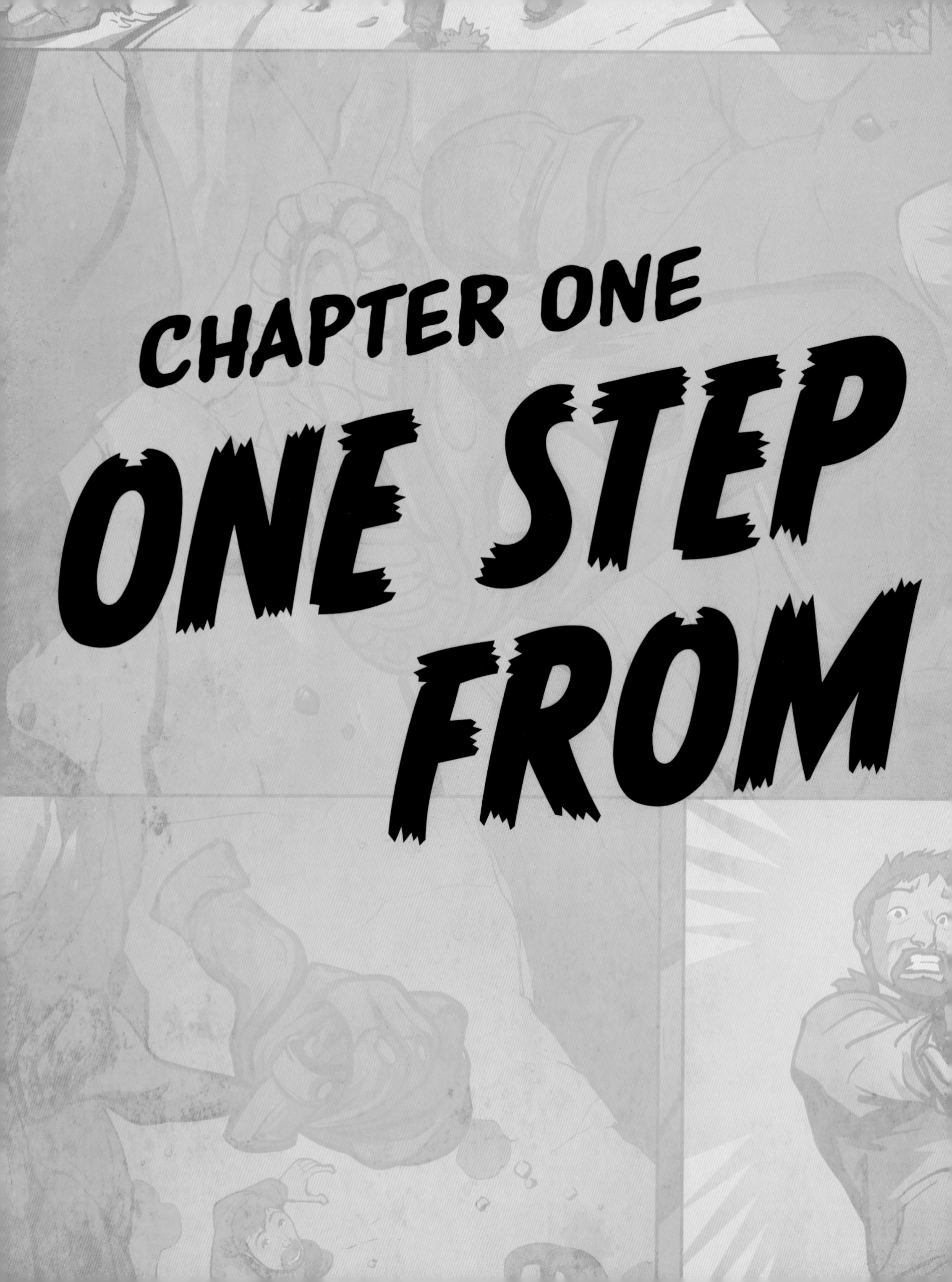

TOTAL DISASTER

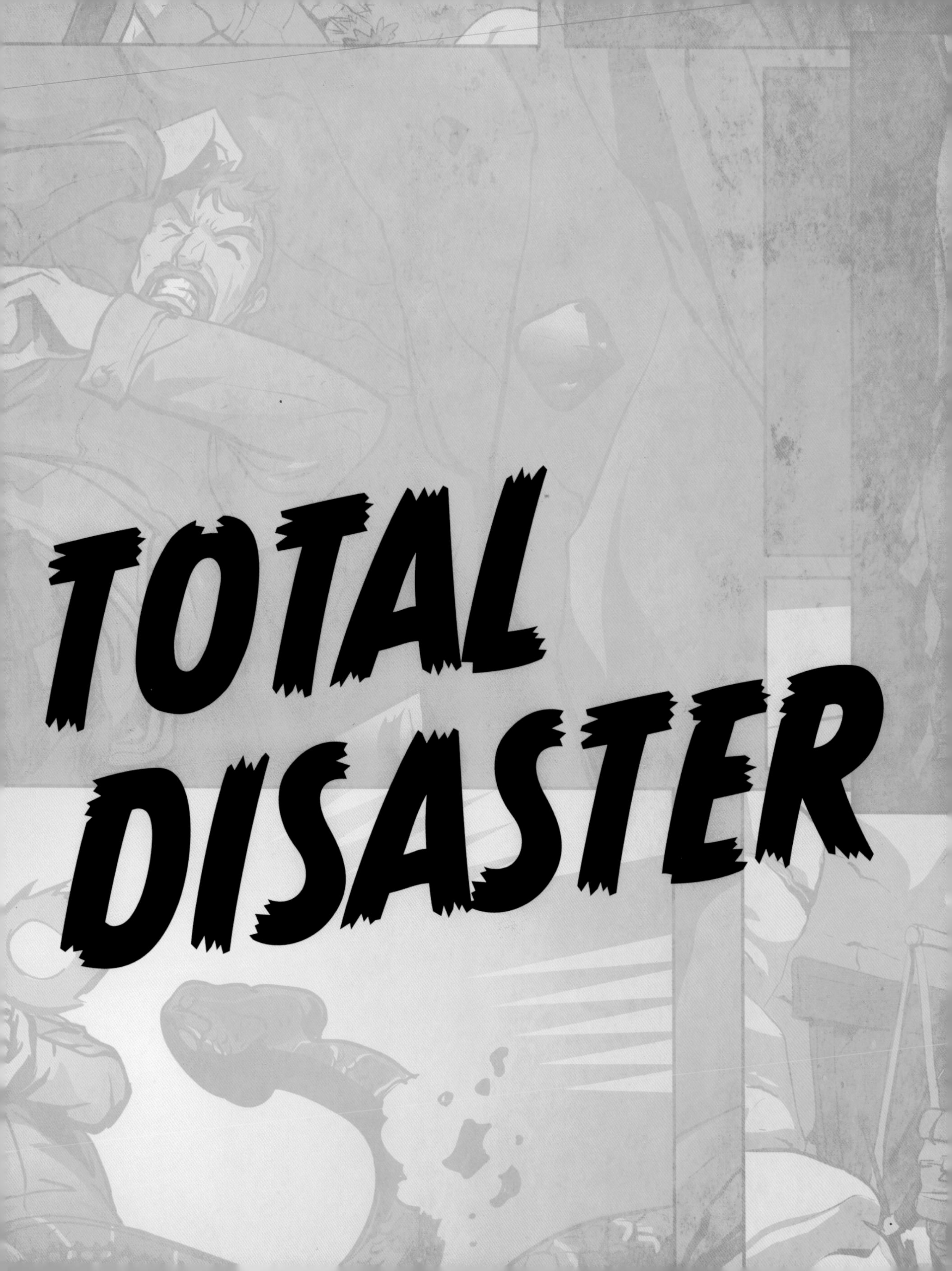

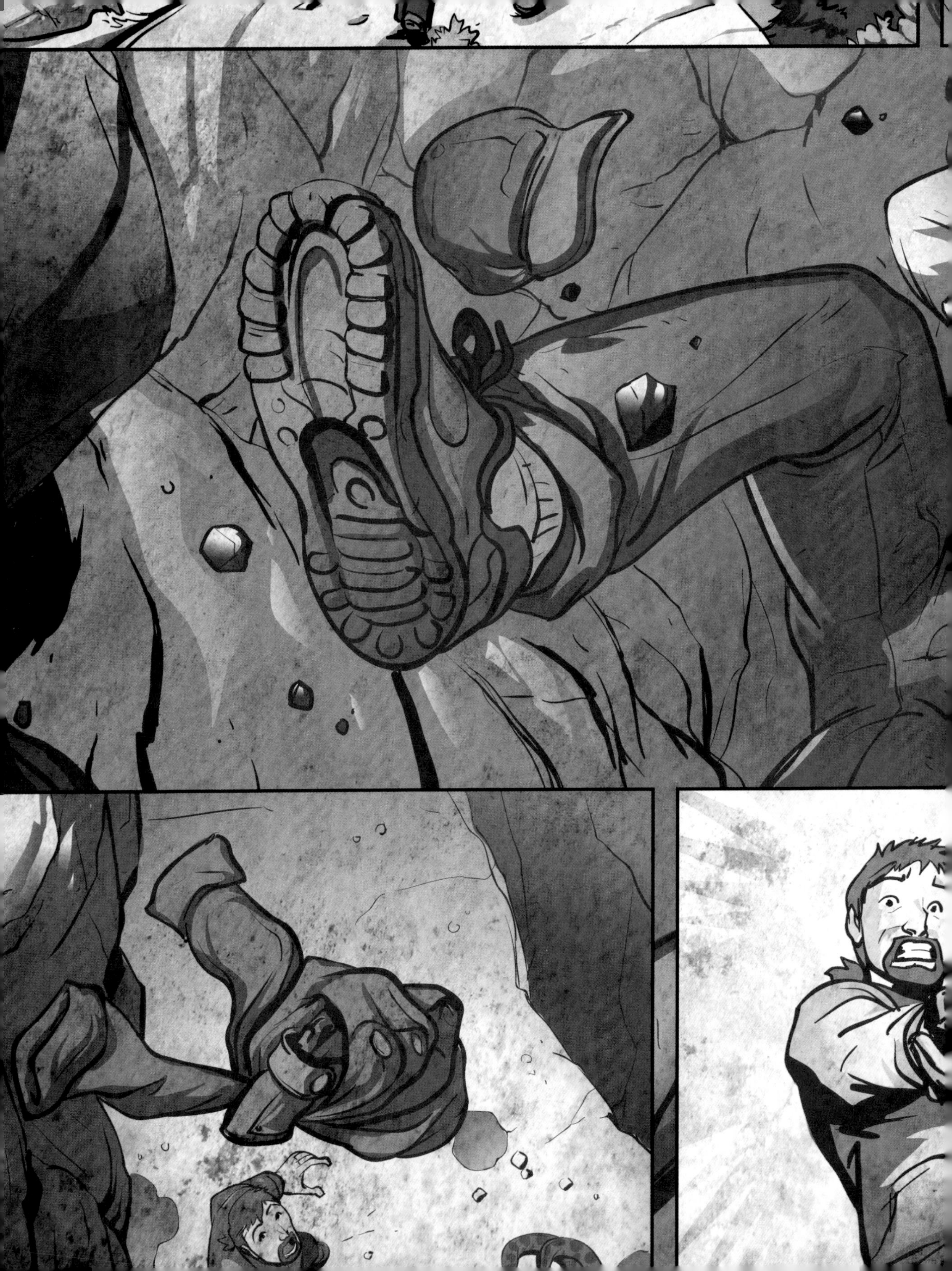

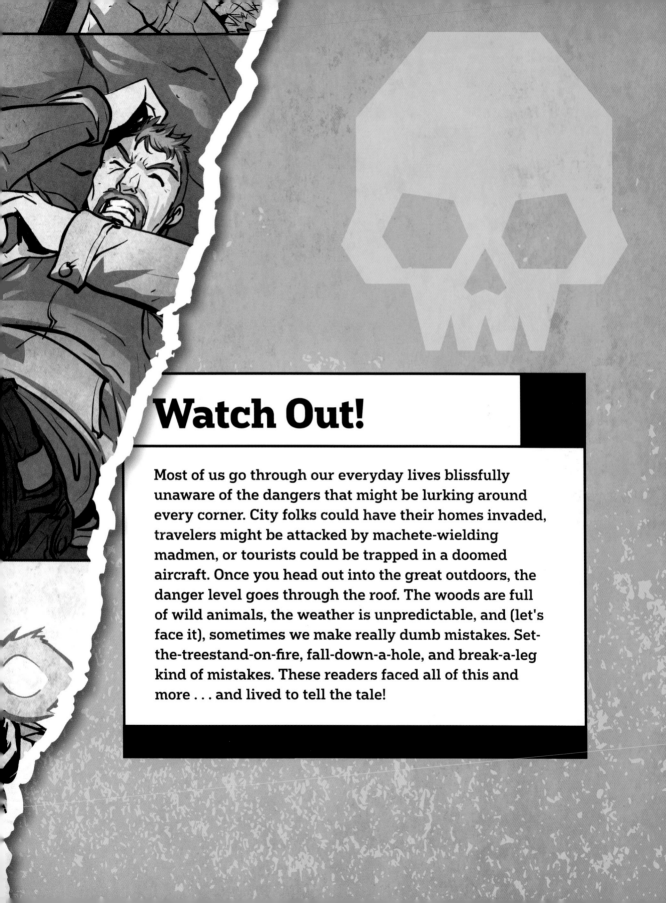

Watch Out!

Most of us go through our everyday lives blissfully unaware of the dangers that might be lurking around every corner. City folks could have their homes invaded, travelers might be attacked by machete-wielding madmen, or tourists could be trapped in a doomed aircraft. Once you head out into the great outdoors, the danger level goes through the roof. The woods are full of wild animals, the weather is unpredictable, and (let's face it), sometimes we make really dumb mistakes. Set-the-treestand-on-fire, fall-down-a-hole, and break-a-leg kind of mistakes. These readers faced all of this and more . . . and lived to tell the tale!

Mine Shafted // by Axel Jonasson, San Jose, CA

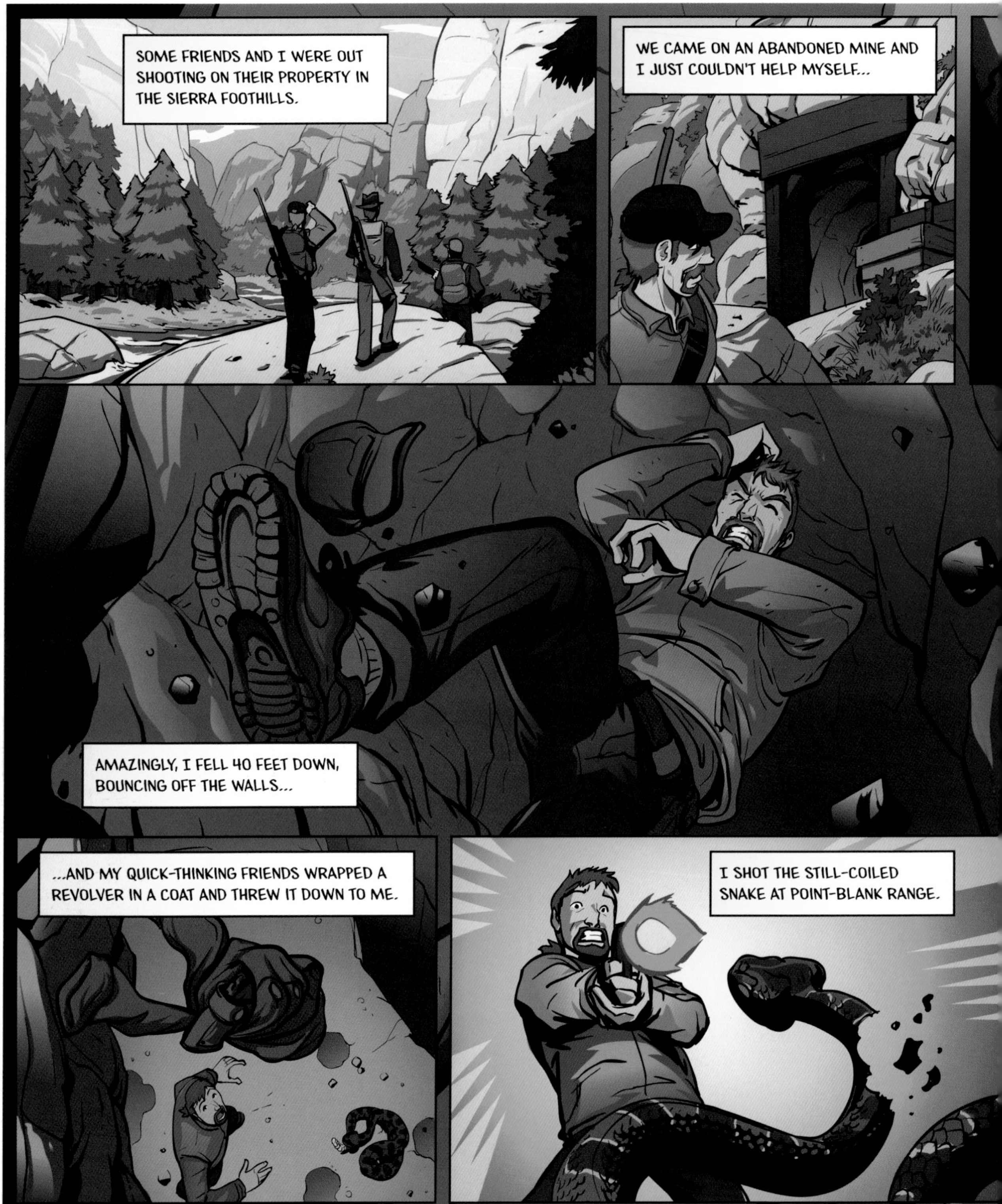
SOME FRIENDS AND I WERE OUT SHOOTING ON THEIR PROPERTY IN THE SIERRA FOOTHILLS.
WE CAME ON AN ABANDONED MINE AND I JUST COULDN'T HELP MYSELF...
AMAZINGLY, I FELL 40 FEET DOWN, BOUNCING OFF THE WALLS...
...AND MY QUICK-THINKING FRIENDS WRAPPED A REVOLVER IN A COAT AND THREW IT DOWN TO ME.
I SHOT THE STILL-COILED SNAKE AT POINT-BLANK RANGE.

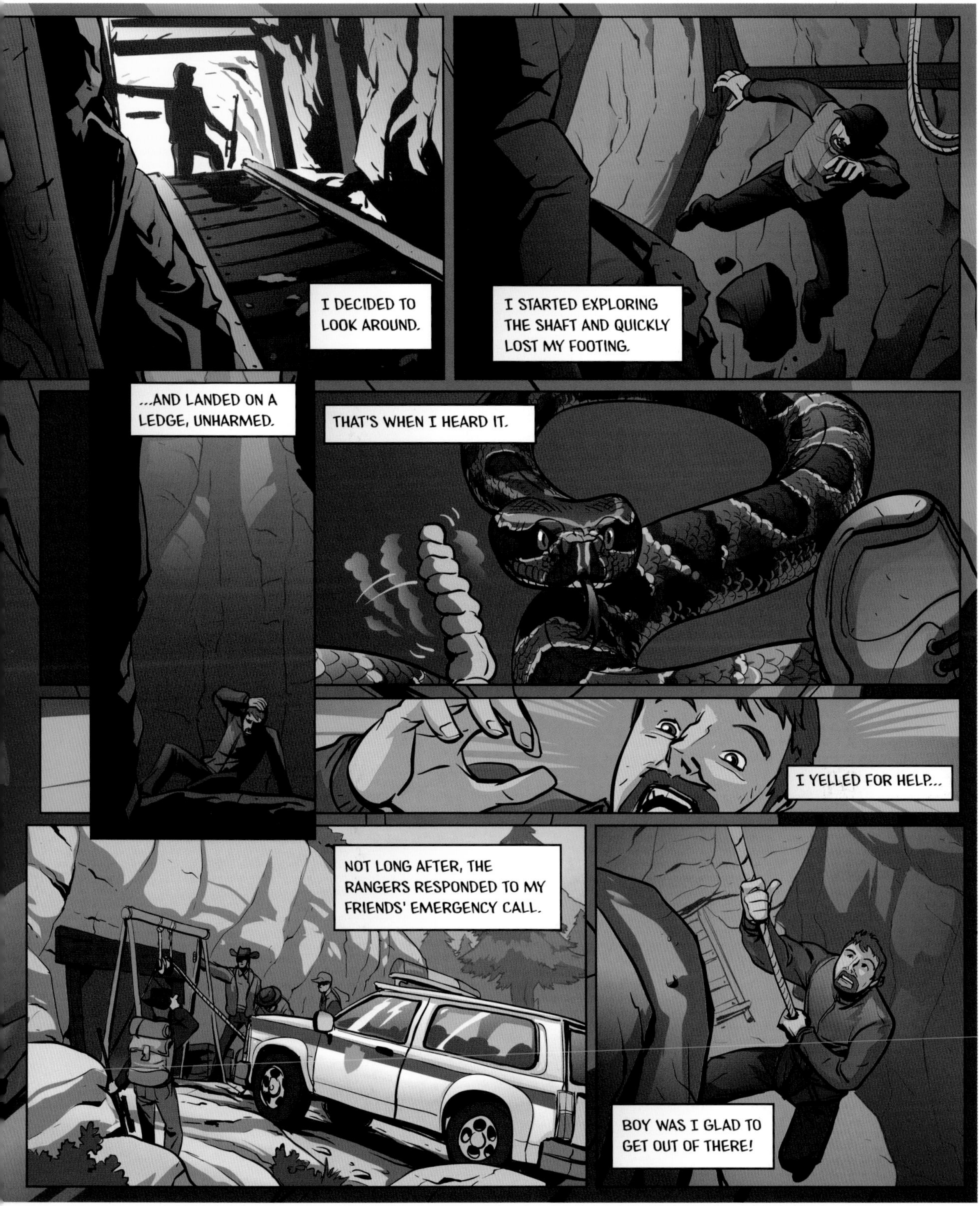
I DECIDED TO LOOK AROUND.
I STARTED EXPLORING THE SHAFT AND QUICKLY LOST MY FOOTING.
...AND LANDED ON A LEDGE, UNHARMED.
THAT'S WHEN I HEARD IT.
I YELLED FOR HELP...
NOT LONG AFTER, THE RANGERS RESPONDED TO MY FRIENDS' EMERGENCY CALL.
BOY WAS I GLAD TO GET OUT OF THERE!

Blown Away // by Marty Kehoe, Schenectady, NY

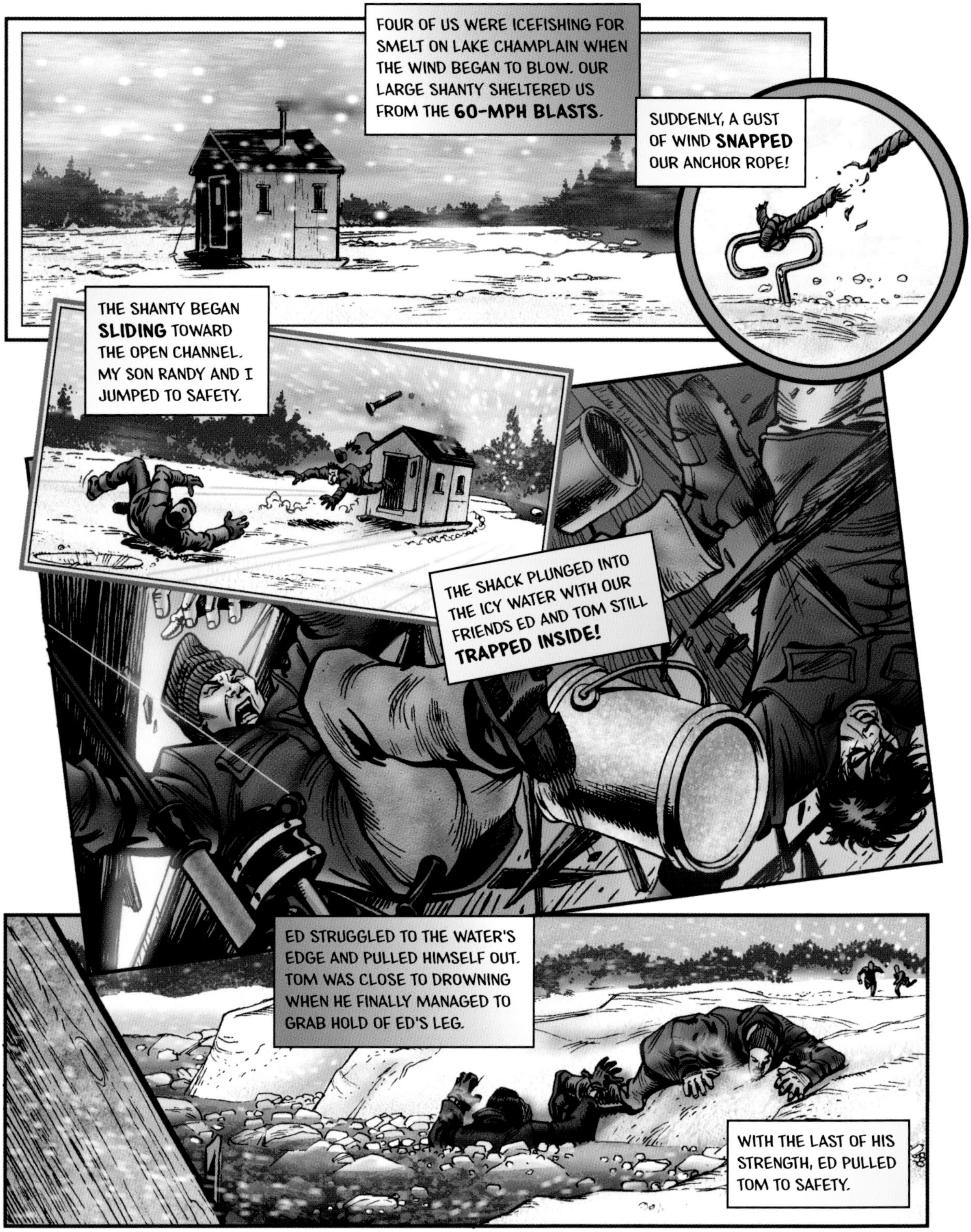
FOUR OF US WERE ICEFISHING FOR SMELT ON LAKE CHAMPLAIN WHEN THE WIND BEGAN TO BLOW. OUR LARGE SHANTY SHELTERED US FROM THE **60-MPH BLASTS**.
SUDDENLY, A GUST OF WIND **SNAPPED** OUR ANCHOR ROPE!
THE SHANTY BEGAN **SLIDING** TOWARD THE OPEN CHANNEL. MY SON RANDY AND I JUMPED TO SAFETY.
THE SHACK PLUNGED INTO THE ICY WATER WITH OUR FRIENDS ED AND TOM STILL **TRAPPED INSIDE!**
ED STRUGGLED TO THE WATER'S EDGE AND PULLED HIMSELF OUT. TOM WAS CLOSE TO DROWNING WHEN HE FINALLY MANAGED TO GRAB HOLD OF ED'S LEG.
WITH THE LAST OF HIS STRENGTH, ED PULLED TOM TO SAFETY.

Handling Hypothermia

COLD AS ICE As I'm sure you remember from grade school, the ideal temperature for the human body is 98.6°F. If a person's temperature drops below 95°F, you've got a case of hypothermia on your hands. Symptoms range from mild chills to coma and even death, depending on how low that body temperature drops.

FIRST THINGS FIRST While hypothermia can be deadly, you're lucky in that treating it is relatively simple, once you've hauled yourself or your buddy out of the drink. Start by making sure you're warm and out of danger before you do anything else—if the environment is cold enough to cause hypothermia in the victim, then it's cold enough to put you at risk, too.

GET COMFY (RELATIVELY SPEAKING) Once you've got a secure base set up, even if it's just a tent or the interior of your car, get the victim out of the cold and remove any wet clothing.

RESTORE WARMTH You'll want to wrap the victim in blankets or coats and, if possible, place warm water bottles or chemical warmers in his or her armpits and groin, and on their stomach. A warm, sweet drink will help—just avoid the old adage about drinking warm booze, as alcohol is not your friend right now (it actually causes you to lose heat and dehydrate). Your next duty is to get your friend to a hospital as quickly as possible.

SNUGGLE UP If you can't get out right away (say, you need to wait until the morning or until a storm passes), then it's time to get close and share whatever warmth you can. Body heat will do you both good, and you can swear to never speak of it again once you return to civilization.

KNOW THE NUMBERS:
Falling

1,000 FEET Distance fallen from a cliff by very, very lucky hiker Adam Potter, resulting in only minor injuries.

33,300 FEET Longest fall from an aircraft, survived without a parachute. Flight Attendant Vesna Vulovic was grievously injured when the plane she was on broke up in midair; she recovered after 17 months and went back to work with the airline.

40,230 FEET Depth of the world's deepest hole.

80,380 FEET Longest freefall parachute jump.

12 SECONDS Amount of time it takes a human body to reach terminal velocity.

1,500 FEET Approximate distance to reach terminal velocity.

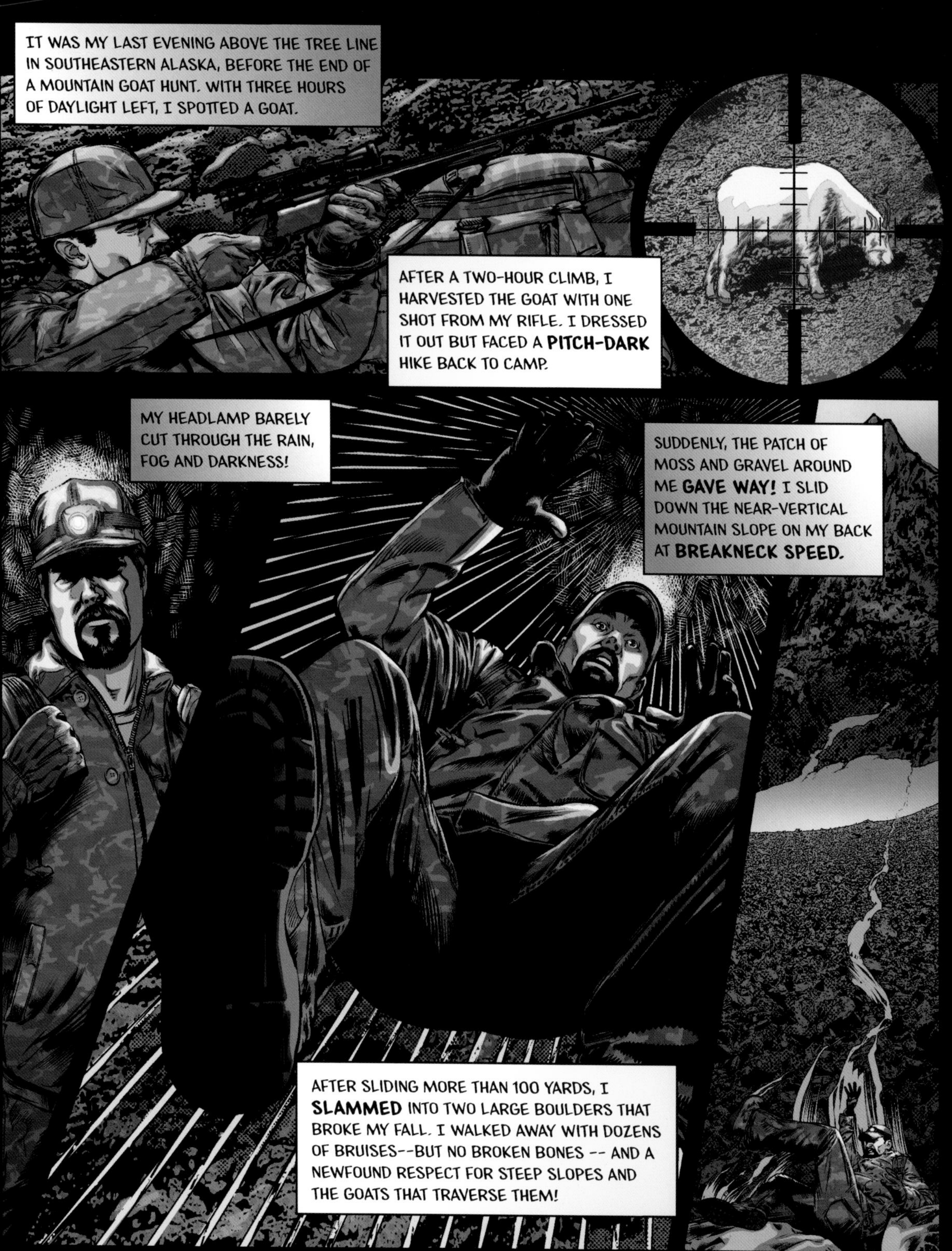
IT WAS MY LAST EVENING ABOVE THE TREE LINE IN SOUTHEASTERN ALASKA, BEFORE THE END OF A MOUNTAIN GOAT HUNT. WITH THREE HOURS OF DAYLIGHT LEFT, I SPOTTED A GOAT.
AFTER A TWO-HOUR CLIMB, I HARVESTED THE GOAT WITH ONE SHOT FROM MY RIFLE. I DRESSED IT OUT BUT FACED A PITCH-DARK HIKE BACK TO CAMP.
MY HEADLAMP BARELY CUT THROUGH THE RAIN, FOG AND DARKNESS!
SUDDENLY, THE PATCH OF MOSS AND GRAVEL AROUND ME GAVE WAY! I SLID DOWN THE NEAR-VERTICAL MOUNTAIN SLOPE ON MY BACK AT BREAKNECK SPEED.
AFTER SLIDING MORE THAN 100 YARDS, I SLAMMED INTO TWO LARGE BOULDERS THAT BROKE MY FALL. I WALKED AWAY WITH DOZENS OF BRUISES--BUT NO BROKEN BONES -- AND A NEWFOUND RESPECT FOR STEEP SLOPES AND THE GOATS THAT TRAVERSE THEM!

Fire and Ice // by Bruce Christian, Tomahawk, WI

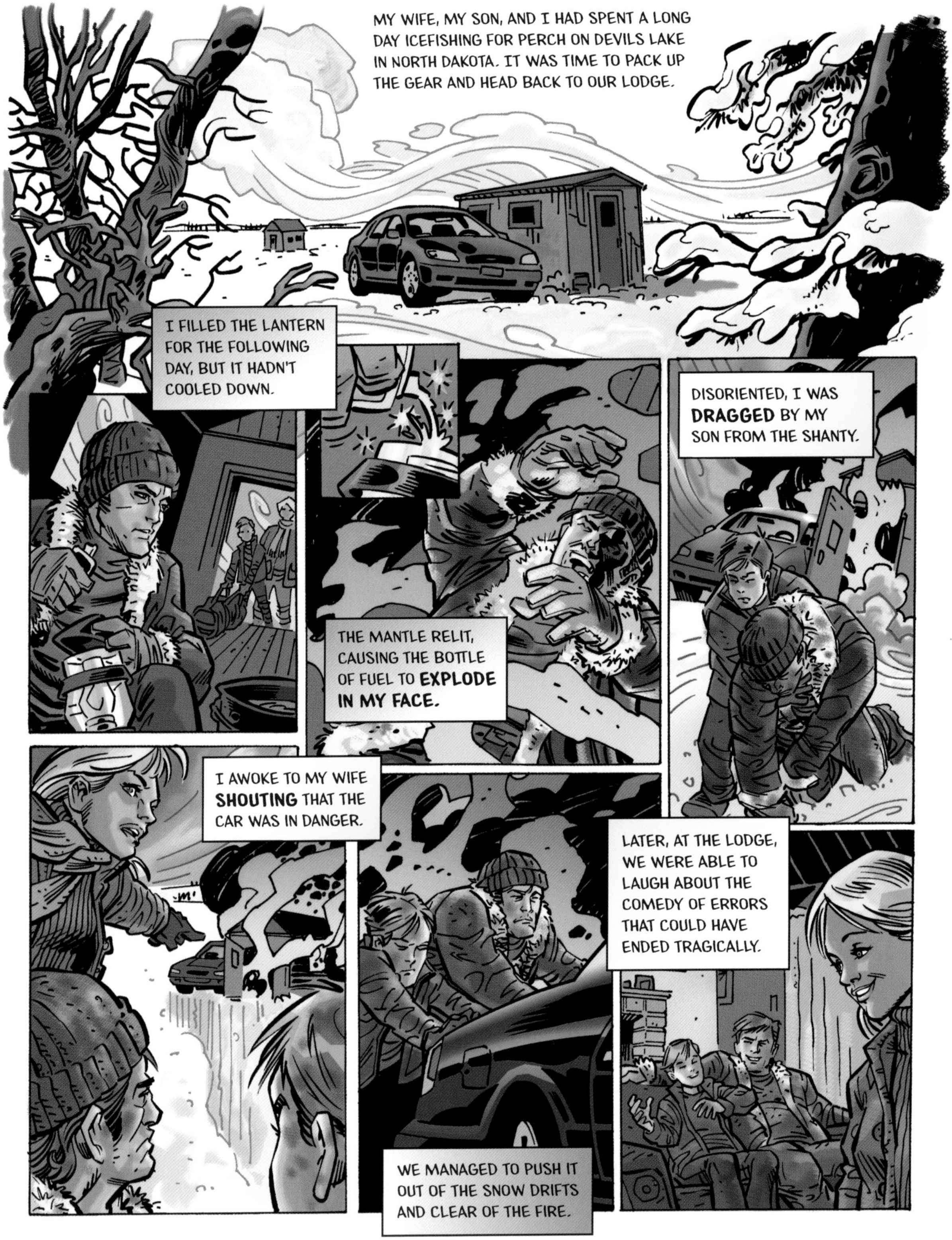
MY WIFE, MY SON, AND I HAD SPENT A LONG DAY ICEFISHING FOR PERCH ON DEVILS LAKE IN NORTH DAKOTA. IT WAS TIME TO PACK UP THE GEAR AND HEAD BACK TO OUR LODGE.
I FILLED THE LANTERN FOR THE FOLLOWING DAY, BUT IT HADN'T COOLED DOWN.
THE MANTLE RELIT, CAUSING THE BOTTLE OF FUEL TO EXPLODE IN MY FACE.
DISORIENTED, I WAS DRAGGED BY MY SON FROM THE SHANTY.
I AWOKE TO MY WIFE SHOUTING THAT THE CAR WAS IN DANGER.
WE MANAGED TO PUSH IT OUT OF THE SNOW DRIFTS AND CLEAR OF THE FIRE.
LATER, AT THE LODGE, WE WERE ABLE TO LAUGH ABOUT THE COMEDY OF ERRORS THAT COULD HAVE ENDED TRAGICALLY.

"Winter is nature's way of saying, 'Up yours.' "

—*Robert Byrne*

Tidal Flat Terror! // by James Wilson, Summerville, WV

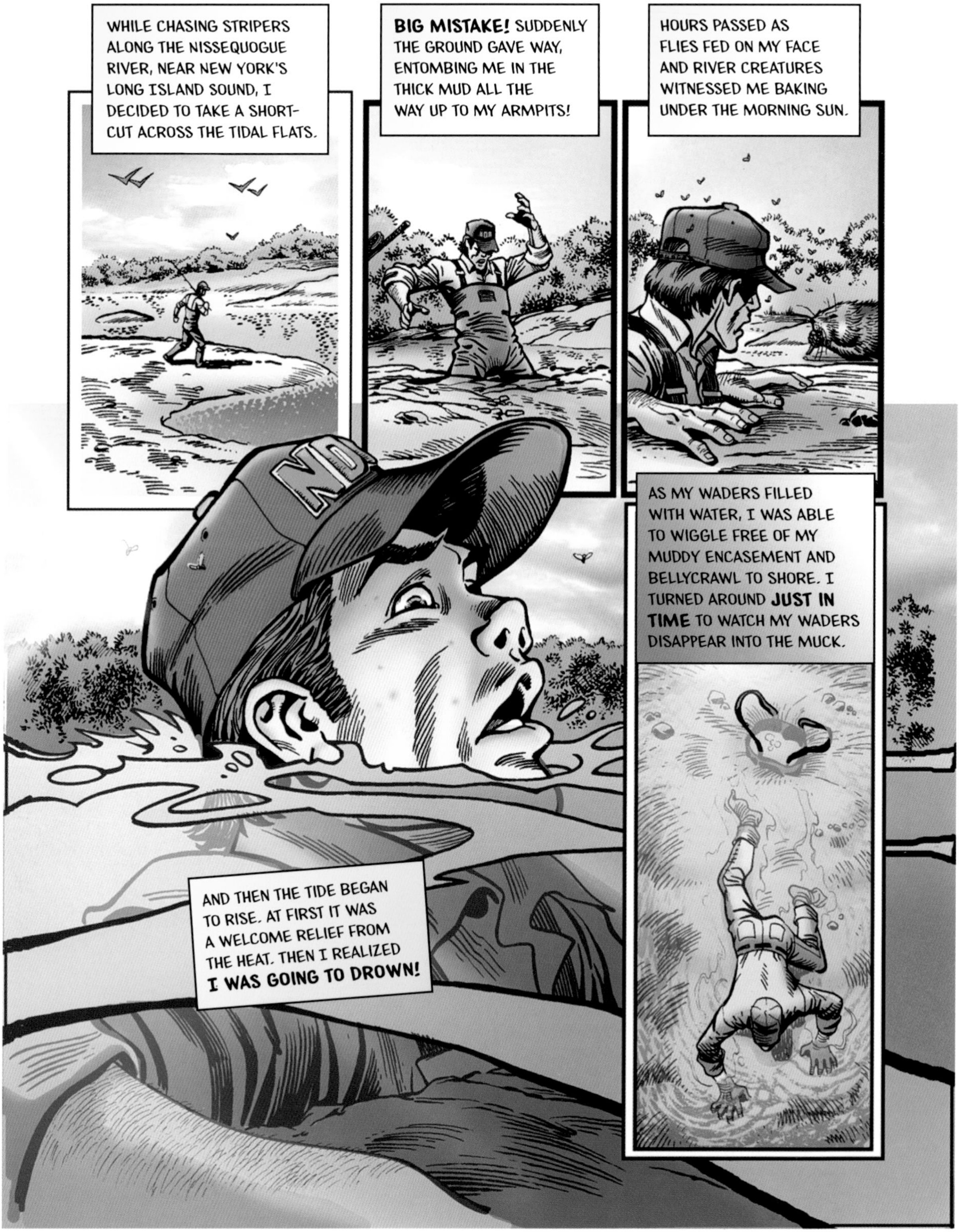

WHILE CHASING STRIPERS ALONG THE NISSEQUOGUE RIVER, NEAR NEW YORK'S LONG ISLAND SOUND, I DECIDED TO TAKE A SHORT-CUT ACROSS THE TIDAL FLATS.
BIG MISTAKE! SUDDENLY THE GROUND GAVE WAY, ENTOMBING ME IN THE THICK MUD ALL THE WAY UP TO MY ARMPITS!
HOURS PASSED AS FLIES FED ON MY FACE AND RIVER CREATURES WITNESSED ME BAKING UNDER THE MORNING SUN.
AND THEN THE TIDE BEGAN TO RISE. AT FIRST IT WAS A WELCOME RELIEF FROM THE HEAT. THEN I REALIZED I WAS GOING TO DROWN!
AS MY WADERS FILLED WITH WATER, I WAS ABLE TO WIGGLE FREE OF MY MUDDY ENCASEMENT AND BELLYCRAWL TO SHORE. I TURNED AROUND JUST IN TIME TO WATCH MY WADERS DISAPPEAR INTO THE MUCK.

One Rocky Ride // by Al Shade, Myerstown, PA

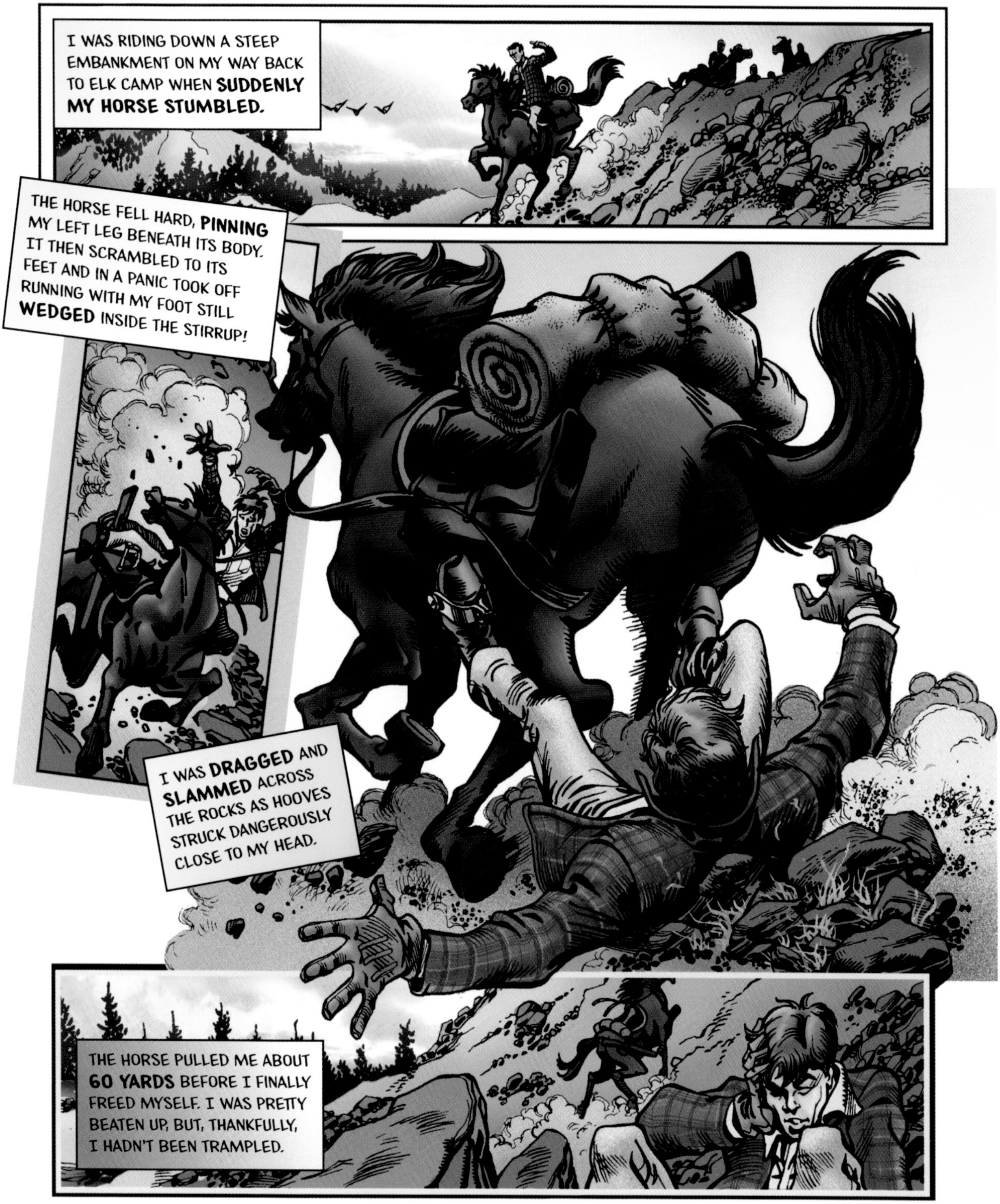
I WAS RIDING DOWN A STEEP EMBANKMENT ON MY WAY BACK TO ELK CAMP WHEN SUDDENLY MY HORSE STUMBLED.
THE HORSE FELL HARD, PINNING MY LEFT LEG BENEATH ITS BODY. IT THEN SCRAMBLED TO ITS FEET AND IN A PANIC TOOK OFF RUNNING WITH MY FOOT STILL WEDGED INSIDE THE STIRRUP!
I WAS DRAGGED AND SLAMMED ACROSS THE ROCKS AS HOOVES STRUCK DANGEROUSLY CLOSE TO MY HEAD.
THE HORSE PULLED ME ABOUT 60 YARDS BEFORE I FINALLY FREED MYSELF. I WAS PRETTY BEATEN UP, BUT, THANKFULLY, I HADN'T BEEN TRAMPLED.

Trapped in a Canyon // by Nat Judd, Provo, UT

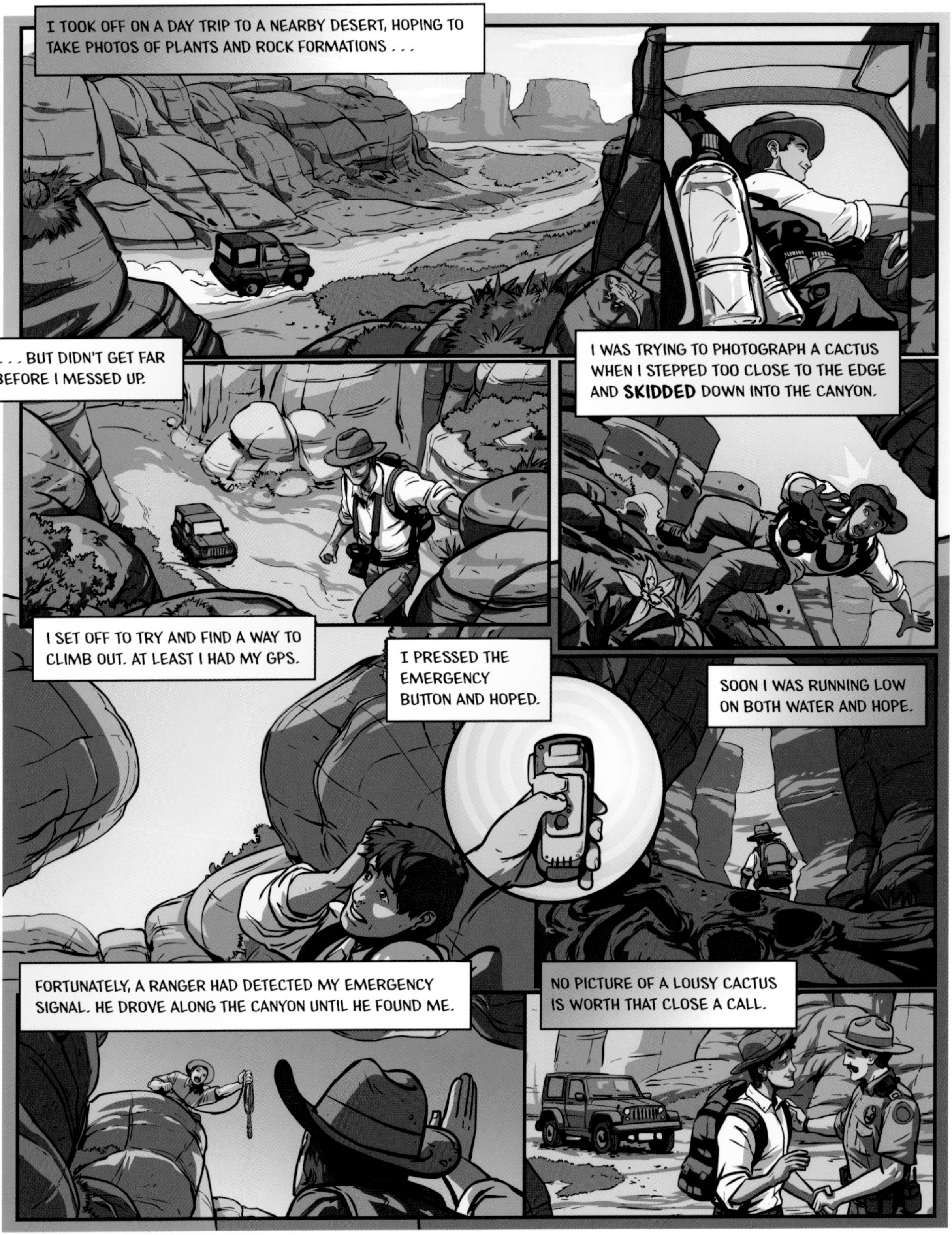

I TOOK OFF ON A DAY TRIP TO A NEARBY DESERT, HOPING TO TAKE PHOTOS OF PLANTS AND ROCK FORMATIONS . . .
. . . BUT DIDN'T GET FAR BEFORE I MESSED UP.
I WAS TRYING TO PHOTOGRAPH A CACTUS WHEN I STEPPED TOO CLOSE TO THE EDGE AND **SKIDDED** DOWN INTO THE CANYON.
I SET OFF TO TRY AND FIND A WAY TO CLIMB OUT. AT LEAST I HAD MY GPS.
I PRESSED THE EMERGENCY BUTTON AND HOPED.
SOON I WAS RUNNING LOW ON BOTH WATER AND HOPE.
FORTUNATELY, A RANGER HAD DETECTED MY EMERGENCY SIGNAL. HE DROVE ALONG THE CANYON UNTIL HE FOUND ME.
NO PICTURE OF A LOUSY CACTUS IS WORTH THAT CLOSE A CALL.

Stay the Course

WHERE ARE YOU? We've all strayed off a trail or two, but losing your way when you're far from civilization is one of the foremost ways to wind up in deep trouble. It's surprisingly easy to get lost . . . the good news is, it's also pretty easy to avoid. You just need to stay aware and follow a few simple guidelines.

TELL A FRIEND Always make sure somebody responsible knows where you're going and when you're supposed to be coming back.

KNOW THE TERRAIN Get a map of the area in which you'll be traveling, and study it before your trip.

STAY ORIENTED Use the map and a compass or GPS while you're there, so you can constantly check (and re-check) and verify your position.

USE YOUR BRAIN Keep a map in your mind, too. Imagine what the terrain would look like from a bird's-eye view and visualize your place in that terrain. Think of that little "You Are Here" arrow on the big map at the trailhead, and keep it updated in your mind.

BE AWARE Take note of any prominent topographical features near your location and keep them in view as much as possible. Look back frequently and remember the landmarks behind you—especially if you'll be returning in that direction on your way out of the area.

STAY ON THE STRAIGHT AND NARROW When venturing off marked trails, use a compass or keep an eye on distant features like mountains or canyons to help you travel in straight lines.

Mudslides

130 SQUARE MILES Largest area covered by a mudslide.

738 BILLION GALLONS Largest volume of mud from a single slide in modern times.

23,000 Largest confirmed mudslide death toll, caused by a 1985 slide in Colombia.

30,000 Largest estimated death toll for a single mudslide, which happened in Venezuela in 1999.

MORE THAN 90% Percentage of mudslides triggered by heavy rainfall or storms.

35% Percentage of mudslides that are influenced by human activities such as building construction and scrub-clearing.

210 Average number of yearly landslide events that impact human beings.

40 MILES PER HOUR Average speed of a mudslide.

200 MILES PER HOUR Fastest recorded speed of a mudslide.

Swept Off Our Feet // by John Lusk, Highlands Ranch, CO

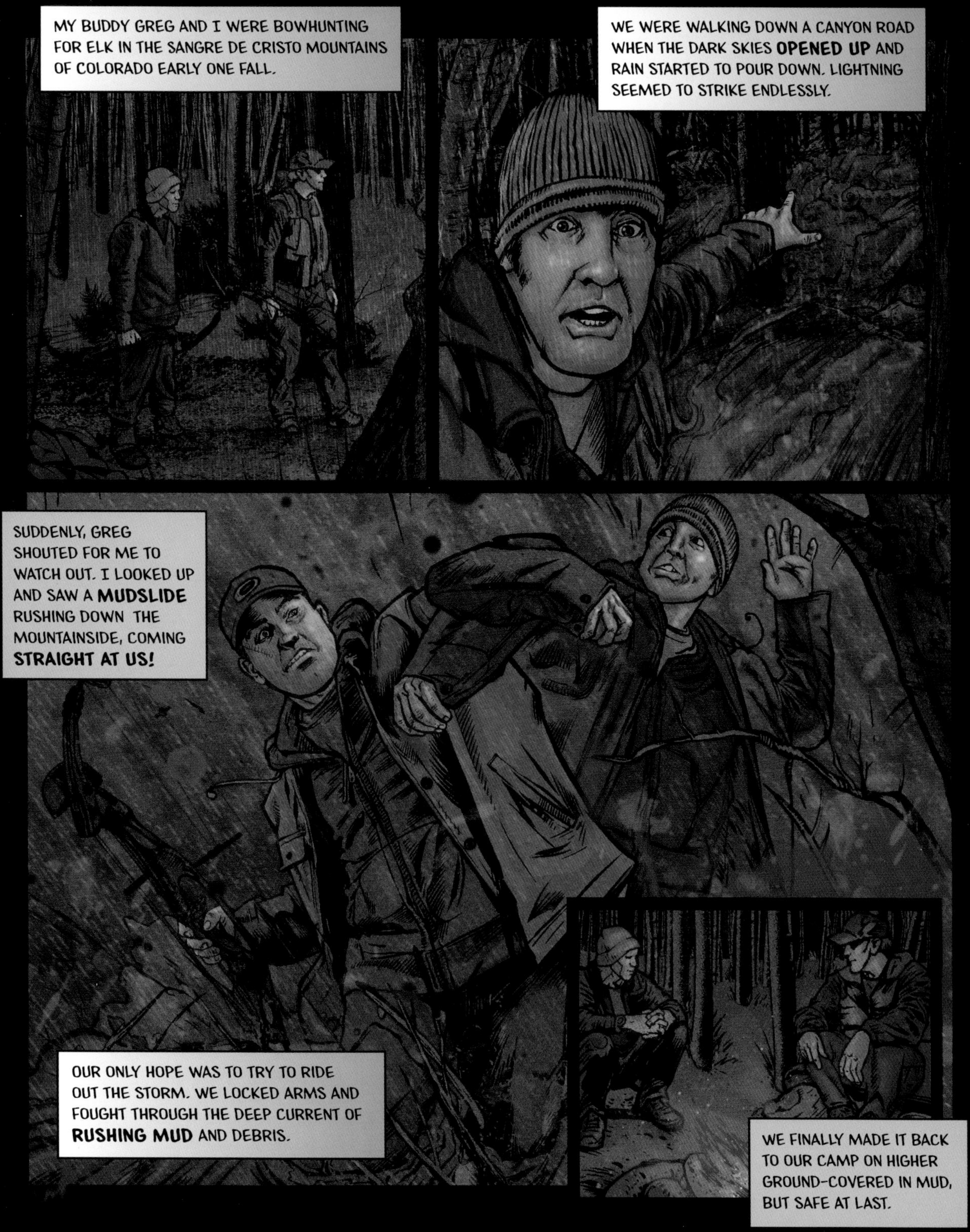

MY BUDDY GREG AND I WERE BOWHUNTING FOR ELK IN THE SANGRE DE CRISTO MOUNTAINS OF COLORADO EARLY ONE FALL.
WE WERE WALKING DOWN A CANYON ROAD WHEN THE DARK SKIES **OPENED UP** AND RAIN STARTED TO POUR DOWN. LIGHTNING SEEMED TO STRIKE ENDLESSLY.
SUDDENLY, GREG SHOUTED FOR ME TO WATCH OUT. I LOOKED UP AND SAW A **MUDSLIDE** RUSHING DOWN THE MOUNTAINSIDE, COMING **STRAIGHT AT US!**
OUR ONLY HOPE WAS TO TRY TO RIDE OUT THE STORM. WE LOCKED ARMS AND FOUGHT THROUGH THE DEEP CURRENT OF **RUSHING MUD** AND DEBRIS.
WE FINALLY MADE IT BACK TO OUR CAMP ON HIGHER GROUND—COVERED IN MUD, BUT SAFE AT LAST.

Saved by the Stringer! // by Julie Livingston, North Port, FL

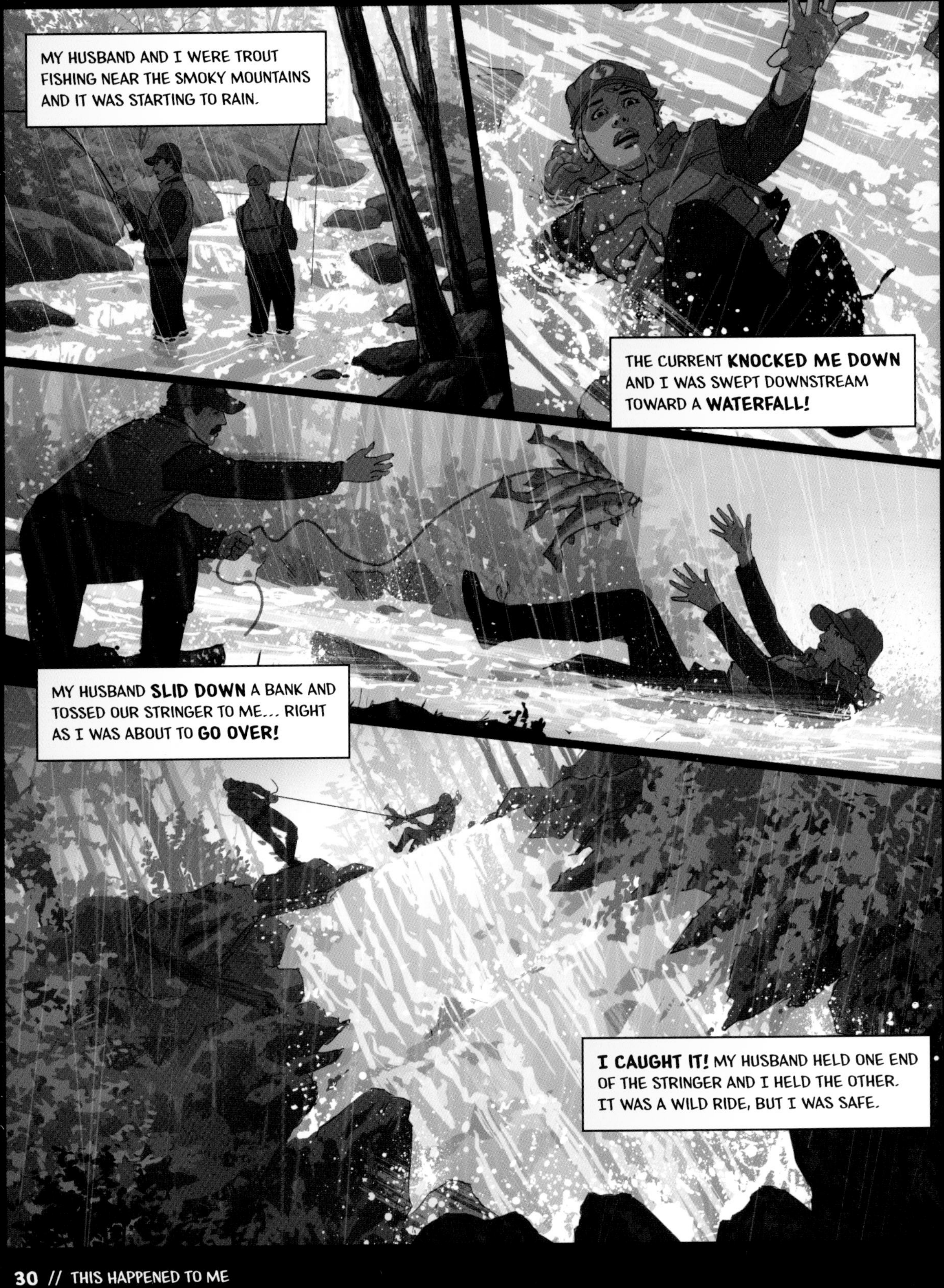
MY HUSBAND AND I WERE TROUT FISHING NEAR THE SMOKY MOUNTAINS AND IT WAS STARTING TO RAIN.
THE CURRENT KNOCKED ME DOWN AND I WAS SWEPT DOWNSTREAM TOWARD A WATERFALL!
MY HUSBAND SLID DOWN A BANK AND TOSSED OUR STRINGER TO ME... RIGHT AS I WAS ABOUT TO GO OVER!
I CAUGHT IT! MY HUSBAND HELD ONE END OF THE STRINGER AND I HELD THE OTHER. IT WAS A WILD RIDE, BUT I WAS SAFE.

"When you're drowning you don't think, I would be incredibly pleased if someone would notice I'm drowning and come and rescue me. You just scream."

—*John Lennon*

Panic in the Air // by Evan Kelly, Hilo, HI

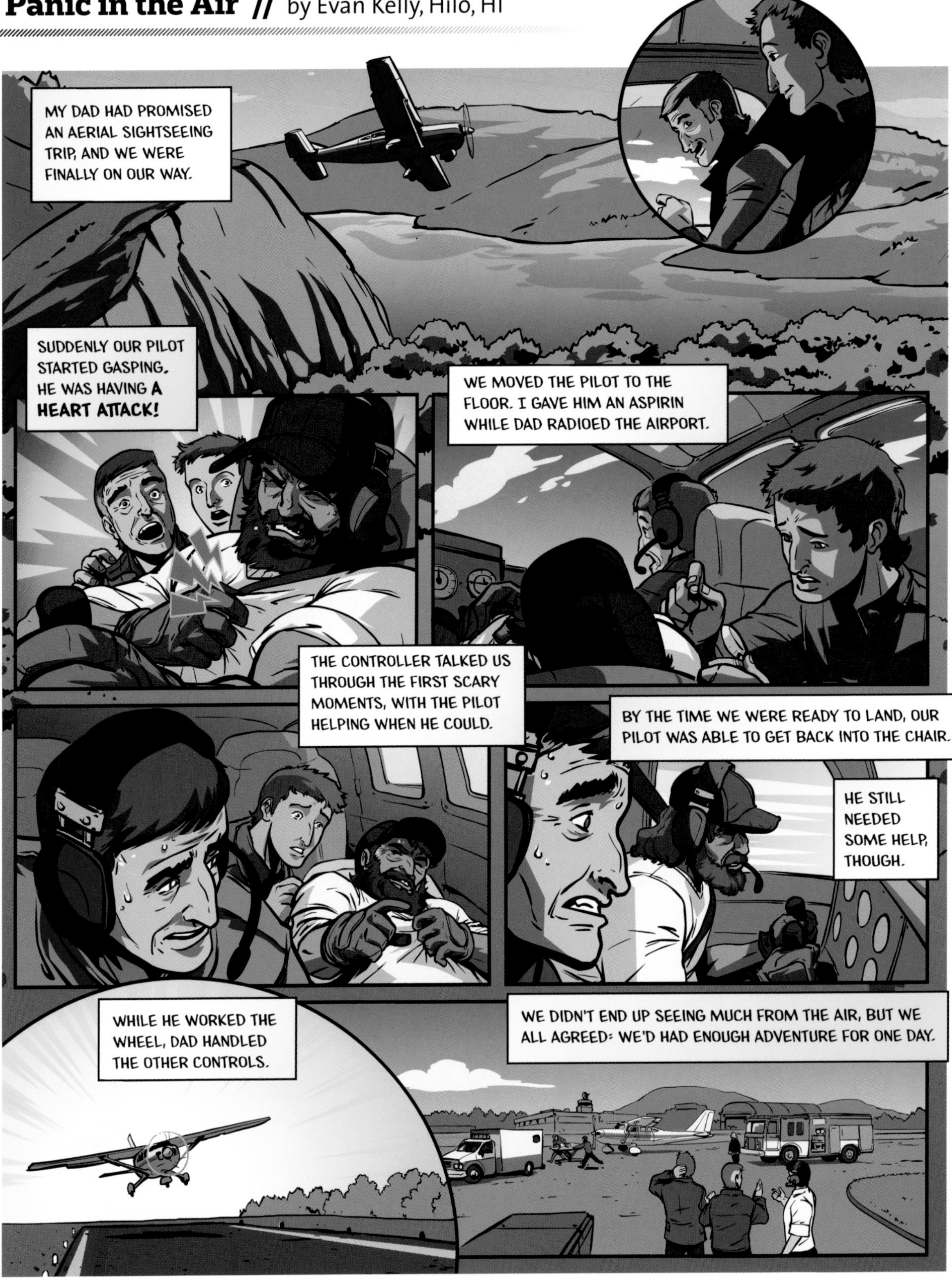

MY DAD HAD PROMISED AN AERIAL SIGHTSEEING TRIP, AND WE WERE FINALLY ON OUR WAY.
SUDDENLY OUR PILOT STARTED GASPING. HE WAS HAVING **A HEART ATTACK!**
WE MOVED THE PILOT TO THE FLOOR. I GAVE HIM AN ASPIRIN WHILE DAD RADIOED THE AIRPORT.
THE CONTROLLER TALKED US THROUGH THE FIRST SCARY MOMENTS, WITH THE PILOT HELPING WHEN HE COULD.
BY THE TIME WE WERE READY TO LAND, OUR PILOT WAS ABLE TO GET BACK INTO THE CHAIR.
HE STILL NEEDED SOME HELP, THOUGH.
WHILE HE WORKED THE WHEEL, DAD HANDLED THE OTHER CONTROLS.
WE DIDN'T END UP SEEING MUCH FROM THE AIR, BUT WE ALL AGREED: WE'D HAD ENOUGH ADVENTURE FOR ONE DAY.

Survive After a Plane Crash

EVERYTHING BUT THE POLAR BEAR If you're lucky, airborne danger will end with you landing safely on firm ground . . . or a convenient body of water. However, you may not be so lucky. If a plane goes down, survivors will face the challenge of staying alive until rescuers arrive. Depending on where you crash, help might be just minutes away . . . or it could take days or even weeks for rescuers to find you. In the latter case, it's time to get creative.

SEND OUT AN S.O.S. The first thing you'll want to do is check the cockpit for the plane's radio. If it works, send out a distress call.

TAKE SHELTER If at all possible, use the fuselage as a shelter—unless fuel has spilled, in which case there's a chance of fire, and you should move at least 100 feet away. Speaking of fuel, carefully punch a hole in the fuel tank (usually located in the wings of larger aircraft), drain the fuel into a container, and use it to start a fire.

GET COMFORTABLE If the plane has broken up, put the debris to good use: Carpeting, upholstery, seat cushions, bulkheads, overhead-bin doors, and plastic windows can all become useful parts of a temporary shelter. Look for electrical wires, which you can use to lash together elements of your shelter.

GO SCAVENGING Dig through cargo compartments and luggage bins to find clothing, blankets, pillows, food, and water. Also, nearly all planes carry medical supplies, including automatic defibrillators. Don't leave those critical items behind. Also, sift through the wreckage for reflective materials that could be used as signal mirrors.

Tundra Conundrum // by James Wilson, Summerville, WV

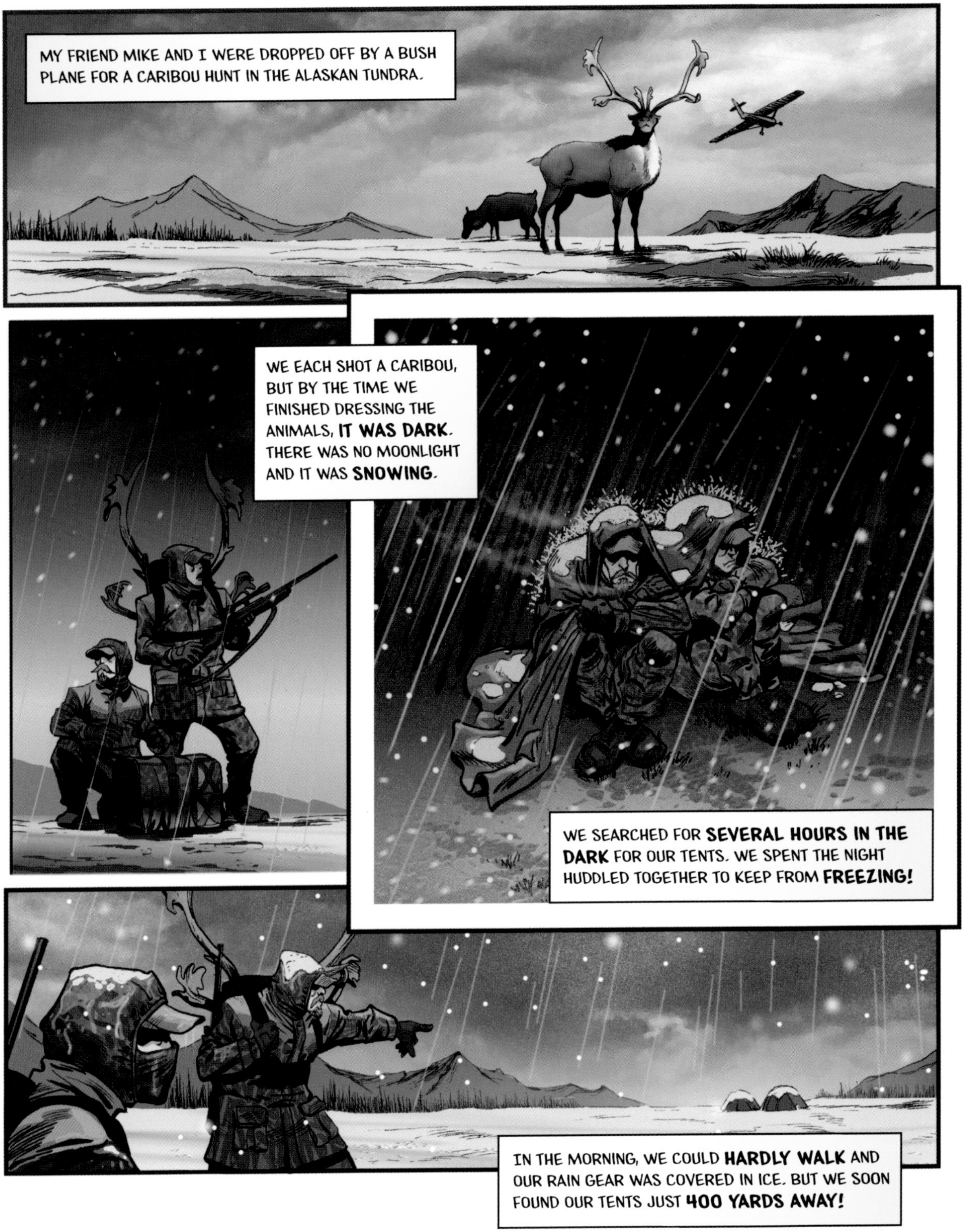
MY FRIEND MIKE AND I WERE DROPPED OFF BY A BUSH PLANE FOR A CARIBOU HUNT IN THE ALASKAN TUNDRA.
WE EACH SHOT A CARIBOU, BUT BY THE TIME WE FINISHED DRESSING THE ANIMALS, IT WAS DARK. THERE WAS NO MOONLIGHT AND IT WAS SNOWING.
WE SEARCHED FOR SEVERAL HOURS IN THE DARK FOR OUR TENTS. WE SPENT THE NIGHT HUDDLED TOGETHER TO KEEP FROM FREEZING!
IN THE MORNING, WE COULD HARDLY WALK AND OUR RAIN GEAR WAS COVERED IN ICE. BUT WE SOON FOUND OUR TENTS JUST 400 YARDS AWAY!

Great Balls of Fire // by Jim Jukich, Hibbing, MN

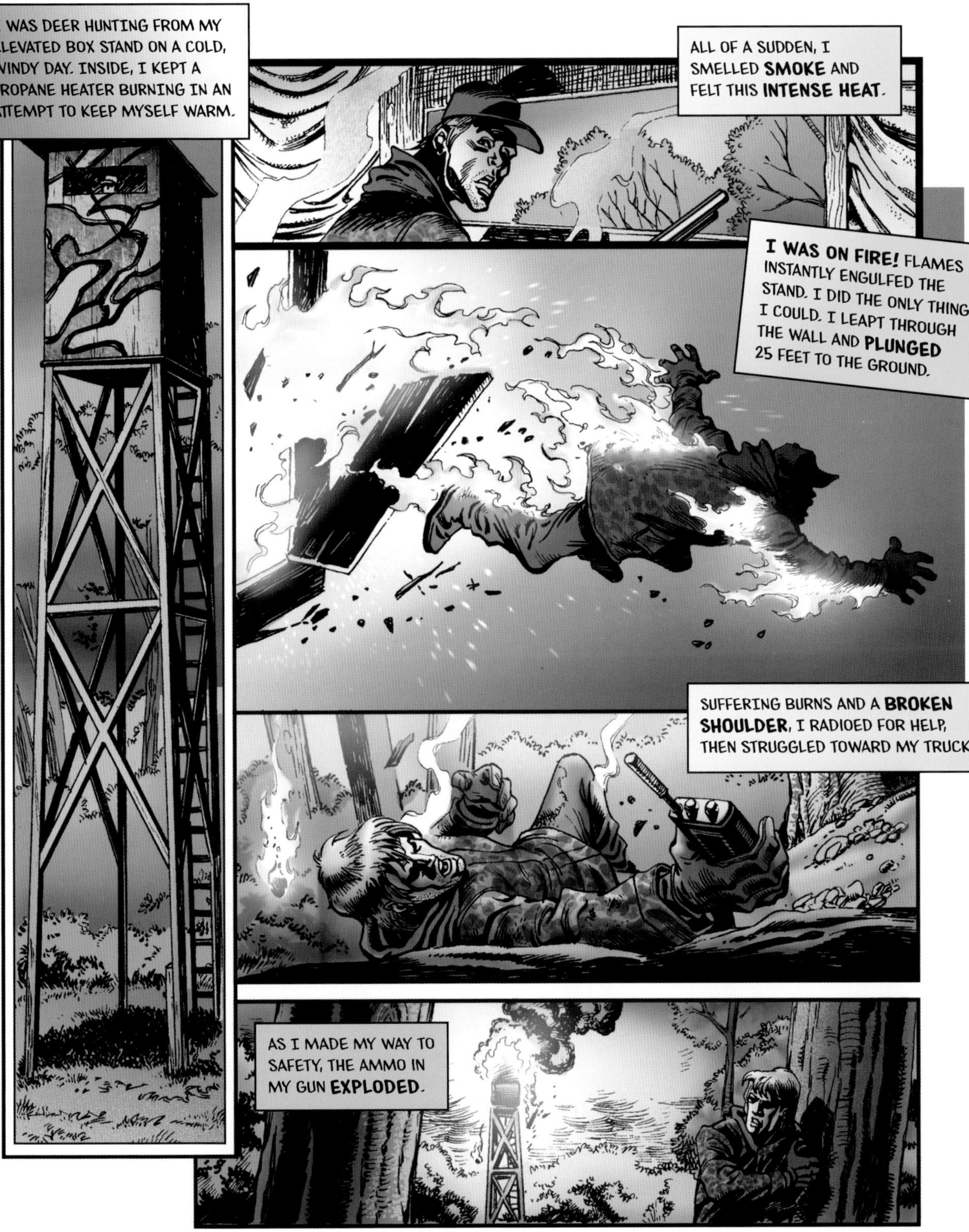
I WAS DEER HUNTING FROM MY ELEVATED BOX STAND ON A COLD, WINDY DAY. INSIDE, I KEPT A PROPANE HEATER BURNING IN AN ATTEMPT TO KEEP MYSELF WARM.
ALL OF A SUDDEN, I SMELLED **SMOKE** AND FELT THIS **INTENSE HEAT**.
I WAS ON FIRE! FLAMES INSTANTLY ENGULFED THE STAND. I DID THE ONLY THING I COULD. I LEAPT THROUGH THE WALL AND **PLUNGED** 25 FEET TO THE GROUND.
SUFFERING BURNS AND A **BROKEN SHOULDER**, I RADIOED FOR HELP, THEN STRUGGLED TOWARD MY TRUCK.
AS I MADE MY WAY TO SAFETY, THE AMMO IN MY GUN **EXPLODED**.

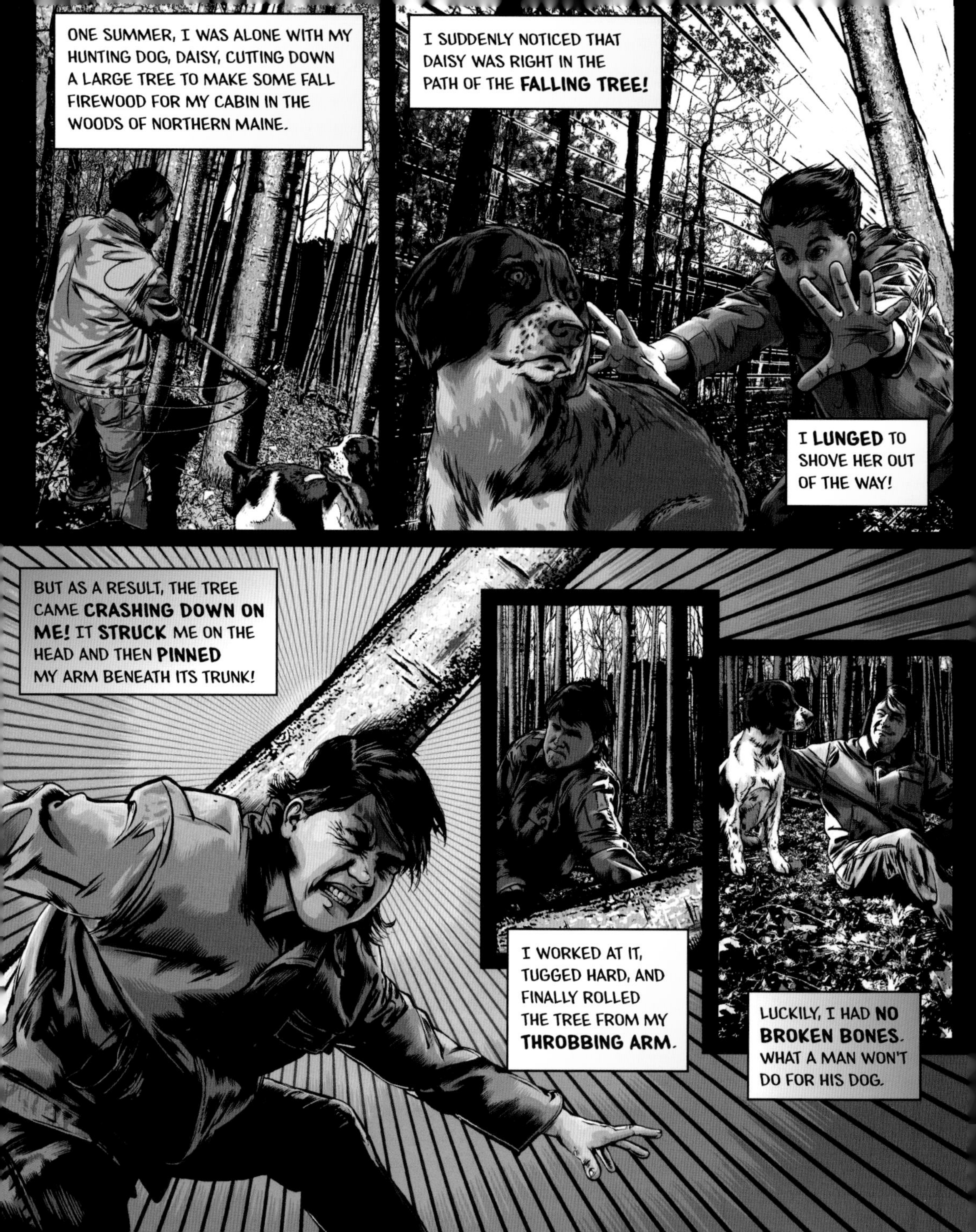
ONE SUMMER, I WAS ALONE WITH MY HUNTING DOG, DAISY, CUTTING DOWN A LARGE TREE TO MAKE SOME FALL FIREWOOD FOR MY CABIN IN THE WOODS OF NORTHERN MAINE.
I SUDDENLY NOTICED THAT DAISY WAS RIGHT IN THE PATH OF THE **FALLING TREE!**
I **LUNGED** TO SHOVE HER OUT OF THE WAY!
BUT AS A RESULT, THE TREE CAME **CRASHING DOWN ON ME!** IT **STRUCK** ME ON THE HEAD AND THEN **PINNED** MY ARM BENEATH ITS TRUNK!
I WORKED AT IT, TUGGED HARD, AND FINALLY ROLLED THE TREE FROM MY **THROBBING ARM**.
LUCKILY, I HAD **NO BROKEN BONES**. WHAT A MAN WON'T DO FOR HIS DOG.

"I've seen a look in dogs' eyes, a quickly vanishing look of amazed contempt, and I am convinced that basically dogs think humans are nuts."

—*John Steinbeck*

One Mean Machete // by John Tee, Baltimore, MD

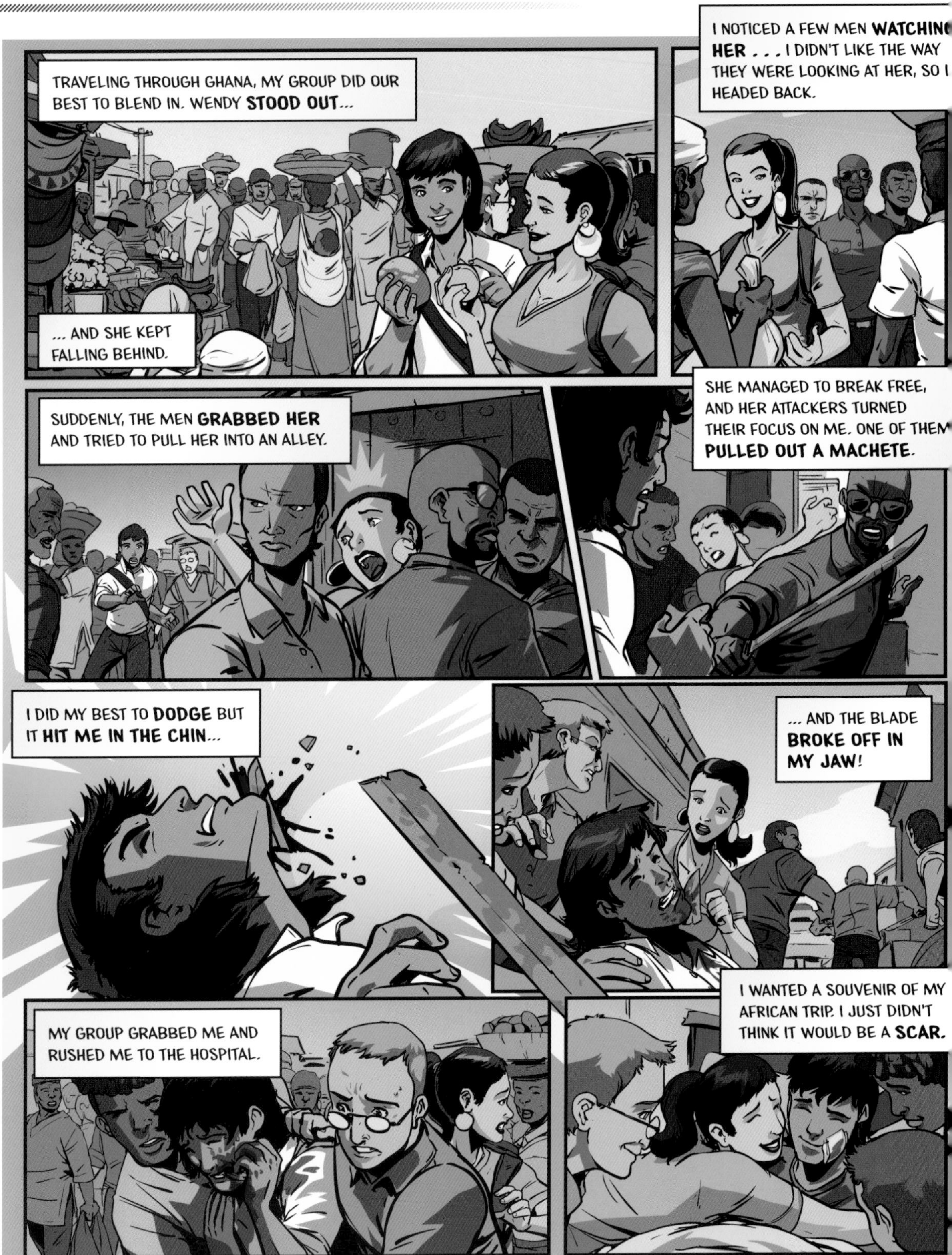
TRAVELING THROUGH GHANA, MY GROUP DID OUR BEST TO BLEND IN. WENDY STOOD OUT...
... AND SHE KEPT FALLING BEHIND.
I NOTICED A FEW MEN WATCHING HER . . . I DIDN'T LIKE THE WAY THEY WERE LOOKING AT HER, SO I HEADED BACK.
SUDDENLY, THE MEN GRABBED HER AND TRIED TO PULL HER INTO AN ALLEY.
SHE MANAGED TO BREAK FREE, AND HER ATTACKERS TURNED THEIR FOCUS ON ME. ONE OF THEM PULLED OUT A MACHETE.
I DID MY BEST TO DODGE BUT IT HIT ME IN THE CHIN...
... AND THE BLADE BROKE OFF IN MY JAW!
MY GROUP GRABBED ME AND RUSHED ME TO THE HOSPITAL.
I WANTED A SOUVENIR OF MY AFRICAN TRIP. I JUST DIDN'T THINK IT WOULD BE A SCAR.

Danger Abroad

HAVE A SAFE TRIP Vacations may be fun, but hitting the road and seeing the world doesn't mean taking a holiday from vigilance—quite the opposite in fact. Sure, you don't want to be a nervous Nelly, but then again you really don't want to wake up in a strange hotel room missing a kidney. So, follow these guidelines for happy, crime-free travels.

MAKE A COPY Before your departure, make copies of all important documents and keep them in multiple locations in case of emergency. Have an itinerary and share it with a trusted friend. Set check-in times. And if your itinerary changes, alert him or her immediately.

BE HOTEL SAFE No matter where you're staying, don't open the hotel door without using the peephole to see who's there—just like at home. Don't allow strangers into your room. Don't display your room keys in public—you don't want strangers knowing your room number.

STASH YOUR CASH Don't carry large quantities of cash or expensive jewelry with you, and don't keep all your valuables or currency together in one place. Any valuables you absolutely have to bring along should be stored in the hotel or room safe-deposit box, if possible.

DRESS DOWN Don't wear things that will easily mark you as a foreigner. For instance, if you're American, avoid wearing fanny packs, baseball caps, tennis shoes, and casual clothing with prominent brand names or logos. Instead, dress a little nicer than you might usually, and wear colors that correspond to those worn by the majority of the host population.

Preseason Plunge // by Glenn Osgood, Durham, ME

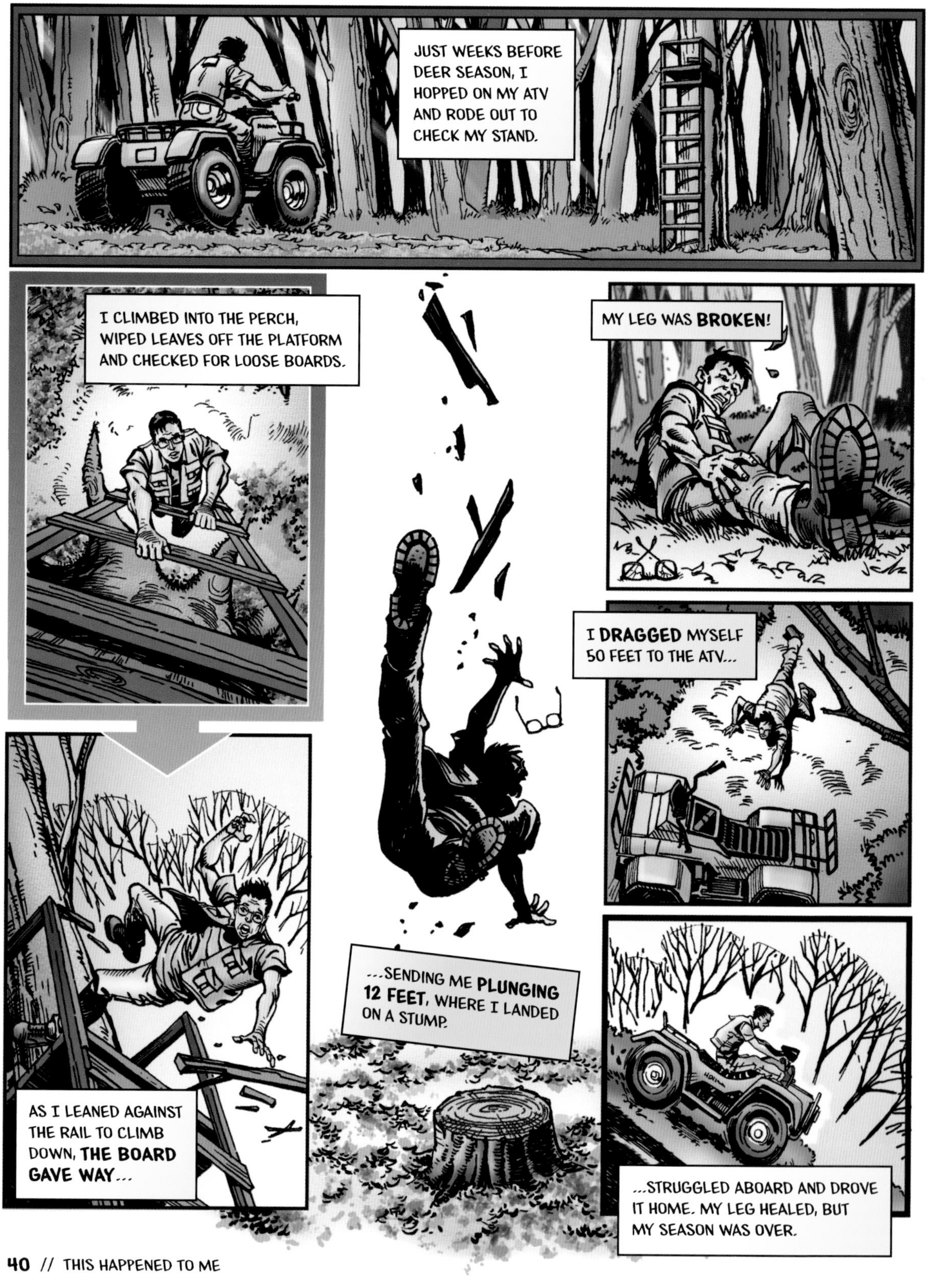
JUST WEEKS BEFORE DEER SEASON, I HOPPED ON MY ATV AND RODE OUT TO CHECK MY STAND.
I CLIMBED INTO THE PERCH, WIPED LEAVES OFF THE PLATFORM AND CHECKED FOR LOOSE BOARDS.
AS I LEANED AGAINST THE RAIL TO CLIMB DOWN, THE BOARD GAVE WAY...
...SENDING ME PLUNGING 12 FEET, WHERE I LANDED ON A STUMP.
MY LEG WAS BROKEN!
I DRAGGED MYSELF 50 FEET TO THE ATV...
...STRUGGLED ABOARD AND DROVE IT HOME. MY LEG HEALED, BUT MY SEASON WAS OVER.

Blown Off the Mountain! // by Ken Jones, Mesa, AZ

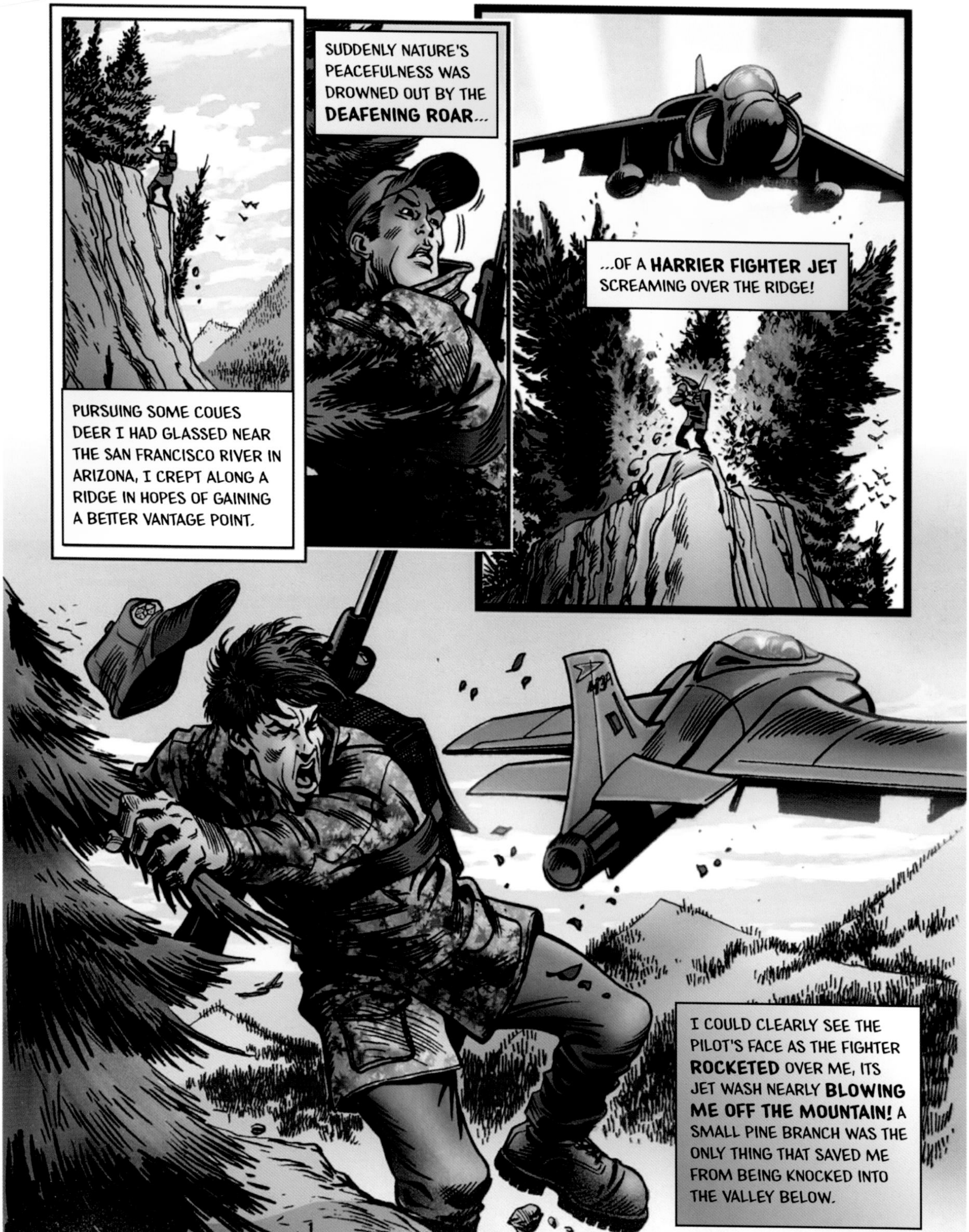

PURSUING SOME COUES DEER I HAD GLASSED NEAR THE SAN FRANCISCO RIVER IN ARIZONA, I CREPT ALONG A RIDGE IN HOPES OF GAINING A BETTER VANTAGE POINT.
SUDDENLY NATURE'S PEACEFULNESS WAS DROWNED OUT BY THE **DEAFENING ROAR**...
...OF A **HARRIER FIGHTER JET** SCREAMING OVER THE RIDGE!
I COULD CLEARLY SEE THE PILOT'S FACE AS THE FIGHTER **ROCKETED** OVER ME, ITS JET WASH NEARLY **BLOWING ME OFF THE MOUNTAIN!** A SMALL PINE BRANCH WAS THE ONLY THING THAT SAVED ME FROM BEING KNOCKED INTO THE VALLEY BELOW.

"You know horses are smarter than people. You never heard of a horse going broke betting on people."

—*Will Rogers*

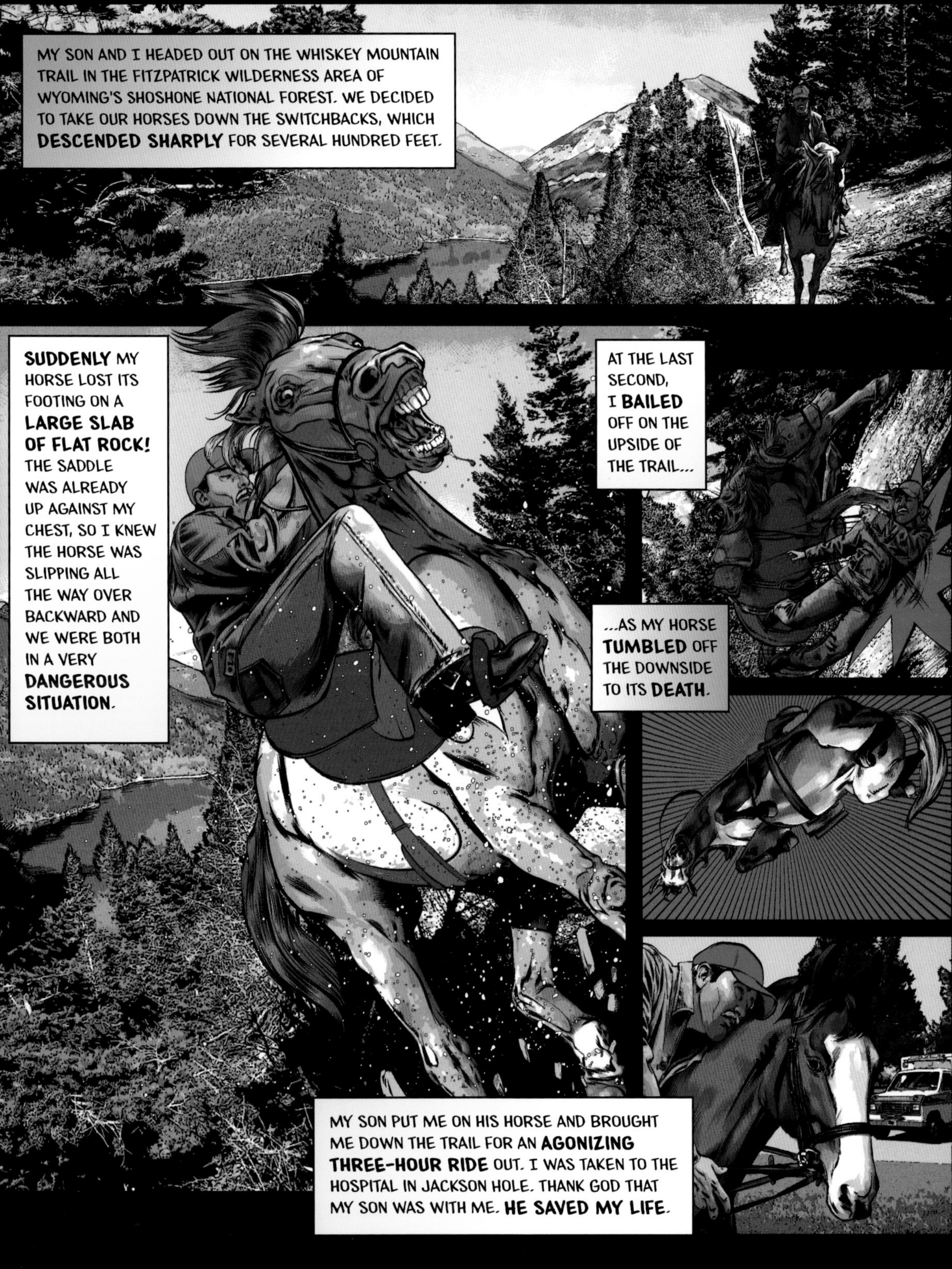
MY SON AND I HEADED OUT ON THE WHISKEY MOUNTAIN TRAIL IN THE FITZPATRICK WILDERNESS AREA OF WYOMING'S SHOSHONE NATIONAL FOREST. WE DECIDED TO TAKE OUR HORSES DOWN THE SWITCHBACKS, WHICH DESCENDED SHARPLY FOR SEVERAL HUNDRED FEET.
SUDDENLY MY HORSE LOST ITS FOOTING ON A LARGE SLAB OF FLAT ROCK! THE SADDLE WAS ALREADY UP AGAINST MY CHEST, SO I KNEW THE HORSE WAS SLIPPING ALL THE WAY OVER BACKWARD AND WE WERE BOTH IN A VERY DANGEROUS SITUATION.
AT THE LAST SECOND, I BAILED OFF ON THE UPSIDE OF THE TRAIL...
...AS MY HORSE TUMBLED OFF THE DOWNSIDE TO ITS DEATH.
MY SON PUT ME ON HIS HORSE AND BROUGHT ME DOWN THE TRAIL FOR AN AGONIZING THREE-HOUR RIDE OUT. I WAS TAKEN TO THE HOSPITAL IN JACKSON HOLE. THANK GOD THAT MY SON WAS WITH ME. HE SAVED MY LIFE.

Shock Gobblers // by James Wilson, Summerville, WV

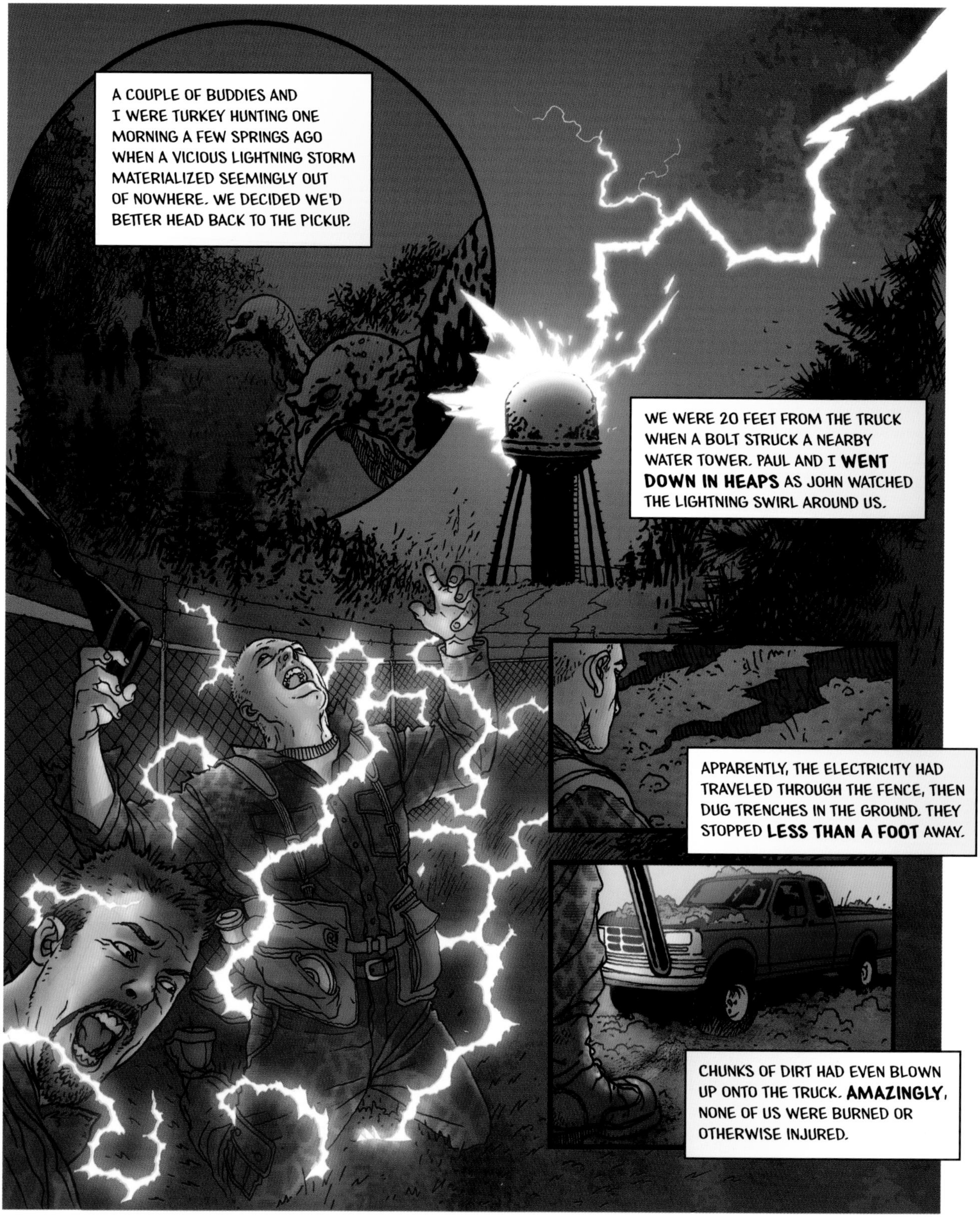

A COUPLE OF BUDDIES AND I WERE TURKEY HUNTING ONE MORNING A FEW SPRINGS AGO WHEN A VICIOUS LIGHTNING STORM MATERIALIZED SEEMINGLY OUT OF NOWHERE. WE DECIDED WE'D BETTER HEAD BACK TO THE PICKUP.
WE WERE 20 FEET FROM THE TRUCK WHEN A BOLT STRUCK A NEARBY WATER TOWER. PAUL AND I **WENT DOWN IN HEAPS** AS JOHN WATCHED THE LIGHTNING SWIRL AROUND US.
APPARENTLY, THE ELECTRICITY HAD TRAVELED THROUGH THE FENCE, THEN DUG TRENCHES IN THE GROUND. THEY STOPPED **LESS THAN A FOOT** AWAY.
CHUNKS OF DIRT HAD EVEN BLOWN UP ONTO THE TRUCK. **AMAZINGLY**, NONE OF US WERE BURNED OR OTHERWISE INJURED.

It's Electrifying!

HIGH VOLTAGE The shocking truth about lightning is that it can travel 140,000 miles per hour—and the bolt's temperature can reach 54,000 °F. But if you're caught in a lightning storm, there are a few steps you can take to save your bacon—or, more accurately, to keep yourself from turning into bacon.

LISTEN FOR TROUBLE BREWING Sometimes lightning strikes without warning, but often there's a big, rumbling tip-off: The sound of thunder. As a storm approaches, thunder lags behind lightning about five seconds for each mile of distance. If you spot lightning, and thunder reaches you ten seconds later, the strike was about 2 miles away. That might sound reassuring, but it's not. A storm can move up to 8 miles between strikes, so you're definitely going to be in the danger zone.

SEEK SHELTER If you can't take shelter, at least head to low ground. Try to avoid water, open fields, and metal objects—especially tall ones like flagpoles. As for trees, standing by a lone tree is a no-no, but sheltering in a stand of trees will bring up your odds of survival.

LOSE THE BLING At the first signs of thunder and lightning, remove all metal objects and jewelry from your body.

HEED THE FINAL WARNING If your hair stands on end or you hear crackling noises, place your feet together, duck your head down, and crouch low with your hands on your knees.

GET LOW If you have one, put an insulating layer like a blanket on the ground, then crouch on it, keeping your hands off the ground to help the strike flow over your body rather than through it. This position is tough to maintain, so think of it as a last-resort move when a strike seems imminent.

Home Invasion // by Jennie James, San Jose, CA

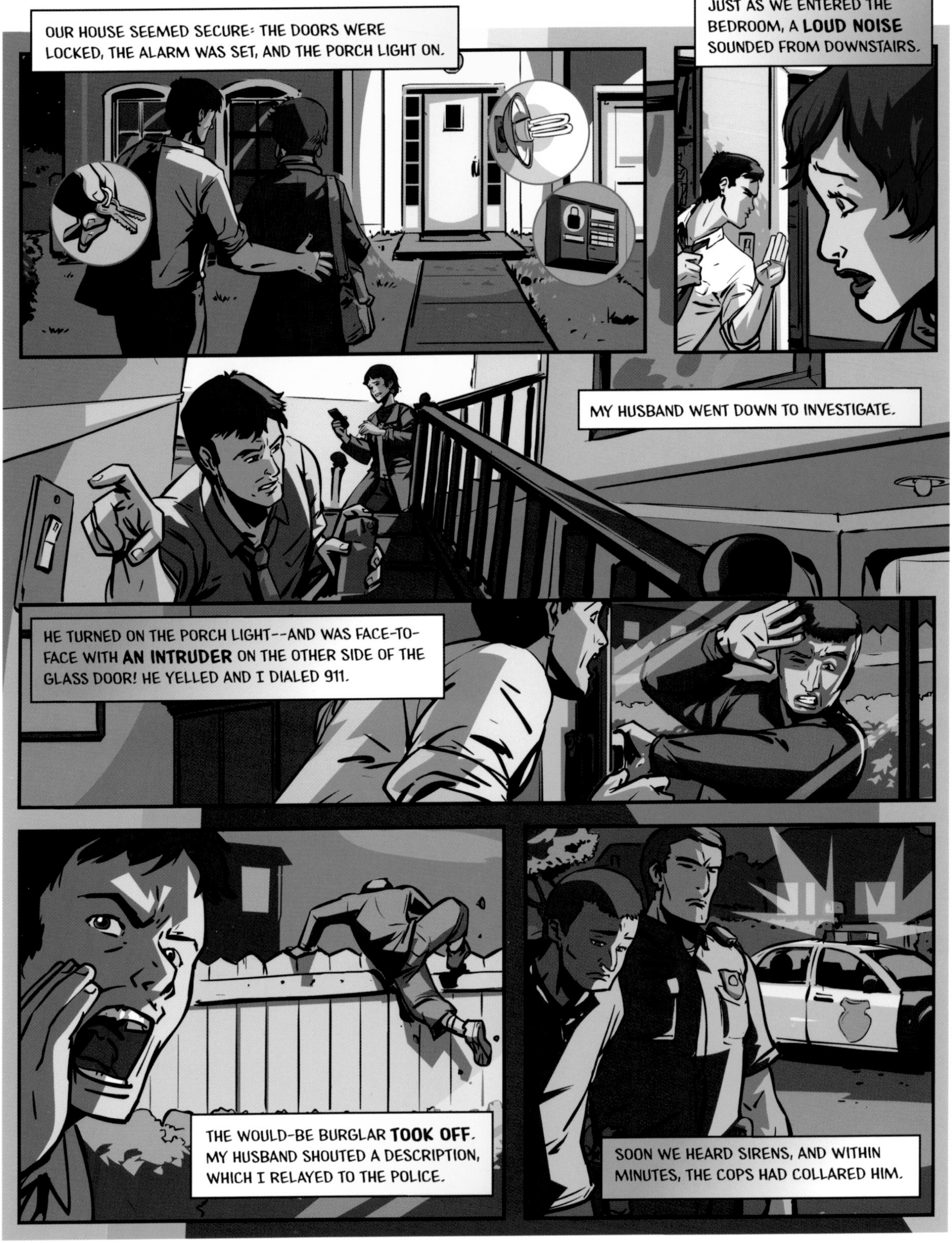
OUR HOUSE SEEMED SECURE: THE DOORS WERE LOCKED, THE ALARM WAS SET, AND THE PORCH LIGHT ON.
JUST AS WE ENTERED THE BEDROOM, A **LOUD NOISE** SOUNDED FROM DOWNSTAIRS.
MY HUSBAND WENT DOWN TO INVESTIGATE.
HE TURNED ON THE PORCH LIGHT--AND WAS FACE-TO-FACE WITH **AN INTRUDER** ON THE OTHER SIDE OF THE GLASS DOOR! HE YELLED AND I DIALED 911.
THE WOULD-BE BURGLAR **TOOK OFF**. MY HUSBAND SHOUTED A DESCRIPTION, WHICH I RELAYED TO THE POLICE.
SOON WE HEARD SIRENS, AND WITHIN MINUTES, THE COPS HAD COLLARED HIM.

KNOW THE NUMBERS:
Home Safety

1 IN 36 Homes in the United States that were broken into and burglarized in 2012.

$2,100 Average value of goods stolen in a burglary.

28% Proportion of home burglaries that have occurred while the house is occupied.

2.2 MILLION Number of burglaries that occur in the United States every year.

60 SECONDS Maximum time taken by the average burglar to break into a house.

Chainsaw Massacre

BUCK UP THERE, BUDDY If you spend enough time in the great outdoors, you're probably going to end up facing a downed tree, armed with only a chainsaw and a vague knowledge of physics. What you want to do here is make like a lumberjack and use the proper technique to cut up a tree on the ground—a process called bucking.

STRIP IT DOWN Your first step is to remove all major branches as close to the trunk as possible. Then, brace the underside of the tree with pieces of wood to keep it stable and off the ground.

CHOP IT UP Standing uphill from the tree, start by cutting the underside of the trunk about one-third of the way through with a chainsaw. Then come back to the top side and finish the cut so it runs all the way through the trunk.

FINISH RIGHT Gravity should pull that trunk section off the tree, but if your saw gets stuck in the cut, shut it off right away. Drive a wedge into the cut to loosen the tension, and then remove the saw. Follow all these steps and you can avoid being "that guy" ... the one the emergency room docs tell stories about. The one with the nickname "Stumpy."

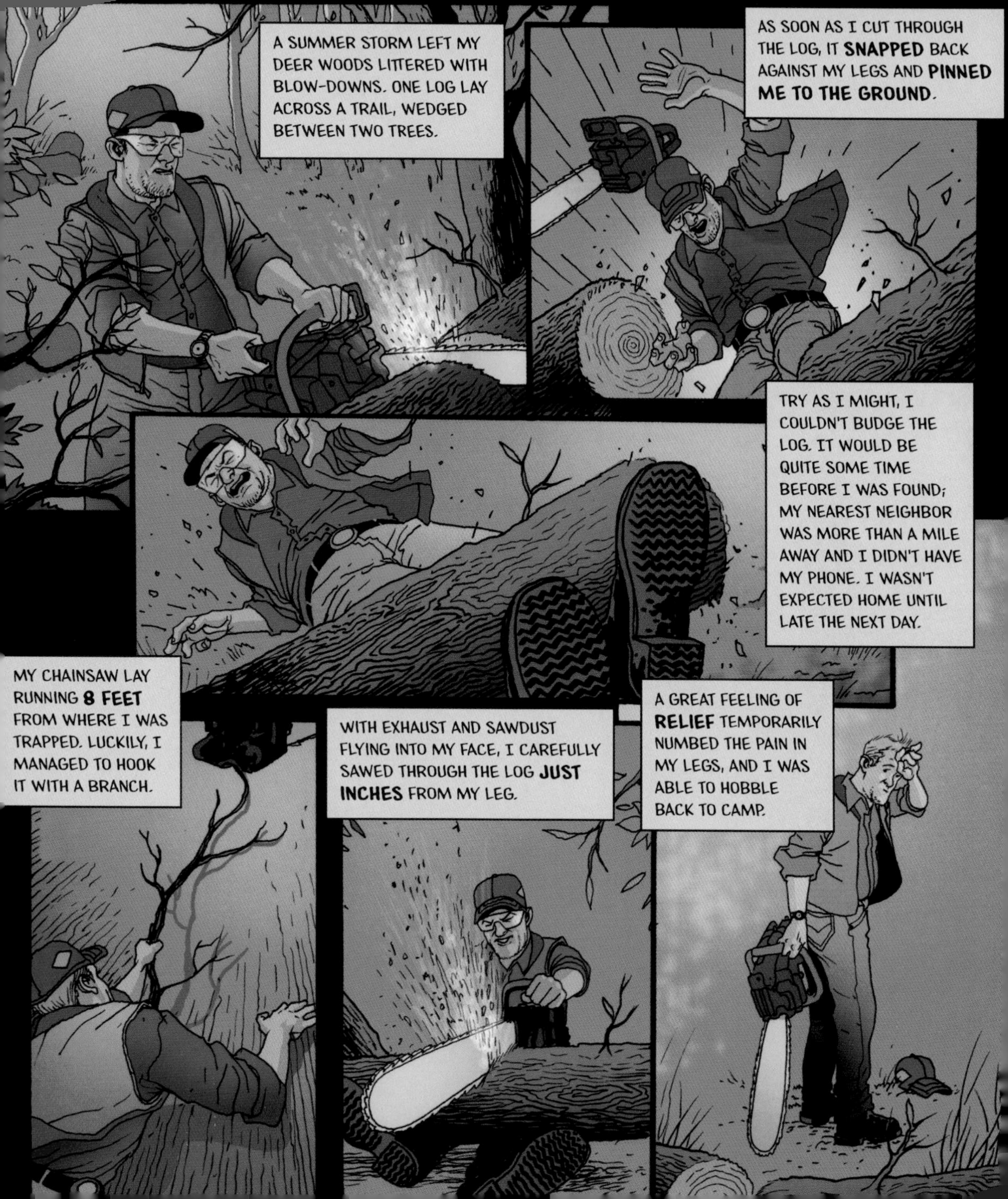
A SUMMER STORM LEFT MY DEER WOODS LITTERED WITH BLOW-DOWNS. ONE LOG LAY ACROSS A TRAIL, WEDGED BETWEEN TWO TREES.
AS SOON AS I CUT THROUGH THE LOG, IT **SNAPPED** BACK AGAINST MY LEGS AND **PINNED ME TO THE GROUND**.
TRY AS I MIGHT, I COULDN'T BUDGE THE LOG. IT WOULD BE QUITE SOME TIME BEFORE I WAS FOUND; MY NEAREST NEIGHBOR WAS MORE THAN A MILE AWAY AND I DIDN'T HAVE MY PHONE. I WASN'T EXPECTED HOME UNTIL LATE THE NEXT DAY.
MY CHAINSAW LAY RUNNING **8 FEET** FROM WHERE I WAS TRAPPED. LUCKILY, I MANAGED TO HOOK IT WITH A BRANCH.
WITH EXHAUST AND SAWDUST FLYING INTO MY FACE, I CAREFULLY SAWED THROUGH THE LOG **JUST INCHES** FROM MY LEG.
A GREAT FEELING OF **RELIEF** TEMPORARILY NUMBED THE PAIN IN MY LEGS, AND I WAS ABLE TO HOBBLE BACK TO CAMP.

Branching Out // by Rick Pellegrini, Palatine, IL

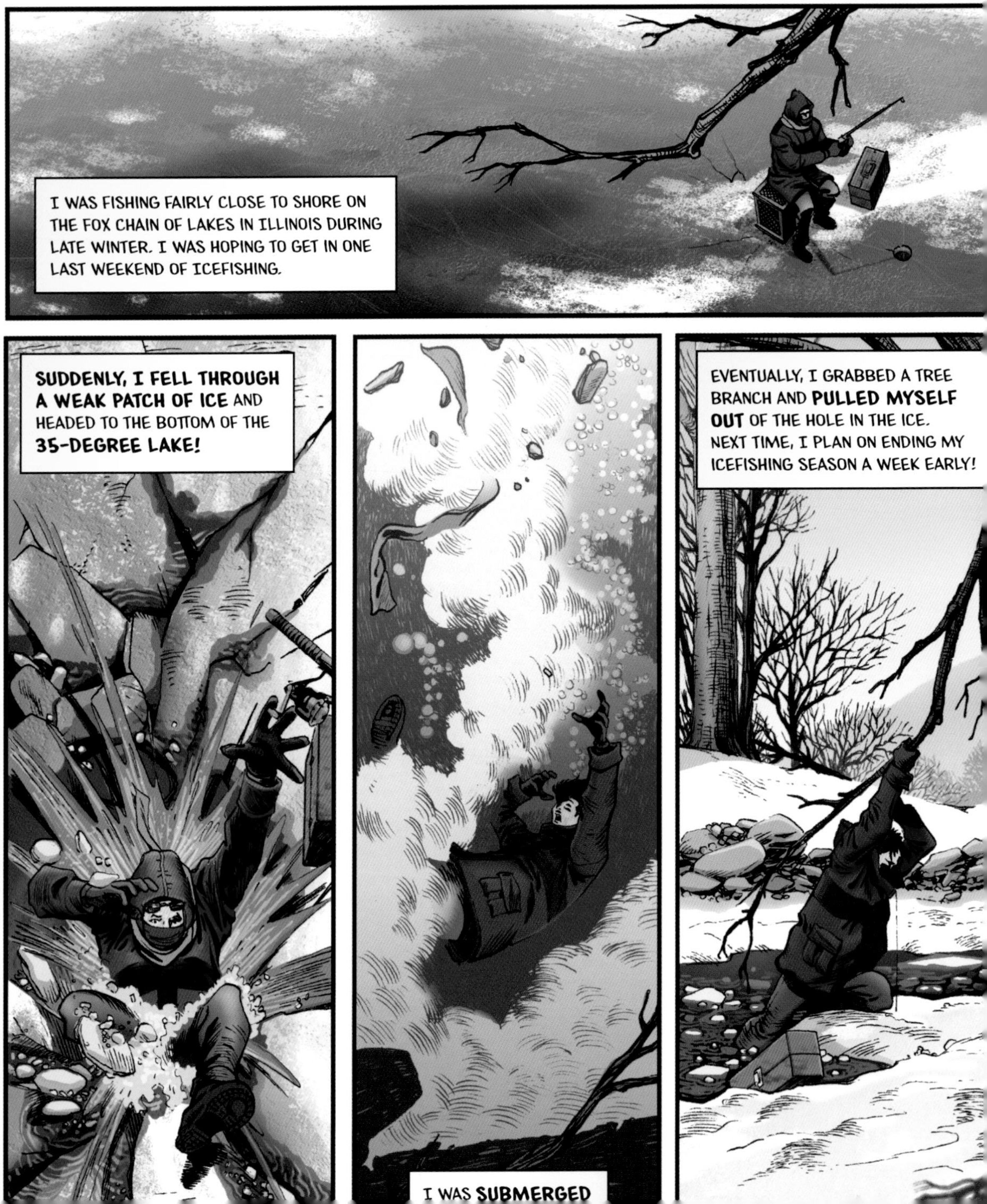
I WAS FISHING FAIRLY CLOSE TO SHORE ON THE FOX CHAIN OF LAKES IN ILLINOIS DURING LATE WINTER. I WAS HOPING TO GET IN ONE LAST WEEKEND OF ICEFISHING.
SUDDENLY, I FELL THROUGH A WEAK PATCH OF ICE AND HEADED TO THE BOTTOM OF THE 35-DEGREE LAKE!
I WAS SUBMERGED
EVENTUALLY, I GRABBED A TREE BRANCH AND PULLED MYSELF OUT OF THE HOLE IN THE ICE. NEXT TIME, I PLAN ON ENDING MY ICEFISHING SEASON A WEEK EARLY!

"**The thinner the ice, the more anxious everyone is to see whether it will bear.**"

—*Josh Billings*

The Alaskan Tent Trample // by Arthur Lenon, Delta Junction, AK

I WAS CAMPING WITH FRIENDS AT PAXSON LAKE, IN ALASKA. WE SET UP A TENT AT A CAMPSITE AND SETTLED IN FOR THE NIGHT.

I WAS AWAKENED WHEN MY TENT BEGAN **SHAKING!** I THOUGHT IT WAS THE WIND, BUT THEN IT BEGAN TO SHAKE EVEN MORE.

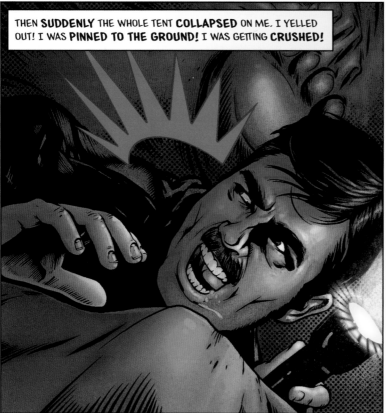

THEN **SUDDENLY** THE WHOLE TENT **COLLAPSED** ON ME. I YELLED OUT! I WAS **PINNED TO THE GROUND!** I WAS GETTING **CRUSHED!**

FINALLY THE WEIGHT LET UP. I EMERGED TO FIND THAT THE TENT POLES WERE ALL BENT. MY WHOLE BODY WAS **THROBBING**, AND I SAW **GRIZZLY TRACKS** LEADING AWAY FROM MY TENT!

Barrel Peril // by Billy R. Hales, Winnsboro, LA

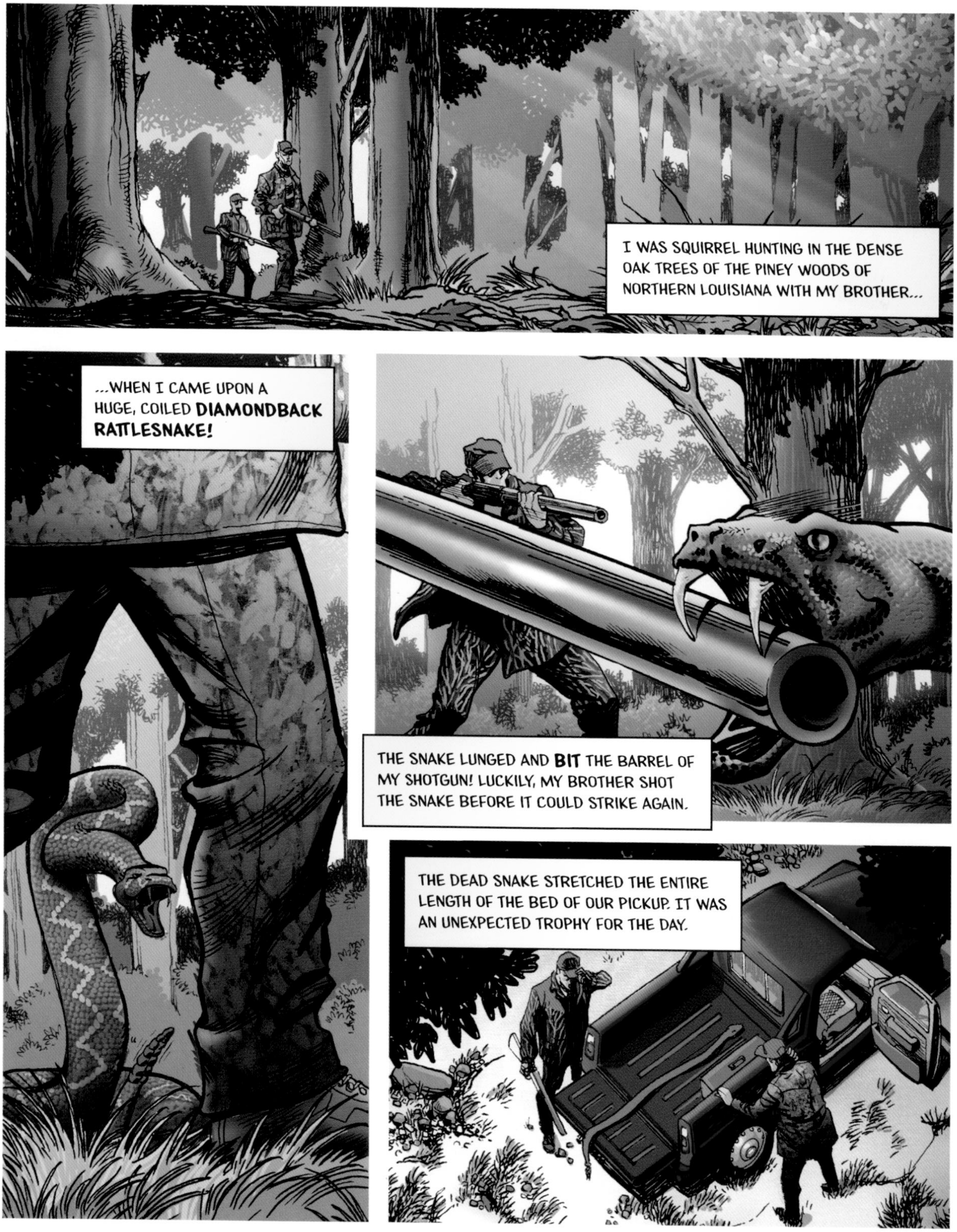
I WAS SQUIRREL HUNTING IN THE DENSE OAK TREES OF THE PINEY WOODS OF NORTHERN LOUISIANA WITH MY BROTHER...
...WHEN I CAME UPON A HUGE, COILED **DIAMONDBACK RATTLESNAKE!**
THE SNAKE LUNGED AND **BIT** THE BARREL OF MY SHOTGUN! LUCKILY, MY BROTHER SHOT THE SNAKE BEFORE IT COULD STRIKE AGAIN.
THE DEAD SNAKE STRETCHED THE ENTIRE LENGTH OF THE BED OF OUR PICKUP. IT WAS AN UNEXPECTED TROPHY FOR THE DAY.

CHAPTER TWO
WHEN

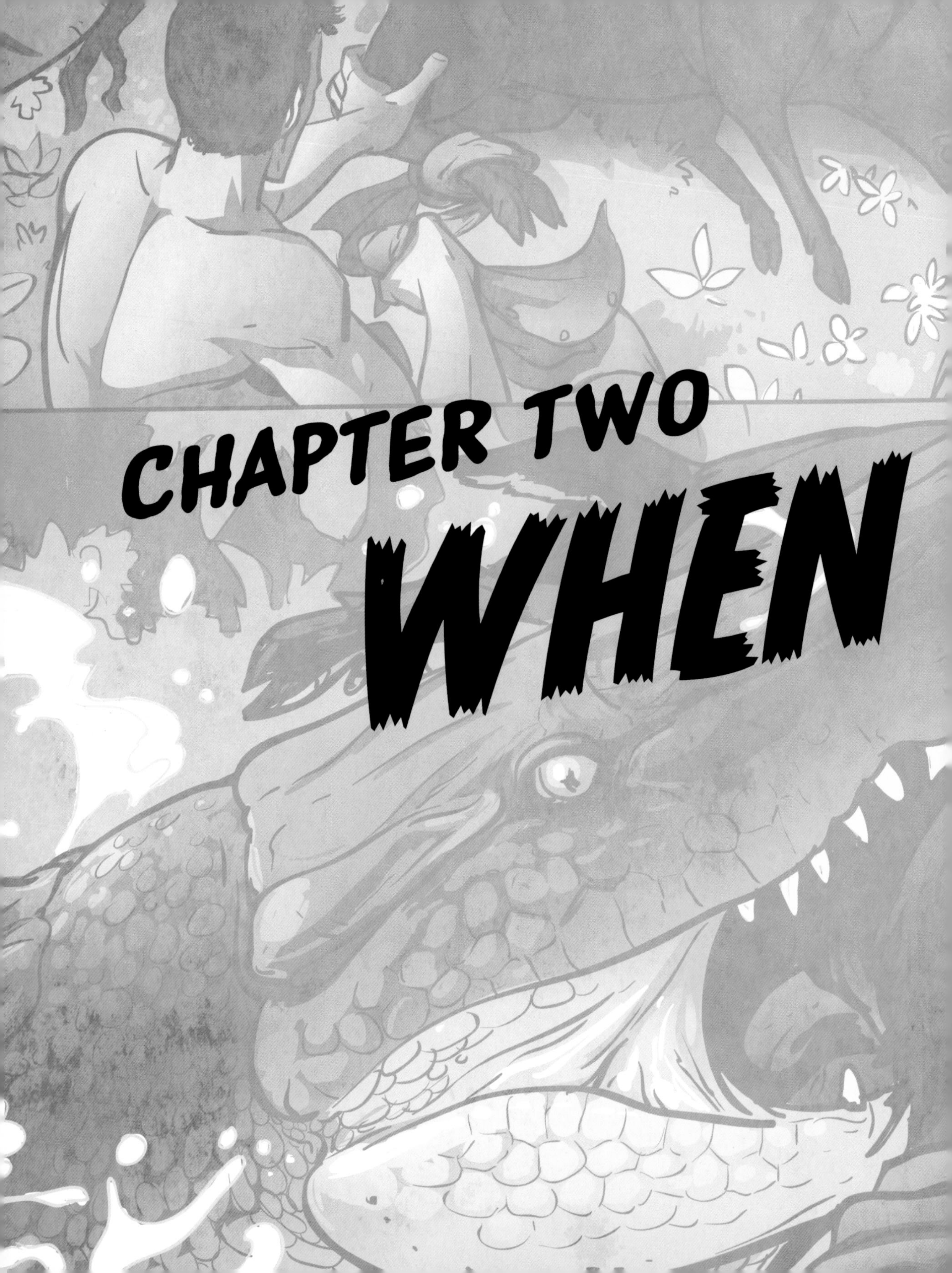

ANIMALS ATTACK

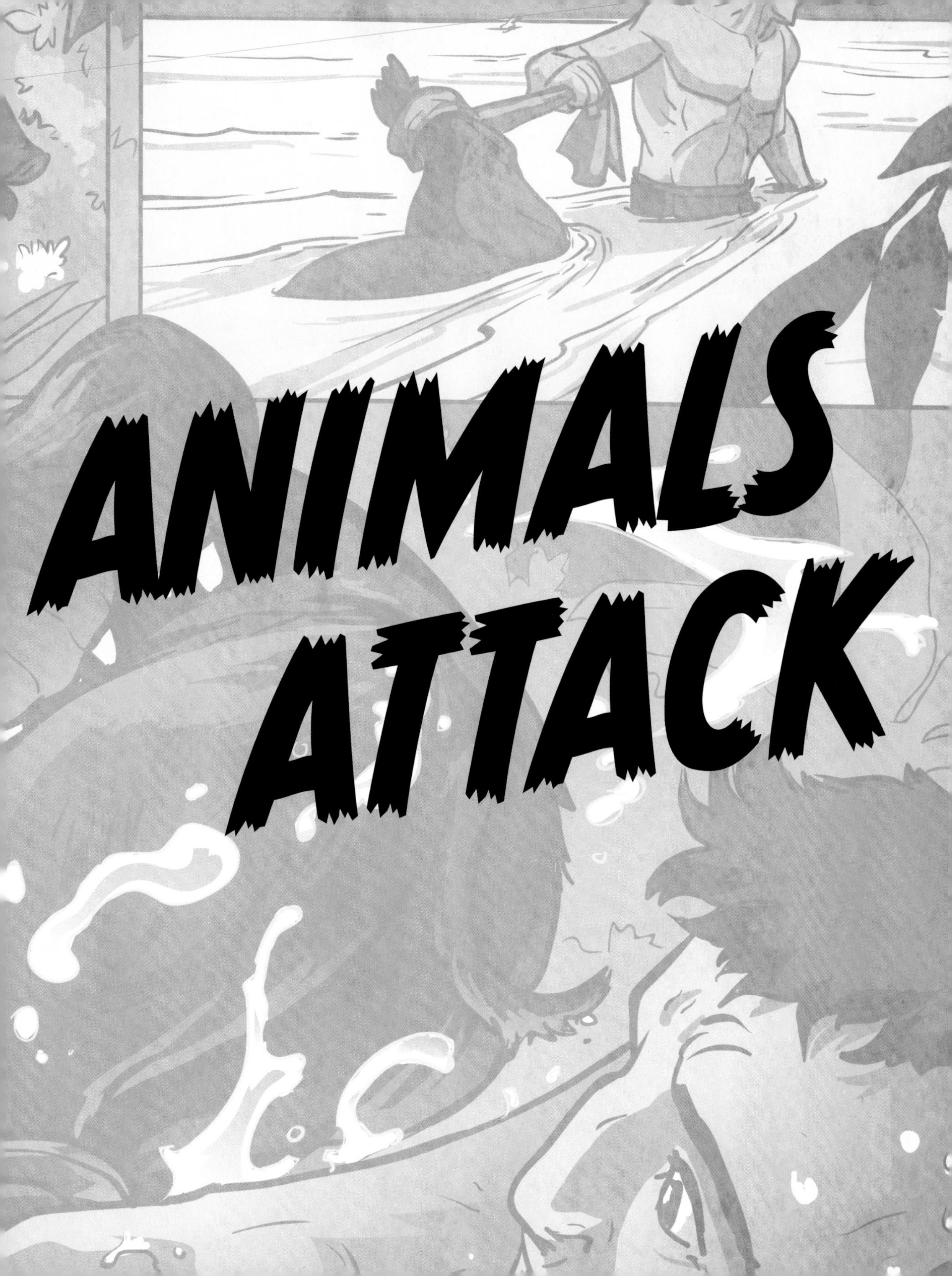

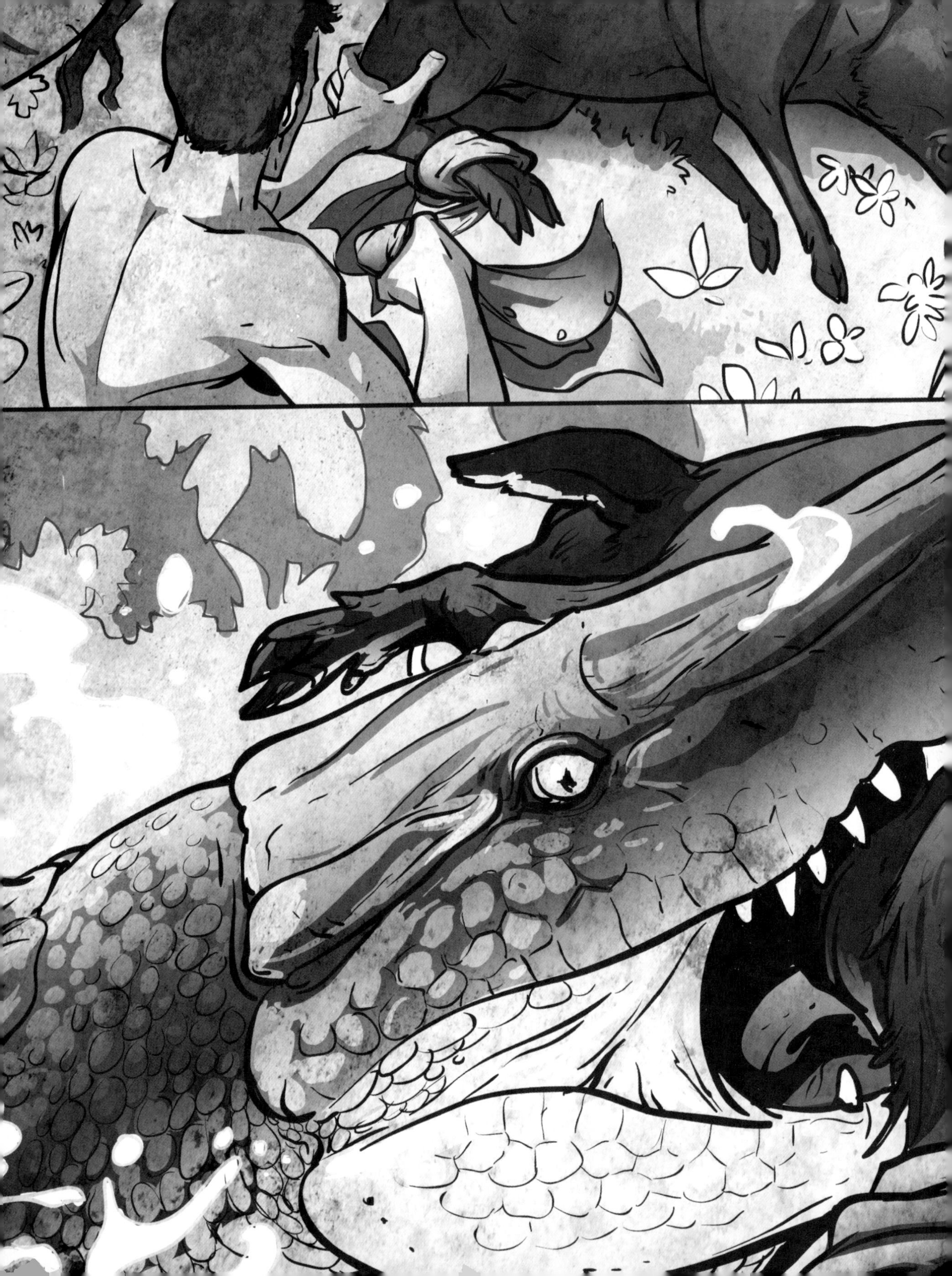

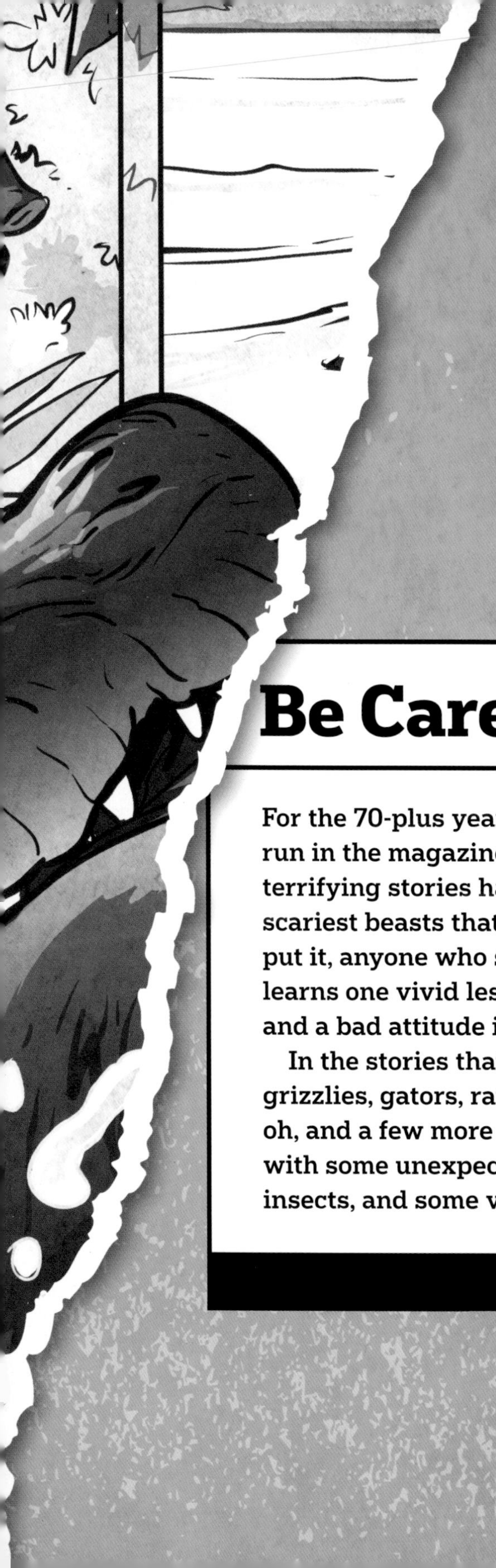

Be Careful!

For the 70-plus years that "This Happened to Me" has run in the magazine, the most consistently exciting and terrifying stories have involved run-ins with the biggest, scariest beasts that nature has to offer. As one writer put it, anyone who survives an encounter with a grizzly learns one vivid lesson: A half-ton Rototiller with claws and a bad attitude is nothing to mess with.

In the stories that follow, brave souls cross paths with grizzlies, gators, rattlesnakes, wild boars, cougars . . . oh, and a few more grizzlies. They also learn not to mess with some unexpected natural terrors, including otters, insects, and some very feisty fish.

What a Croc! // by Captain David F. Harbour, St. Cloud, MN

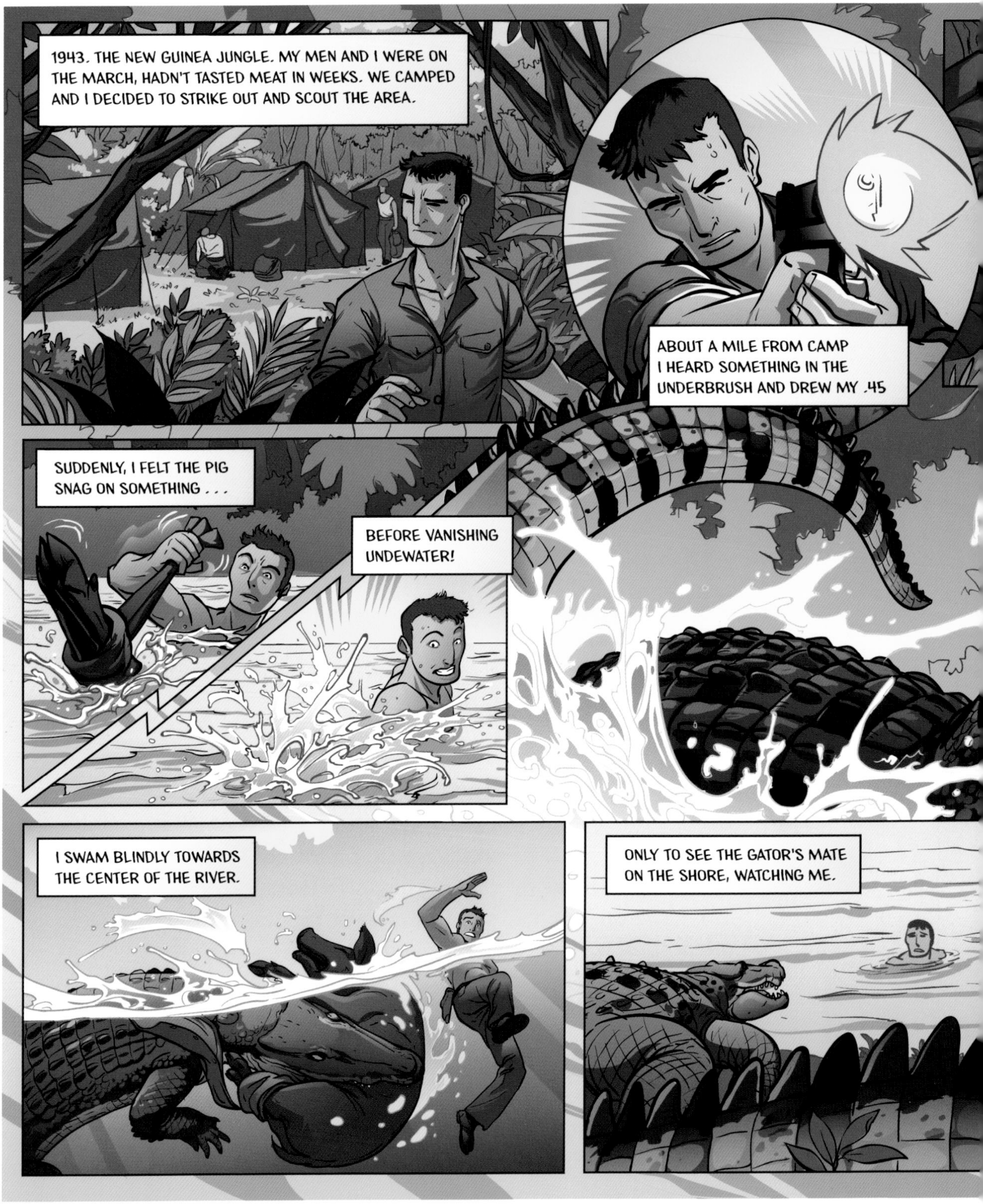

1943. THE NEW GUINEA JUNGLE. MY MEN AND I WERE ON THE MARCH, HADN'T TASTED MEAT IN WEEKS. WE CAMPED AND I DECIDED TO STRIKE OUT AND SCOUT THE AREA.
ABOUT A MILE FROM CAMP I HEARD SOMETHING IN THE UNDERBRUSH AND DREW MY .45
SUDDENLY, I FELT THE PIG SNAG ON SOMETHING . . .
BEFORE VANISHING UNDEWATER!
I SWAM BLINDLY TOWARDS THE CENTER OF THE RIVER.
ONLY TO SEE THE GATOR'S MATE ON THE SHORE, WATCHING ME.

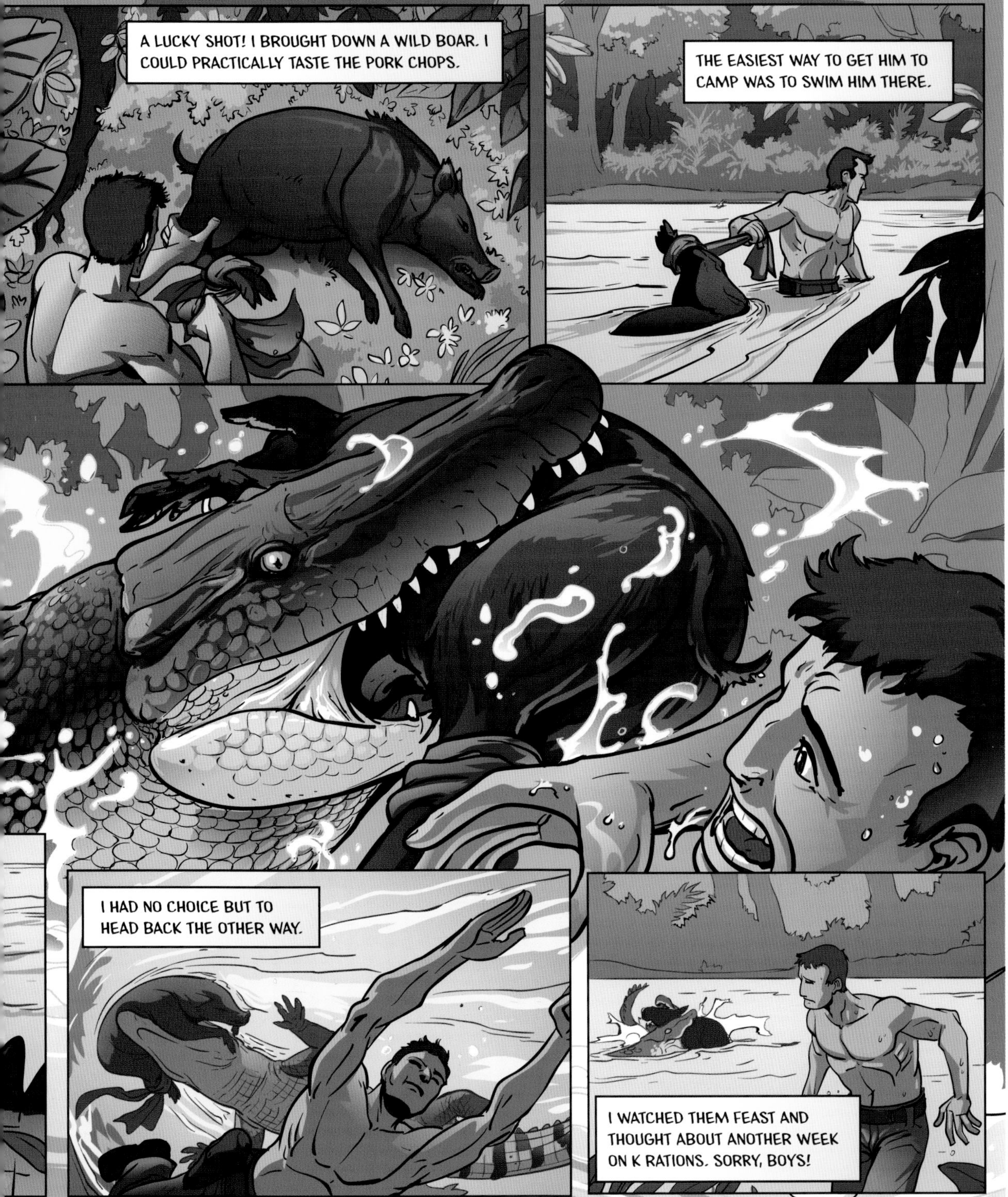
A LUCKY SHOT! I BROUGHT DOWN A WILD BOAR. I COULD PRACTICALLY TASTE THE PORK CHOPS.
THE EASIEST WAY TO GET HIM TO CAMP WAS TO SWIM HIM THERE.
I HAD NO CHOICE BUT TO HEAD BACK THE OTHER WAY.
I WATCHED THEM FEAST AND THOUGHT ABOUT ANOTHER WEEK ON K RATIONS. SORRY, BOYS!

A Nose Job! // by David Ogden, Abbeville, SC

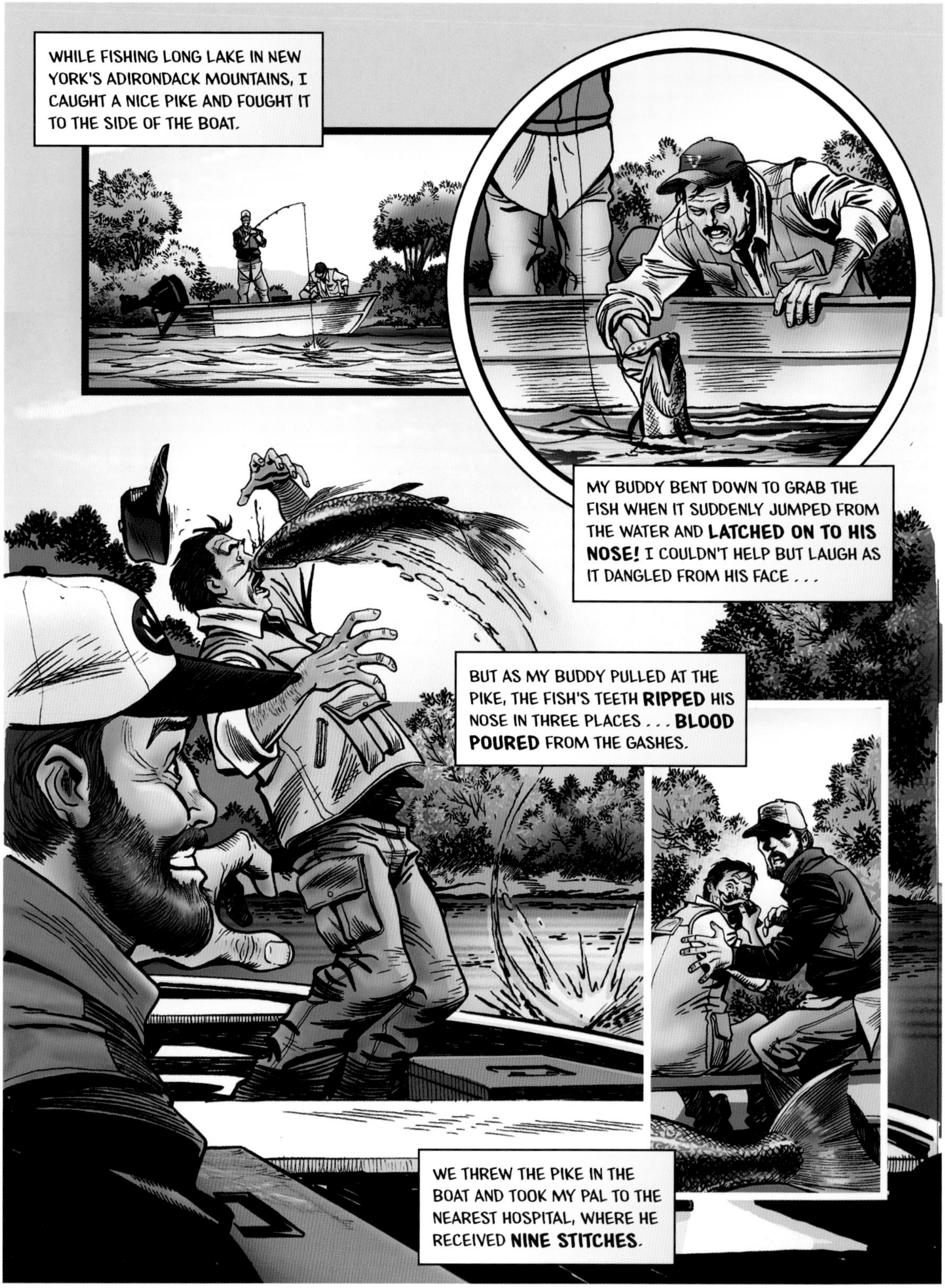
WHILE FISHING LONG LAKE IN NEW YORK'S ADIRONDACK MOUNTAINS, I CAUGHT A NICE PIKE AND FOUGHT IT TO THE SIDE OF THE BOAT.
MY BUDDY BENT DOWN TO GRAB THE FISH WHEN IT SUDDENLY JUMPED FROM THE WATER AND LATCHED ON TO HIS NOSE! I COULDN'T HELP BUT LAUGH AS IT DANGLED FROM HIS FACE . . .
BUT AS MY BUDDY PULLED AT THE PIKE, THE FISH'S TEETH RIPPED HIS NOSE IN THREE PLACES . . . BLOOD POURED FROM THE GASHES.
WE THREW THE PIKE IN THE BOAT AND TOOK MY PAL TO THE NEAREST HOSPITAL, WHERE HE RECEIVED NINE STITCHES.

"Don't tell fish stories where the people know you; but particularly, don't tell them where they know the fish."

—*Mark Twain*

Stinky Situation // by Daryl Frysinger, Forest, OH

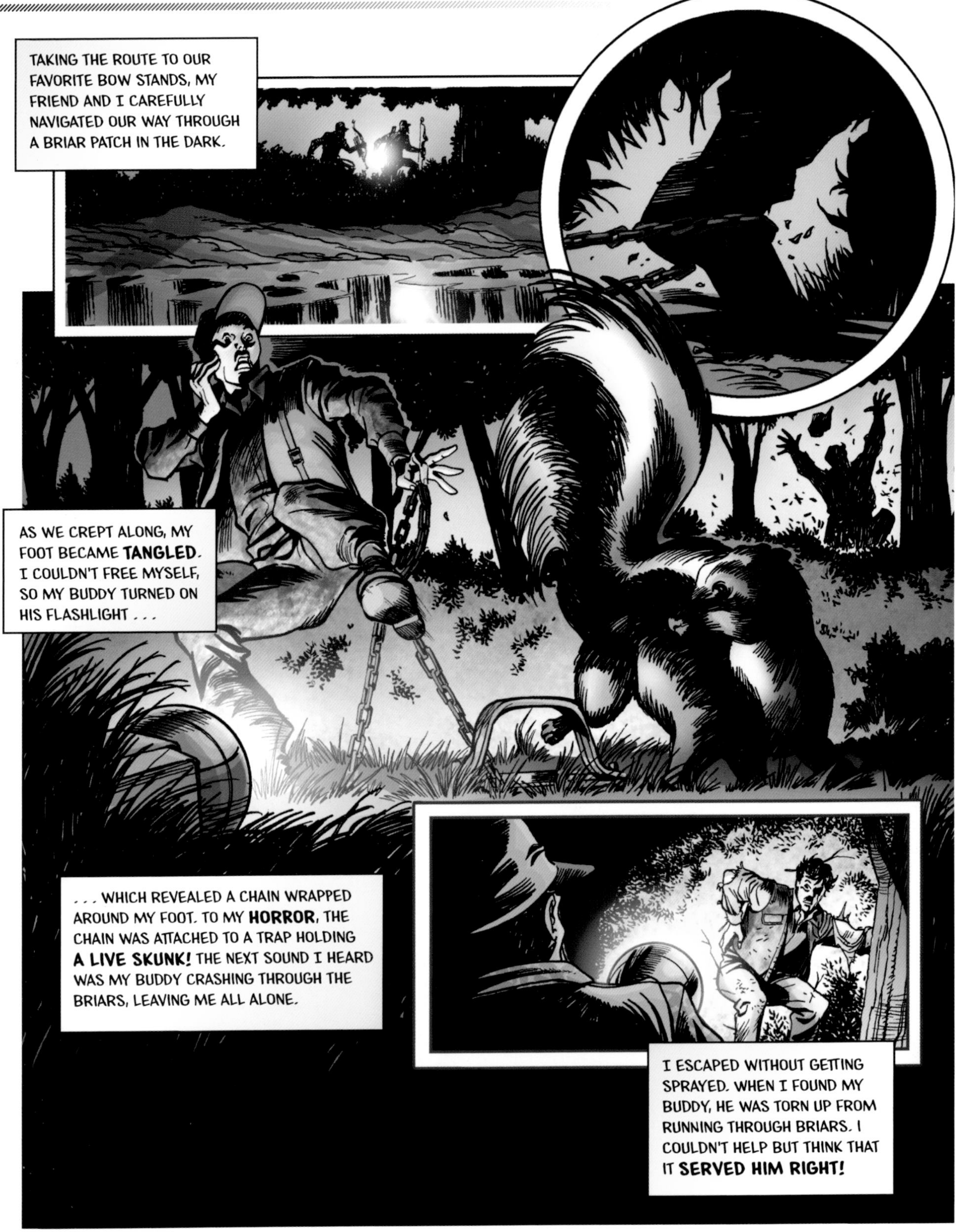
TAKING THE ROUTE TO OUR FAVORITE BOW STANDS, MY FRIEND AND I CAREFULLY NAVIGATED OUR WAY THROUGH A BRIAR PATCH IN THE DARK.
AS WE CREPT ALONG, MY FOOT BECAME **TANGLED**. I COULDN'T FREE MYSELF, SO MY BUDDY TURNED ON HIS FLASHLIGHT . . .
. . . WHICH REVEALED A CHAIN WRAPPED AROUND MY FOOT. TO MY **HORROR**, THE CHAIN WAS ATTACHED TO A TRAP HOLDING **A LIVE SKUNK!** THE NEXT SOUND I HEARD WAS MY BUDDY CRASHING THROUGH THE BRIARS, LEAVING ME ALL ALONE.
I ESCAPED WITHOUT GETTING SPRAYED. WHEN I FOUND MY BUDDY, HE WAS TORN UP FROM RUNNING THROUGH BRIARS. I COULDN'T HELP BUT THINK THAT IT **SERVED HIM RIGHT!**

Rude Awakening // by Bob Hertz, Stevens Point, WI

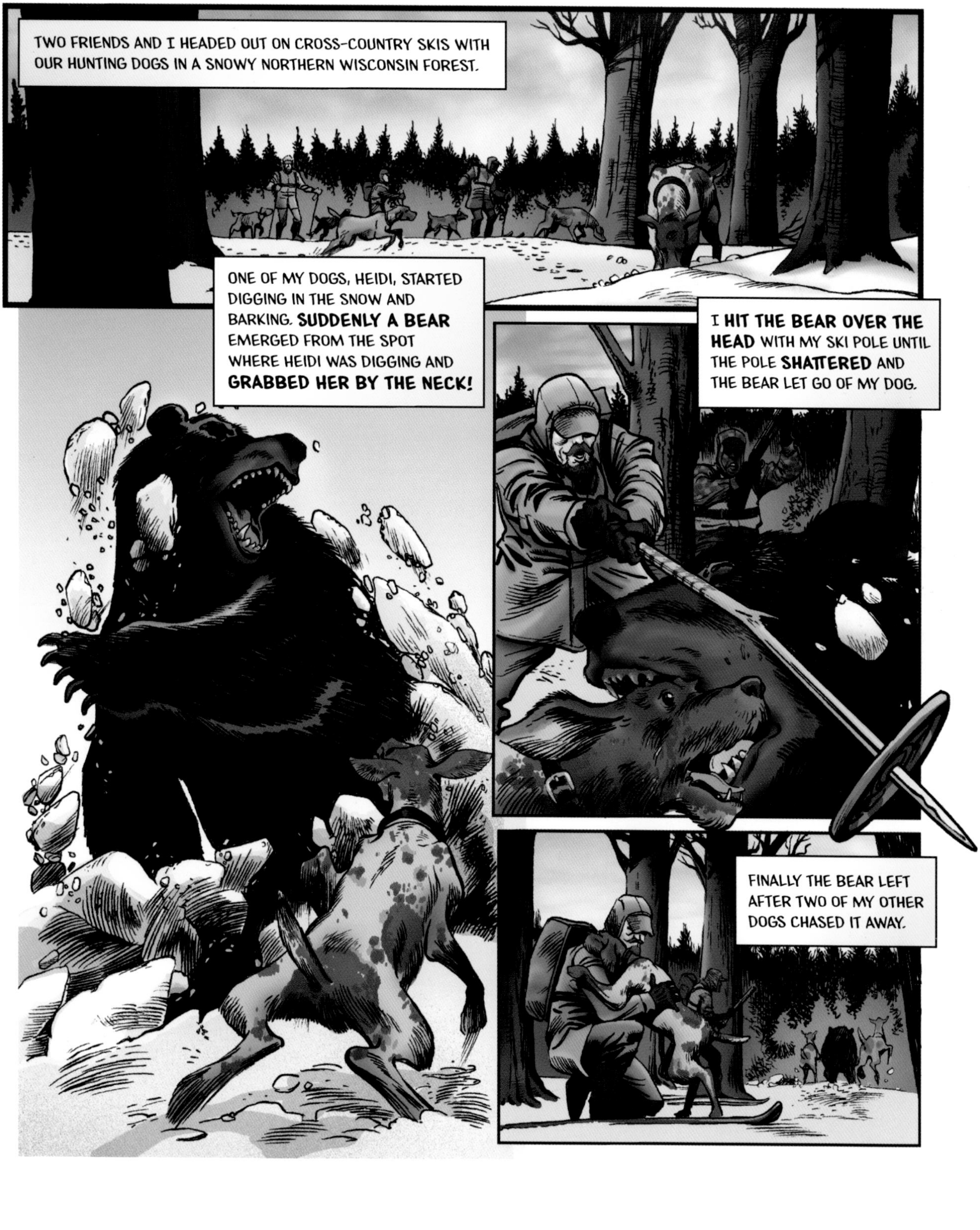

TWO FRIENDS AND I HEADED OUT ON CROSS-COUNTRY SKIS WITH OUR HUNTING DOGS IN A SNOWY NORTHERN WISCONSIN FOREST.
ONE OF MY DOGS, HEIDI, STARTED DIGGING IN THE SNOW AND BARKING. **SUDDENLY A BEAR** EMERGED FROM THE SPOT WHERE HEIDI WAS DIGGING AND **GRABBED HER BY THE NECK!**
I **HIT THE BEAR OVER THE HEAD** WITH MY SKI POLE UNTIL THE POLE **SHATTERED** AND THE BEAR LET GO OF MY DOG.
FINALLY THE BEAR LEFT AFTER TWO OF MY OTHER DOGS CHASED IT AWAY.

Never Boaring // by Marcus Field, Tampa, FL

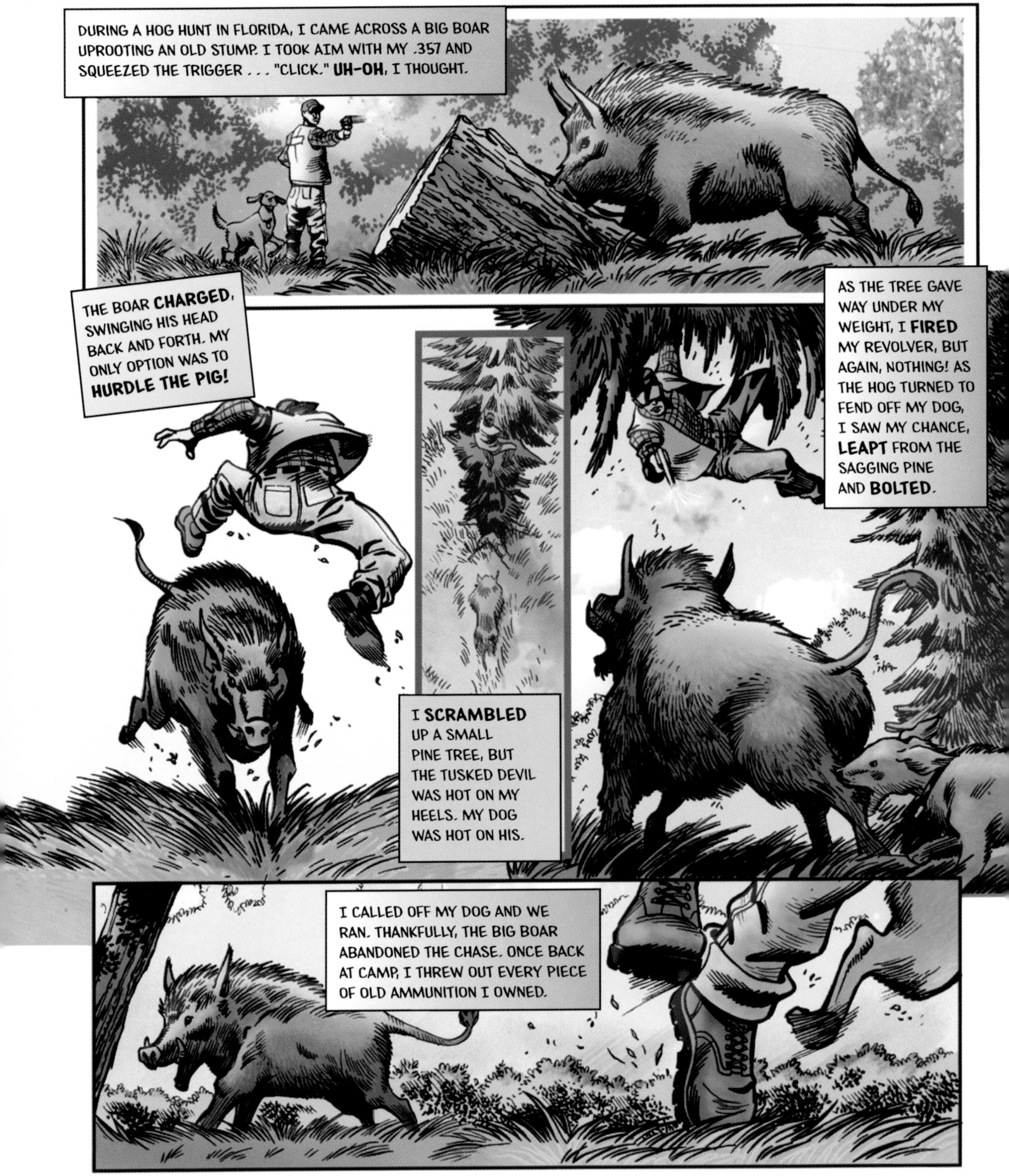
DURING A HOG HUNT IN FLORIDA, I CAME ACROSS A BIG BOAR UPROOTING AN OLD STUMP. I TOOK AIM WITH MY .357 AND SQUEEZED THE TRIGGER . . . "CLICK." UH-OH, I THOUGHT.
THE BOAR CHARGED, SWINGING HIS HEAD BACK AND FORTH. MY ONLY OPTION WAS TO HURDLE THE PIG!
I SCRAMBLED UP A SMALL PINE TREE, BUT THE TUSKED DEVIL WAS HOT ON MY HEELS. MY DOG WAS HOT ON HIS.
AS THE TREE GAVE WAY UNDER MY WEIGHT, I FIRED MY REVOLVER, BUT AGAIN, NOTHING! AS THE HOG TURNED TO FEND OFF MY DOG, I SAW MY CHANCE, LEAPT FROM THE SAGGING PINE AND BOLTED.
I CALLED OFF MY DOG AND WE RAN. THANKFULLY, THE BIG BOAR ABANDONED THE CHASE. ONCE BACK AT CAMP, I THREW OUT EVERY PIECE OF OLD AMMUNITION I OWNED.

Serious Swine

Known as the razorback, the wild boar is native to Europe and Asia, but has spread over the world, with territory across America. Male pigs tend to be solitary; females and young travel in groups called sounders, averaging 20 members. Males' upper canines develop into tusks, used for foraging and defense—they've even reportedly gored tigers to death in Asia.

Boars can:
- Bear litters of up to 14 young
- Grow tusks up to 7 inches long
- Run a 7-minute mile (averaging 18 mph)
- Learn tasks as quickly as chimpanzees

HOG HABITS: Boars are nocturnal or crepuscular (active during evenings or twilight), and are generally inactive during the day. Attacks on humans are not common but have occurred increasingly as boars' natural habitats have been intruded upon or cleared by humans, along with increased aggressive behavior from males during mating season, or when females are defending their young. Some of these attacks have been in self defense, when boars have been hunted and turned on their pursuers. Injuries to humans are usually to the legs and thighs, as boars bite or slash upward with their tusks.

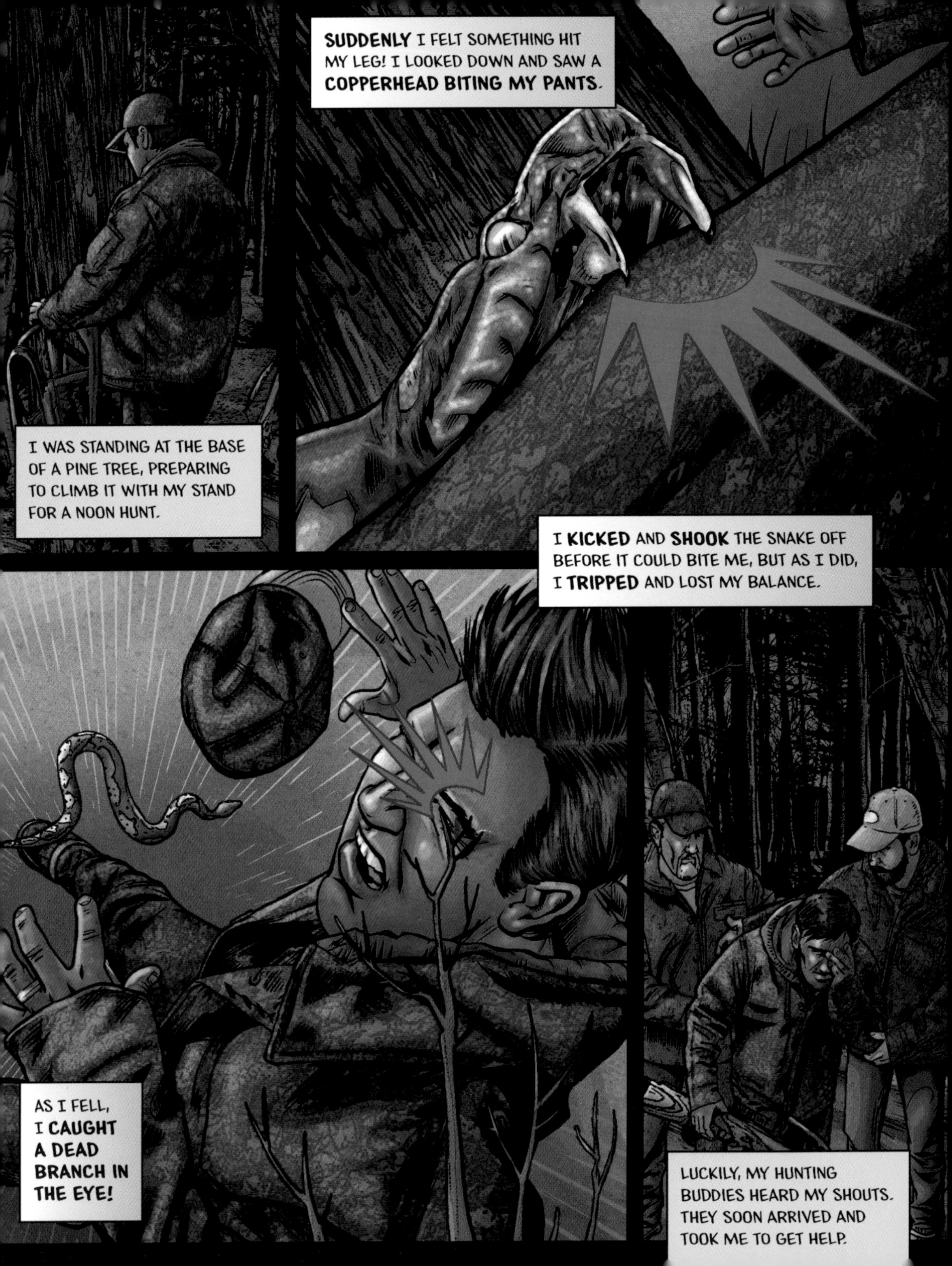
I WAS STANDING AT THE BASE OF A PINE TREE, PREPARING TO CLIMB IT WITH MY STAND FOR A NOON HUNT.
SUDDENLY I FELT SOMETHING HIT MY LEG! I LOOKED DOWN AND SAW A COPPERHEAD BITING MY PANTS.
I KICKED AND SHOOK THE SNAKE OFF BEFORE IT COULD BITE ME, BUT AS I DID, I TRIPPED AND LOST MY BALANCE.
AS I FELL, I CAUGHT A DEAD BRANCH IN THE EYE!
LUCKILY, MY HUNTING BUDDIES HEARD MY SHOUTS. THEY SOON ARRIVED AND TOOK ME TO GET HELP.

"If you see a snake, just kill it—don't appoint a committee on snakes."

—*Ross Perot*

KNOW THE NUMBERS:
Dog Attacks

4.7 MILLION The number of dog bites in the U.S. annually.

800,000 Dog bites requiring medical care yearly in the U.S.

$18,000 Average cost of a dog-bite-related hospital stay.

71% Percentage of bites on limbs.

5% Percentage of hospital ER visits involving dog attacks.

Hell Hounds Attack! // by Clifford Green, Machais, NY

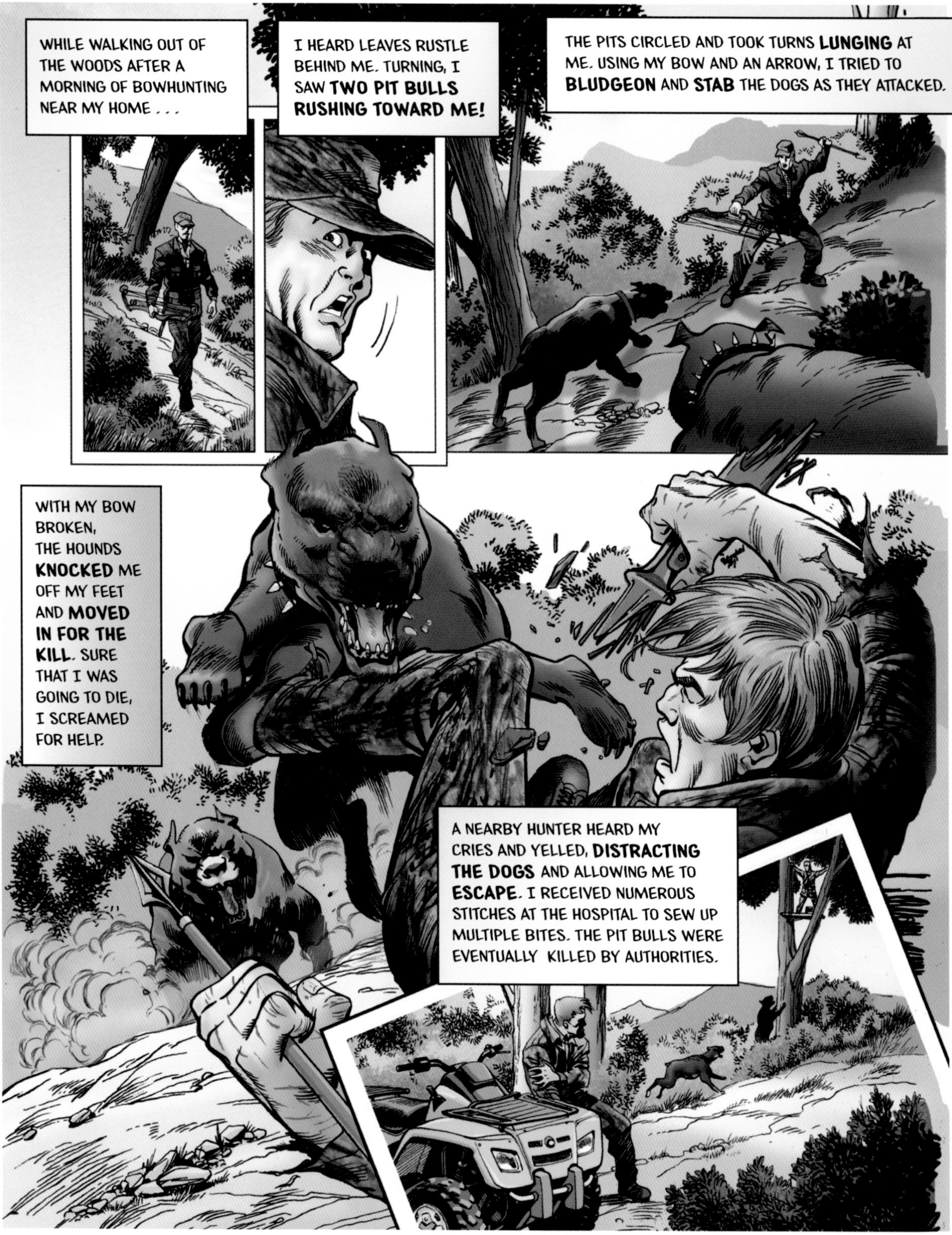
WHILE WALKING OUT OF THE WOODS AFTER A MORNING OF BOWHUNTING NEAR MY HOME . . .
I HEARD LEAVES RUSTLE BEHIND ME. TURNING, I SAW **TWO PIT BULLS RUSHING TOWARD ME!**
THE PITS CIRCLED AND TOOK TURNS **LUNGING** AT ME. USING MY BOW AND AN ARROW, I TRIED TO **BLUDGEON** AND **STAB** THE DOGS AS THEY ATTACKED.
WITH MY BOW BROKEN, THE HOUNDS **KNOCKED** ME OFF MY FEET AND **MOVED IN FOR THE KILL**. SURE THAT I WAS GOING TO DIE, I SCREAMED FOR HELP.
A NEARBY HUNTER HEARD MY CRIES AND YELLED, **DISTRACTING THE DOGS** AND ALLOWING ME TO **ESCAPE**. I RECEIVED NUMEROUS STITCHES AT THE HOSPITAL TO SEW UP MULTIPLE BITES. THE PIT BULLS WERE EVENTUALLY KILLED BY AUTHORITIES.

Hooked! // by Kurt Anderson, Brookston, MN

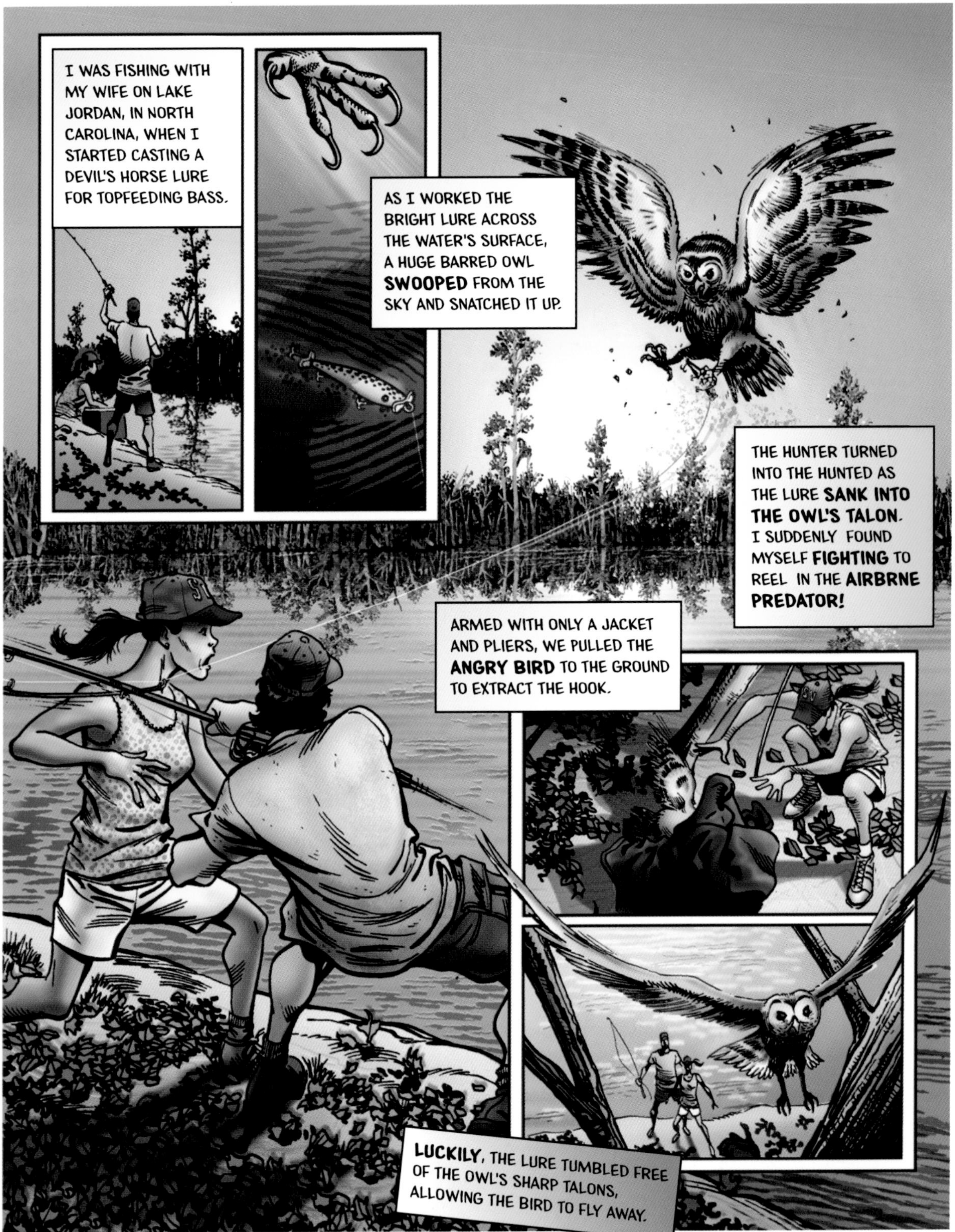

I WAS FISHING WITH MY WIFE ON LAKE JORDAN, IN NORTH CAROLINA, WHEN I STARTED CASTING A DEVIL'S HORSE LURE FOR TOPFEEDING BASS.
AS I WORKED THE BRIGHT LURE ACROSS THE WATER'S SURFACE, A HUGE BARRED OWL SWOOPED FROM THE SKY AND SNATCHED IT UP.
THE HUNTER TURNED INTO THE HUNTED AS THE LURE SANK INTO THE OWL'S TALON. I SUDDENLY FOUND MYSELF FIGHTING TO REEL IN THE AIRBRNE PREDATOR!
ARMED WITH ONLY A JACKET AND PLIERS, WE PULLED THE ANGRY BIRD TO THE GROUND TO EXTRACT THE HOOK.
LUCKILY, THE LURE TUMBLED FREE OF THE OWL'S SHARP TALONS, ALLOWING THE BIRD TO FLY AWAY.

I Otter Get Outta Here! // by Jim Jukich, Stroudsburg, PA

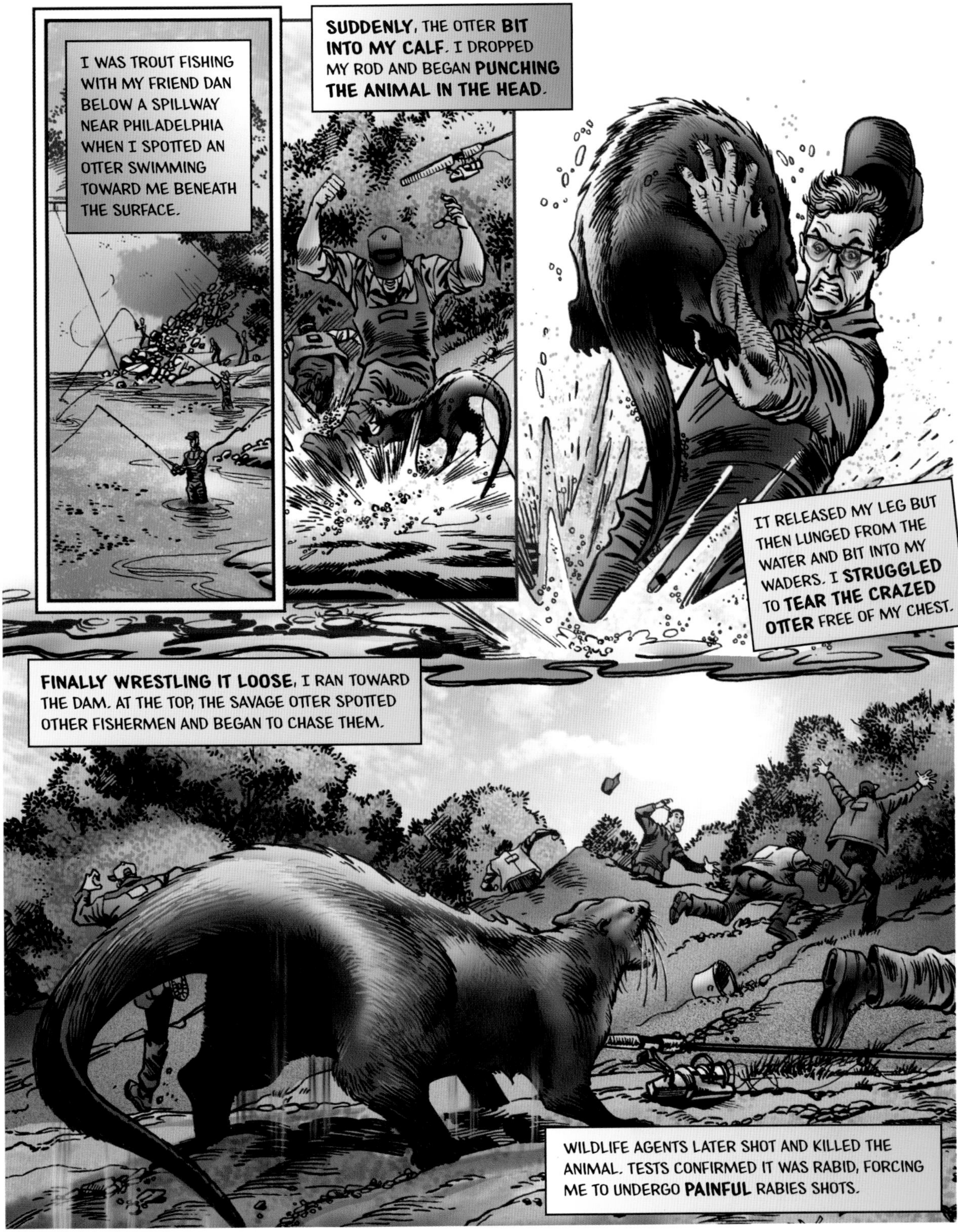
I WAS TROUT FISHING WITH MY FRIEND DAN BELOW A SPILLWAY NEAR PHILADELPHIA WHEN I SPOTTED AN OTTER SWIMMING TOWARD ME BENEATH THE SURFACE.
SUDDENLY, THE OTTER BIT INTO MY CALF. I DROPPED MY ROD AND BEGAN PUNCHING THE ANIMAL IN THE HEAD.
IT RELEASED MY LEG BUT THEN LUNGED FROM THE WATER AND BIT INTO MY WADERS. I STRUGGLED TO TEAR THE CRAZED OTTER FREE OF MY CHEST.
FINALLY WRESTLING IT LOOSE, I RAN TOWARD THE DAM. AT THE TOP, THE SAVAGE OTTER SPOTTED OTHER FISHERMEN AND BEGAN TO CHASE THEM.
WILDLIFE AGENTS LATER SHOT AND KILLED THE ANIMAL. TESTS CONFIRMED IT WAS RABID, FORCING ME TO UNDERGO PAINFUL RABIES SHOTS.

Showdown with a Lion // by Timm McGarry, Dubois, PA

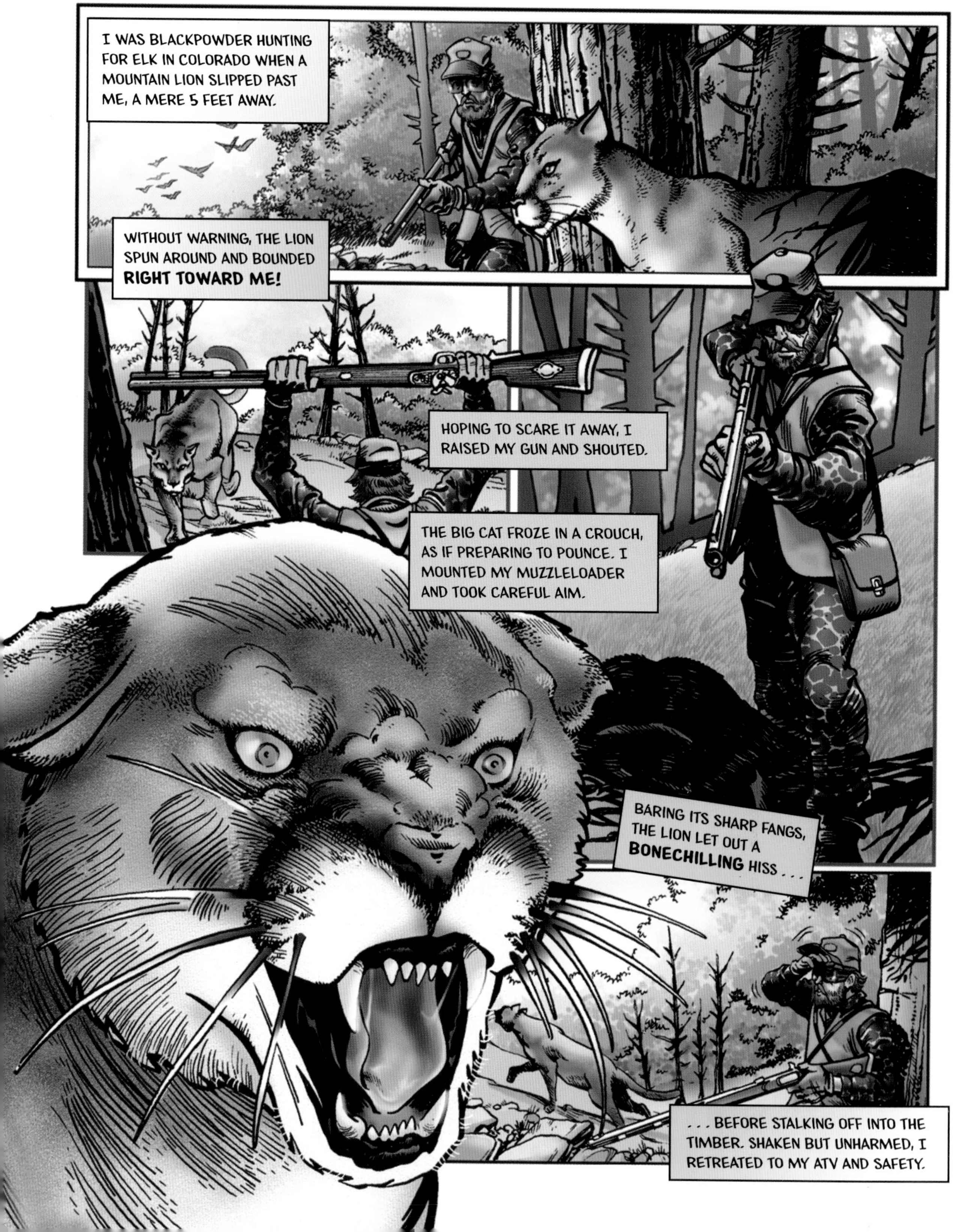

I WAS BLACKPOWDER HUNTING FOR ELK IN COLORADO WHEN A MOUNTAIN LION SLIPPED PAST ME, A MERE 5 FEET AWAY.
WITHOUT WARNING, THE LION SPUN AROUND AND BOUNDED RIGHT TOWARD ME!
HOPING TO SCARE IT AWAY, I RAISED MY GUN AND SHOUTED.
THE BIG CAT FROZE IN A CROUCH, AS IF PREPARING TO POUNCE. I MOUNTED MY MUZZLELOADER AND TOOK CAREFUL AIM.
BARING ITS SHARP FANGS, THE LION LET OUT A BONECHILLING HISS . . .
. . . BEFORE STALKING OFF INTO THE TIMBER. SHAKEN BUT UNHARMED, I RETREATED TO MY ATV AND SAFETY.

Cougar Attack!

American mountain lions are also known as cougars, panthers, and pumas. While cougar attacks are rare, they're on the rise as humans expand further and further into territory that was formerly ruled by these tawny, toothy feline predators.

Mountain lions can:
- Bound up to 40 feet while running
- Leap 15 feet up a tree
- Climb over fences 12 feet in height
- Reach speeds of 50 mph in a sprint

HERE KITTY KITTY: If you're going to be hiking or camping in cougar country, there is strength in numbers. In general, these animals are shy and will rarely approach noise or human activity. They are also nocturnal, so be especially alert during the hours between dusk and dawn.

If you come into contact with a mountain lion, never turn your back or run away. Stay calm and stand your ground. Back away slowly if possible, and pick up small children, but don't bend over (it will make you look like smaller, more tempting prey). Running triggers the cat's predatory response—so don't do it.

Instead, speak firmly and loudly, clap your hands, raise your arms to make yourself look larger, and throw any items that might be handy toward the cougar. Give it room and time to move on. If the lion does attack, you are going to need to fight back with whatever you have at hand. People have successfully fought off aggressive mountain lions with rocks and sticks.

No Rattle for Baby // by Jane Springer, Caddo, OK

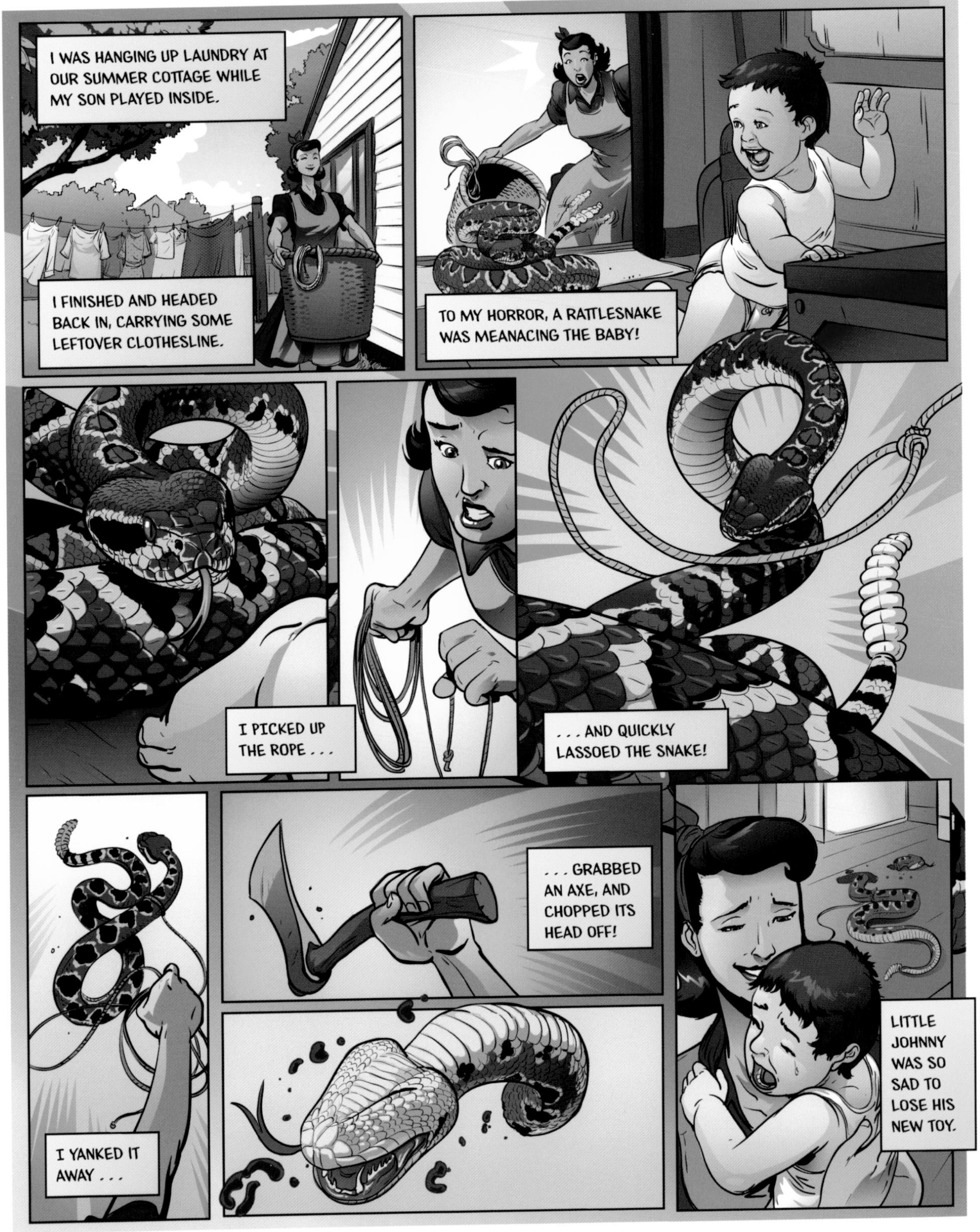
I WAS HANGING UP LAUNDRY AT OUR SUMMER COTTAGE WHILE MY SON PLAYED INSIDE.
I FINISHED AND HEADED BACK IN, CARRYING SOME LEFTOVER CLOTHESLINE.
TO MY HORROR, A RATTLESNAKE WAS MEANACING THE BABY!
I PICKED UP THE ROPE . . .
. . . AND QUICKLY LASSOED THE SNAKE!
I YANKED IT AWAY . . .
. . . GRABBED AN AXE, AND CHOPPED ITS HEAD OFF!
LITTLE JOHNNY WAS SO SAD TO LOSE HIS NEW TOY.

KNOW THE NUMBERS:
Rattlesnakes

7.8 FEET Longest rattlesnake on record (Eastern diamondback or *Crotalus adamanteus*).

8,000 Number of venomous snake bites in the U.S. yearly.

75% Percentage of bites requiring treatment with antivenin.

$1,500 Cost per vial of antivenin. Usually 15–20 doses are needed.

$100,000 TO $150,000 Average cost of hospitalization and treatment for rattlesnake bites.

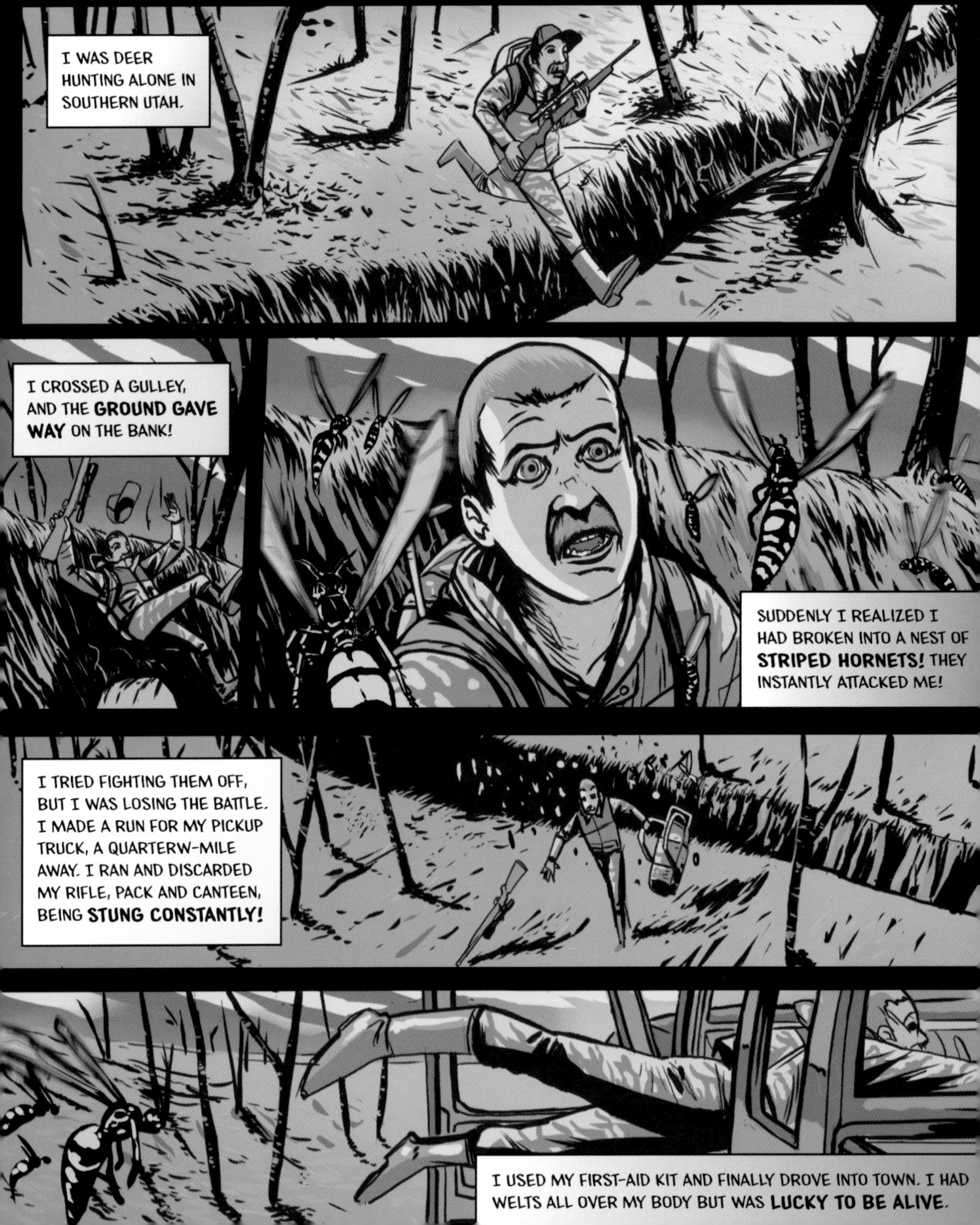
I WAS DEER HUNTING ALONE IN SOUTHERN UTAH.
I CROSSED A GULLEY, AND THE GROUND GAVE WAY ON THE BANK!
SUDDENLY I REALIZED I HAD BROKEN INTO A NEST OF STRIPED HORNETS! THEY INSTANTLY ATTACKED ME!
I TRIED FIGHTING THEM OFF, BUT I WAS LOSING THE BATTLE. I MADE A RUN FOR MY PICKUP TRUCK, A QUARTERW-MILE AWAY. I RAN AND DISCARDED MY RIFLE, PACK AND CANTEEN, BEING STUNG CONSTANTLY!
I USED MY FIRST-AID KIT AND FINALLY DROVE INTO TOWN. I HAD WELTS ALL OVER MY BODY BUT WAS LUCKY TO BE ALIVE.

Terror from Above // by Chuck Holland, Jim Thorpe, PA

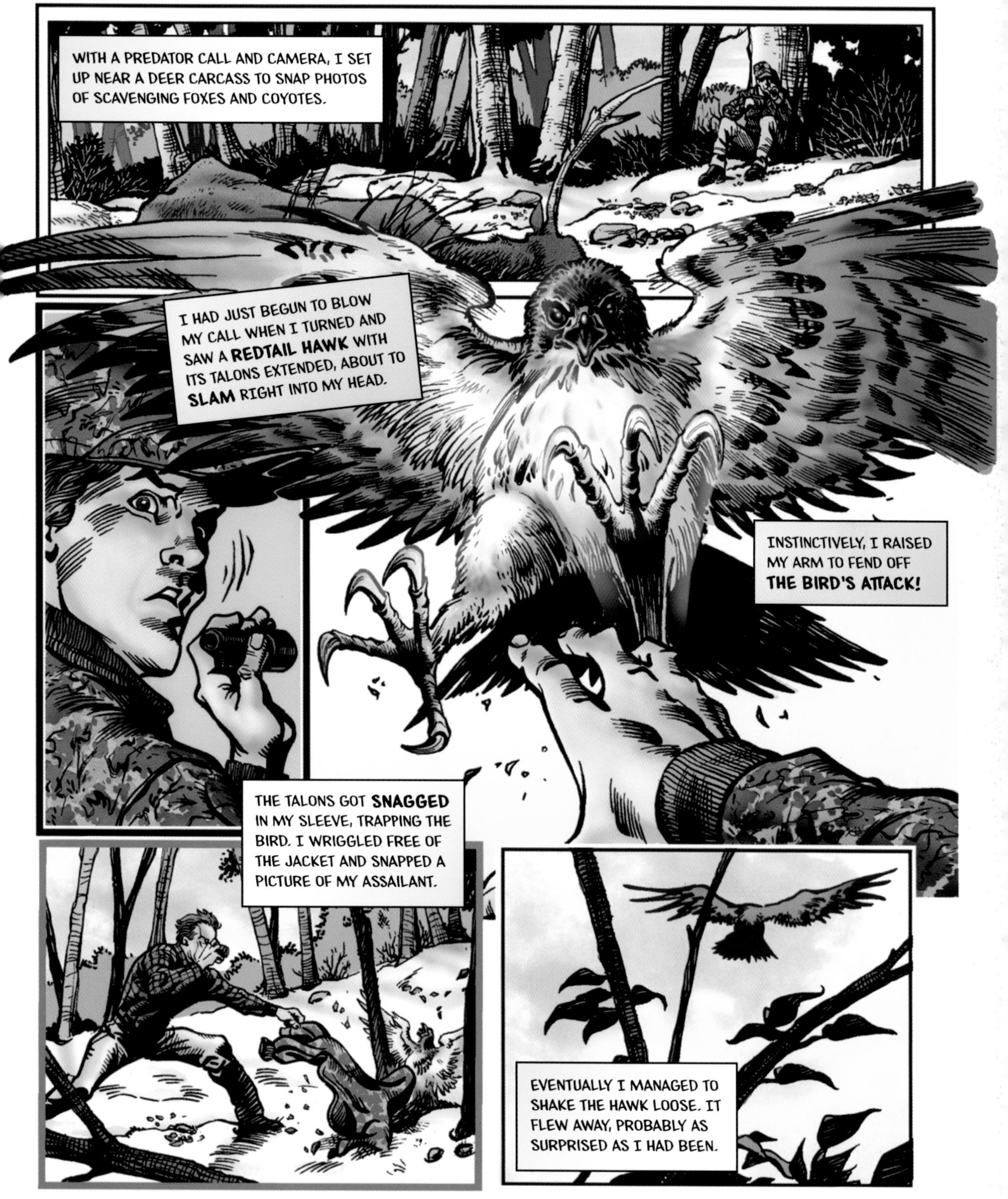

WITH A PREDATOR CALL AND CAMERA, I SET UP NEAR A DEER CARCASS TO SNAP PHOTOS OF SCAVENGING FOXES AND COYOTES.
I HAD JUST BEGUN TO BLOW MY CALL WHEN I TURNED AND SAW A REDTAIL HAWK WITH ITS TALONS EXTENDED, ABOUT TO SLAM RIGHT INTO MY HEAD.
INSTINCTIVELY, I RAISED MY ARM TO FEND OFF THE BIRD'S ATTACK!
THE TALONS GOT SNAGGED IN MY SLEEVE, TRAPPING THE BIRD. I WRIGGLED FREE OF THE JACKET AND SNAPPED A PICTURE OF MY ASSAILANT.
EVENTUALLY I MANAGED TO SHAKE THE HAWK LOOSE. IT FLEW AWAY, PROBABLY AS SURPRISED AS I HAD BEEN.

Faceoff! // by Michael Caltagirone, Old Forge, NY

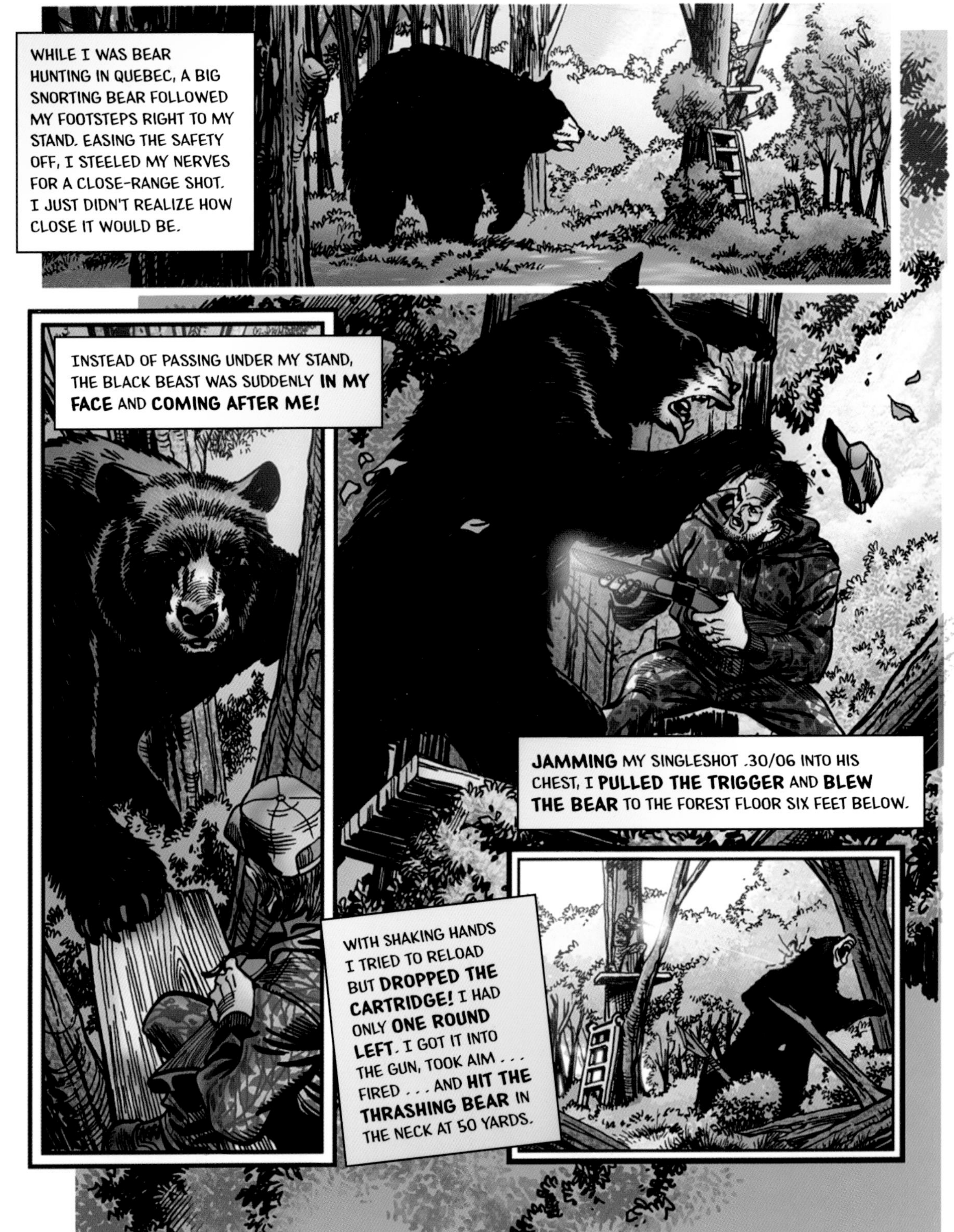

WHILE I WAS BEAR HUNTING IN QUEBEC, A BIG SNORTING BEAR FOLLOWED MY FOOTSTEPS RIGHT TO MY STAND. EASING THE SAFETY OFF, I STEELED MY NERVES FOR A CLOSE-RANGE SHOT. I JUST DIDN'T REALIZE HOW CLOSE IT WOULD BE.
INSTEAD OF PASSING UNDER MY STAND, THE BLACK BEAST WAS SUDDENLY IN MY FACE AND COMING AFTER ME!
JAMMING MY SINGLESHOT .30/06 INTO HIS CHEST, I PULLED THE TRIGGER AND BLEW THE BEAR TO THE FOREST FLOOR SIX FEET BELOW.
WITH SHAKING HANDS I TRIED TO RELOAD BUT DROPPED THE CARTRIDGE! I HAD ONLY ONE ROUND LEFT. I GOT IT INTO THE GUN, TOOK AIM . . . FIRED . . . AND HIT THE THRASHING BEAR IN THE NECK AT 50 YARDS.

Big Bruins

Black bears historically lived across much of North America, and can still be found in many regions of the northern United States, Canada, and Alaska. Despite their name, black bears' fur color can actually range through black, cinnamon brown, and blonde. They are intelligent, curious animals, with a surprisingly good long-term memory.

Black bears can:
- Live up to 30 years in the wild, and up to 44 years in captivity
- Eat up to 45% of their body weight to prepare for hibernation
- Give birth to 2 or 3 cubs every year (while the mother is hibernating)

STAY AWAY FROM SMOKEY Black bears tend to keep their distance from humans, but should be considered unpredictable. Encroaching on black bears' territory can both teach them to associate humans with food and provoke them. Do not give bears water or food, and keep pets, food, and garbage secured.

If you encounter a black bear, keep your distance, and retreat if it hasn't noticed you. If it approaches, don't run away. Make yourself as large and loud as possible: Stand upright, wave your arms or jacket, and yell and bang on objects such as pots and pans. If it doesn't leave, keep facing the bear while you back away slowly, giving the animal a chance to depart.

If the bear becomes aggressive, use pepper spray if you have it, or fight back in any other way you can. Use rocks, sticks, or even your fists, aiming for the eyes and snout. Black bears (unlike the larger brown or grizzly bears) can be discouraged from attacking if their target fights back.

"The coyote is a living,
breathing allegory of want.
He is always hungry.
He is always poor, out of
luck, and friendless."

—*Mark Twain*

Furred Fury // by Darrell Rogers, Live Oak, FL

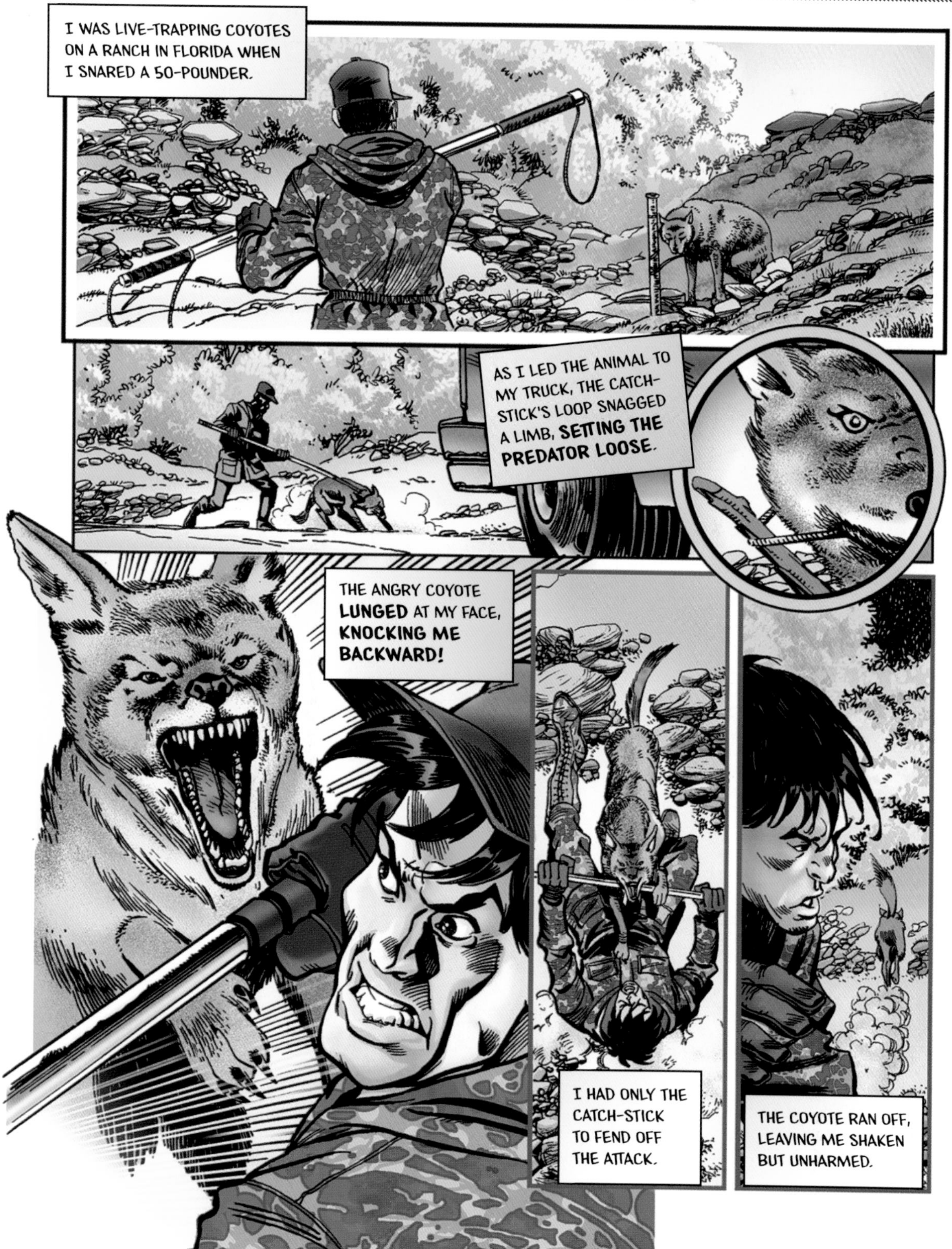

I WAS LIVE-TRAPPING COYOTES ON A RANCH IN FLORIDA WHEN I SNARED A 50-POUNDER.
AS I LED THE ANIMAL TO MY TRUCK, THE CATCH-STICK'S LOOP SNAGGED A LIMB, SETTING THE PREDATOR LOOSE.
THE ANGRY COYOTE LUNGED AT MY FACE, KNOCKING ME BACKWARD!
I HAD ONLY THE CATCH-STICK TO FEND OFF THE ATTACK.
THE COYOTE RAN OFF, LEAVING ME SHAKEN BUT UNHARMED.

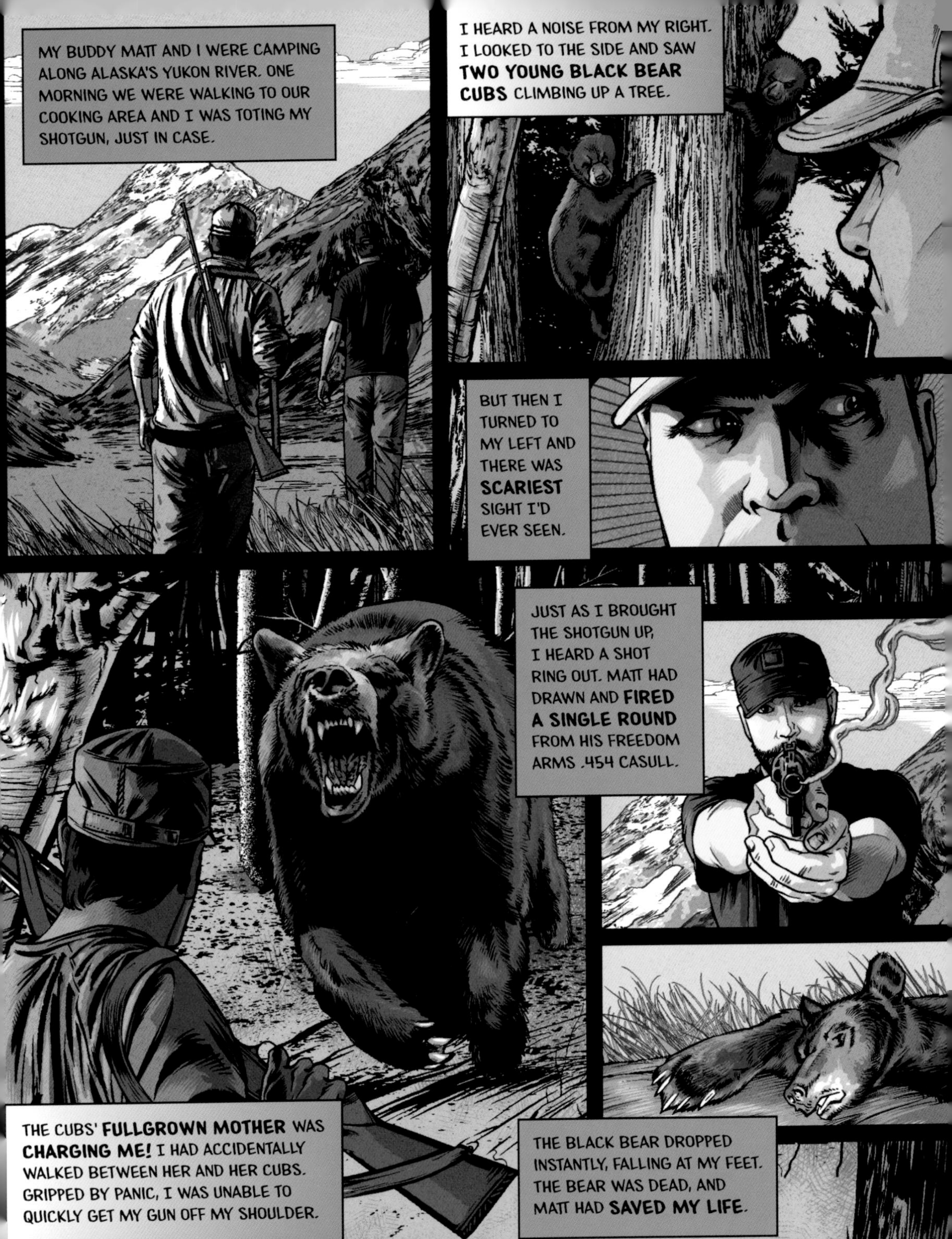
MY BUDDY MATT AND I WERE CAMPING ALONG ALASKA'S YUKON RIVER. ONE MORNING WE WERE WALKING TO OUR COOKING AREA AND I WAS TOTING MY SHOTGUN, JUST IN CASE.
I HEARD A NOISE FROM MY RIGHT. I LOOKED TO THE SIDE AND SAW TWO YOUNG BLACK BEAR CUBS CLIMBING UP A TREE.
BUT THEN I TURNED TO MY LEFT AND THERE WAS SCARIEST SIGHT I'D EVER SEEN.
THE CUBS' FULLGROWN MOTHER WAS CHARGING ME! I HAD ACCIDENTALLY WALKED BETWEEN HER AND HER CUBS. GRIPPED BY PANIC, I WAS UNABLE TO QUICKLY GET MY GUN OFF MY SHOULDER.
JUST AS I BROUGHT THE SHOTGUN UP, I HEARD A SHOT RING OUT. MATT HAD DRAWN AND FIRED A SINGLE ROUND FROM HIS FREEDOM ARMS .454 CASULL.
THE BLACK BEAR DROPPED INSTANTLY, FALLING AT MY FEET. THE BEAR WAS DEAD, AND MATT HAD SAVED MY LIFE.

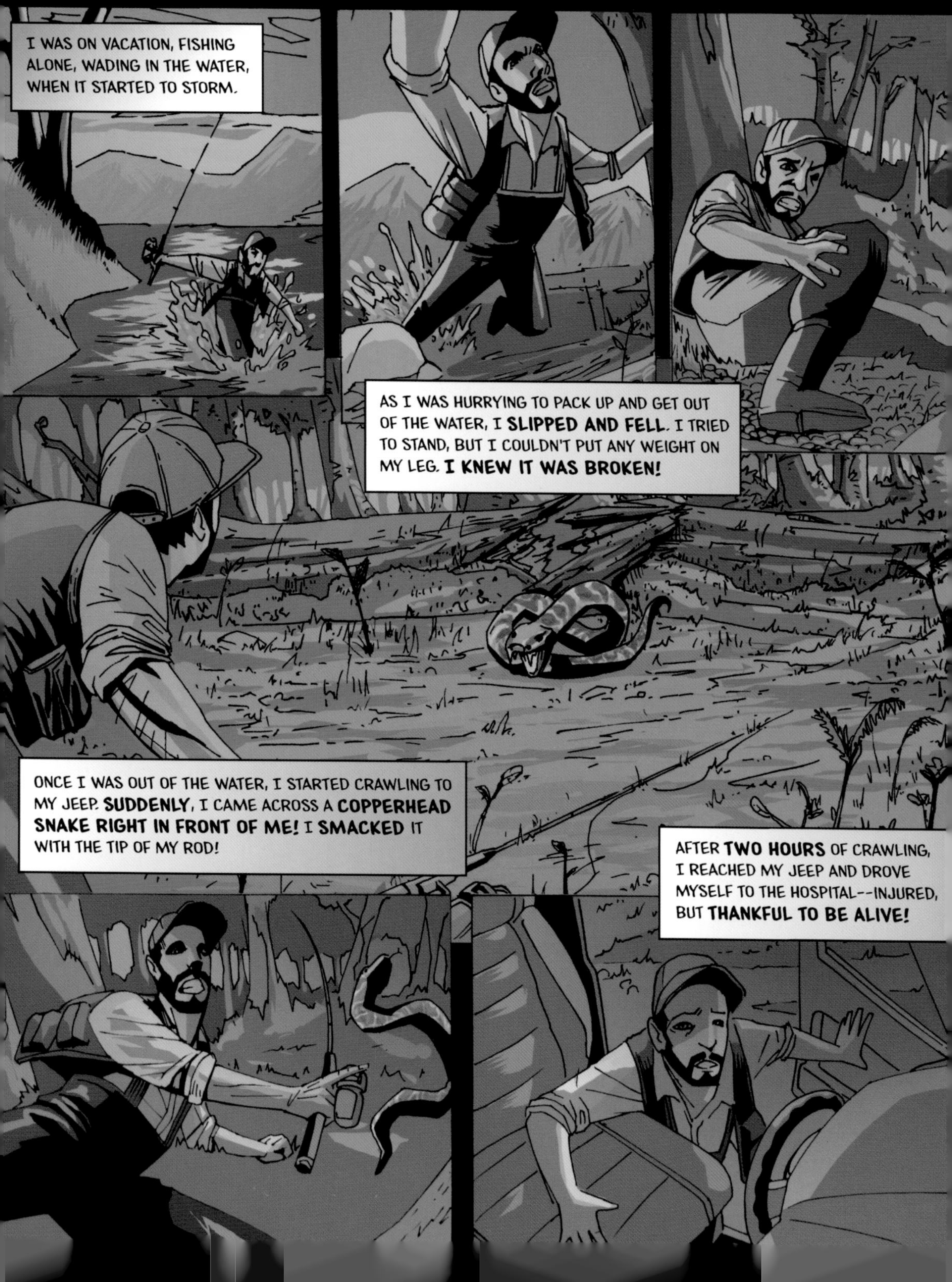
I WAS ON VACATION, FISHING ALONE, WADING IN THE WATER, WHEN IT STARTED TO STORM.
AS I WAS HURRYING TO PACK UP AND GET OUT OF THE WATER, I SLIPPED AND FELL. I TRIED TO STAND, BUT I COULDN'T PUT ANY WEIGHT ON MY LEG. I KNEW IT WAS BROKEN!
ONCE I WAS OUT OF THE WATER, I STARTED CRAWLING TO MY JEEP. SUDDENLY, I CAME ACROSS A COPPERHEAD SNAKE RIGHT IN FRONT OF ME! I SMACKED IT WITH THE TIP OF MY ROD!
AFTER TWO HOURS OF CRAWLING, I REACHED MY JEEP AND DROVE MYSELF TO THE HOSPITAL--INJURED, BUT THANKFUL TO BE ALIVE!

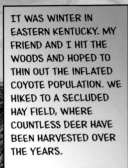

IT WAS WINTER IN EASTERN KENTUCKY. MY FRIEND AND I HIT THE WOODS AND HOPED TO THIN OUT THE INFLATED COYOTE POPULATION. WE HIKED TO A SECLUDED HAY FIELD, WHERE COUNTLESS DEER HAVE BEEN HARVESTED OVER THE YEARS.

I BLEW INTO MY COYOTE CALL AND LET OUT **A LOUD RODENT SQUEAL** . . . AND HEARD LEAVES RUSTLE BEHIND ME.

I TURNED TO SEE THE MOST **TERRIFYING** IMAGE. A BOBCAT WAS **LEAPING TOWARD ME**, COMING FOR THE "DYING RODENT" THAT I WAS HOLDING IN MY MOUTH!

THE CAT **SLAMMED** INTO MY FACE, **SLICED MY SKIN** AND BROKE THE CALL. I TRIED DESPERATELY TO **SHAKE IT OFF!**

THE CAT JUMPED OFF AND DARTED AWAY, REALIZING THE CALL WAS NOT A REAL RODENT AFTER ALL. MY BUDDY AND I WERE BOTH IN SHOCK BUT **GLAD TO BE OKAY.**

This Kitty Has Claws

Bobcats are the most common wild cat in North America, ranging over nearly the entire continental United States, southern Canada, and Mexico. Twice the size of an average housecat, their name is derived from their short, 'bobbed' tail. They can live almost anywhere, from deserts to swamps, and have also been found skulking around the suburbs. They are most active in the evenings, are very stealthy, and are rarely seen.

Bobcats can:
- Leap up to 10 feet horizontally to pounce on prey
- Hunt and kill animals up to 8 times their weight, including deer and sheep
- See up to six times as clearly as humans in dim light
- Live up to 15 years in the wild and 30 years in captivity

FEROCIOUS FELINE Bobcats are not often known to attack humans, but do hunt a variety of animals. Avoid feeding any of the local wildlife, since predatory animals like the bobcat will follow after anything they view as prey. Keep pets indoors at night, too: Bobcats have been known to attack housepets including dogs up to the size of a cocker spaniel.

If you keep small animals such as poultry, completely enclose outdoor pens with 1-inch or smaller chicken wire. Predator guards around tree trunks will also keep bobcats from climbing trees to get to animals. Since bobcats have been known to leap 6 vertical feet or more, try adding electrical wires to the top and bottom of tall wire fences for a little extra discouragement.

KNOW THE NUMBERS:
Wild Horses

31,500 Number of wild horses roaming the United States today.

17.1 HANDS (69 INCHES) Tallest height of a horse at the shoulder.

10,000 NEWTONS Greatest force generated by a kick from a horse.

2,200 POUNDS Maximum weight of a wild mustang.

34 MILES PER HOUR Top speed of a wild horse at full gallop.

Stallion Stampede // by Larry Koznek, Atascadero, CA

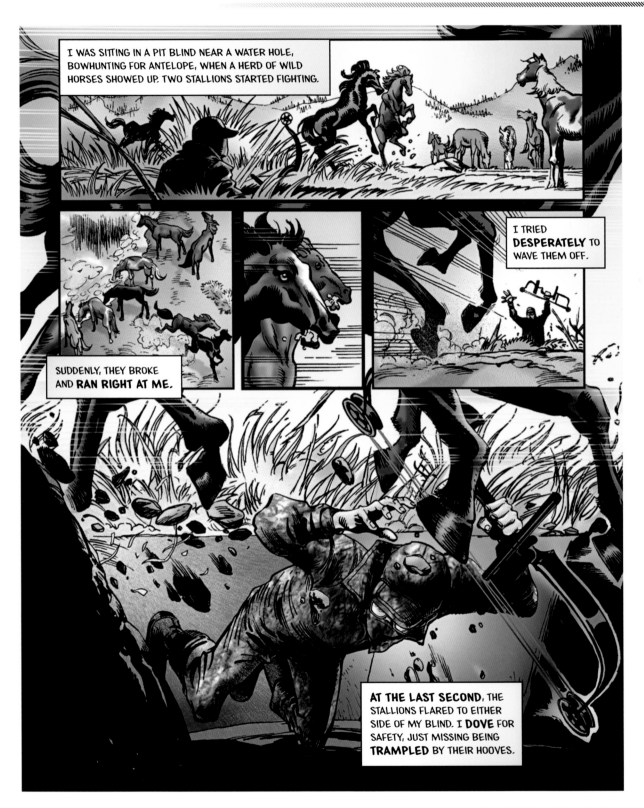

I WAS SITTING IN A PIT BLIND NEAR A WATER HOLE, BOWHUNTING FOR ANTELOPE, WHEN A HERD OF WILD HORSES SHOWED UP. TWO STALLIONS STARTED FIGHTING.

SUDDENLY, THEY BROKE AND **RAN RIGHT AT ME.**

I TRIED **DESPERATELY** TO WAVE THEM OFF.

AT THE LAST SECOND, THE STALLIONS FLARED TO EITHER SIDE OF MY BLIND. I **DOVE** FOR SAFETY, JUST MISSING BEING **TRAMPLED** BY THEIR HOOVES.

Hook, Line . . . and Mink // by Dana Sue Helmandollar, Sevierville, TN

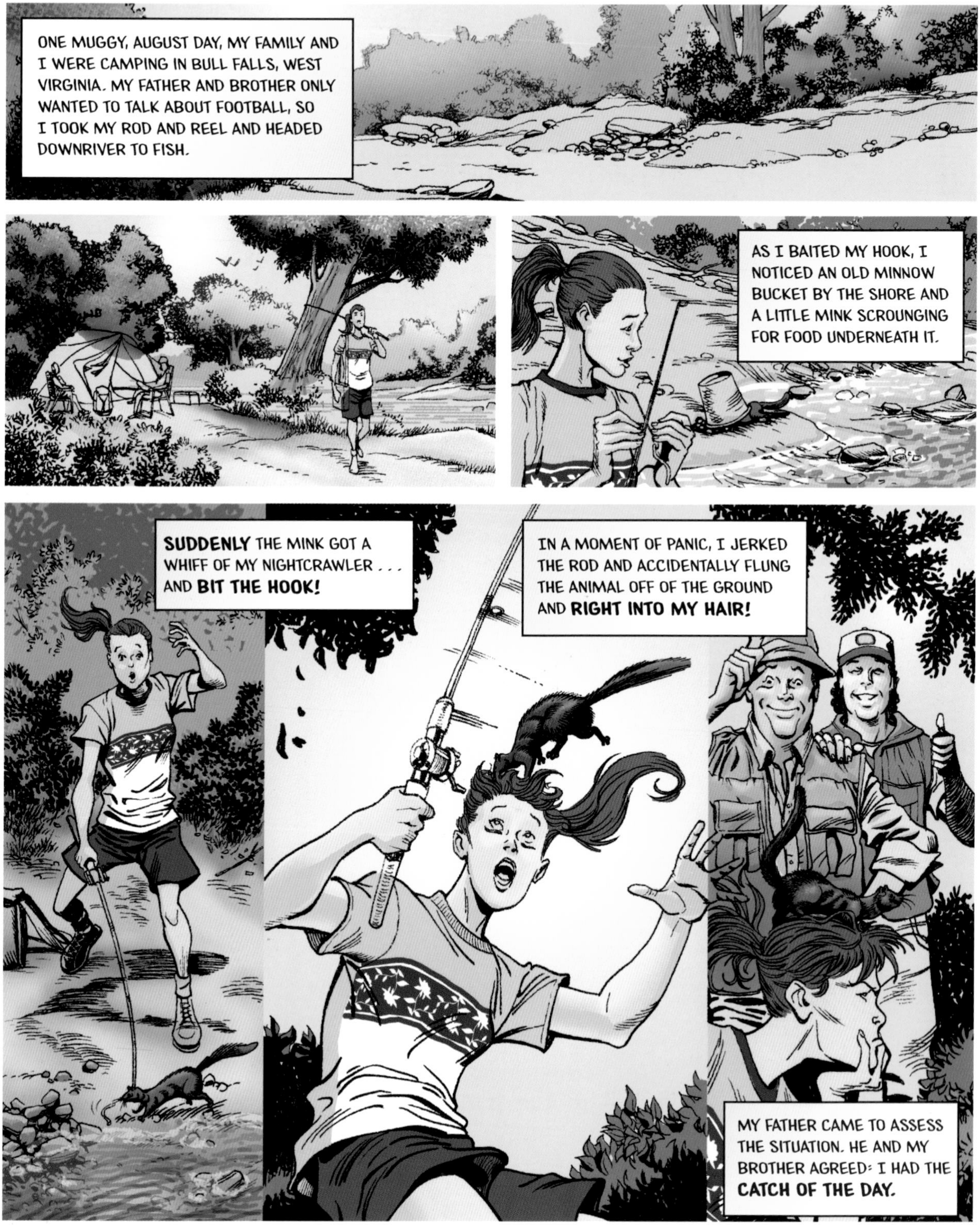

ONE MUGGY, AUGUST DAY, MY FAMILY AND I WERE CAMPING IN BULL FALLS, WEST VIRGINIA. MY FATHER AND BROTHER ONLY WANTED TO TALK ABOUT FOOTBALL, SO I TOOK MY ROD AND REEL AND HEADED DOWNRIVER TO FISH.
AS I BAITED MY HOOK, I NOTICED AN OLD MINNOW BUCKET BY THE SHORE AND A LITTLE MINK SCROUNGING FOR FOOD UNDERNEATH IT.
SUDDENLY THE MINK GOT A WHIFF OF MY NIGHTCRAWLER . . . AND **BIT THE HOOK!**
IN A MOMENT OF PANIC, I JERKED THE ROD AND ACCIDENTALLY FLUNG THE ANIMAL OFF OF THE GROUND AND **RIGHT INTO MY HAIR!**
MY FATHER CAME TO ASSESS THE SITUATION. HE AND MY BROTHER AGREED: I HAD THE **CATCH OF THE DAY.**

Hunted by a Lion // by Judy Davis, Trenton, TN

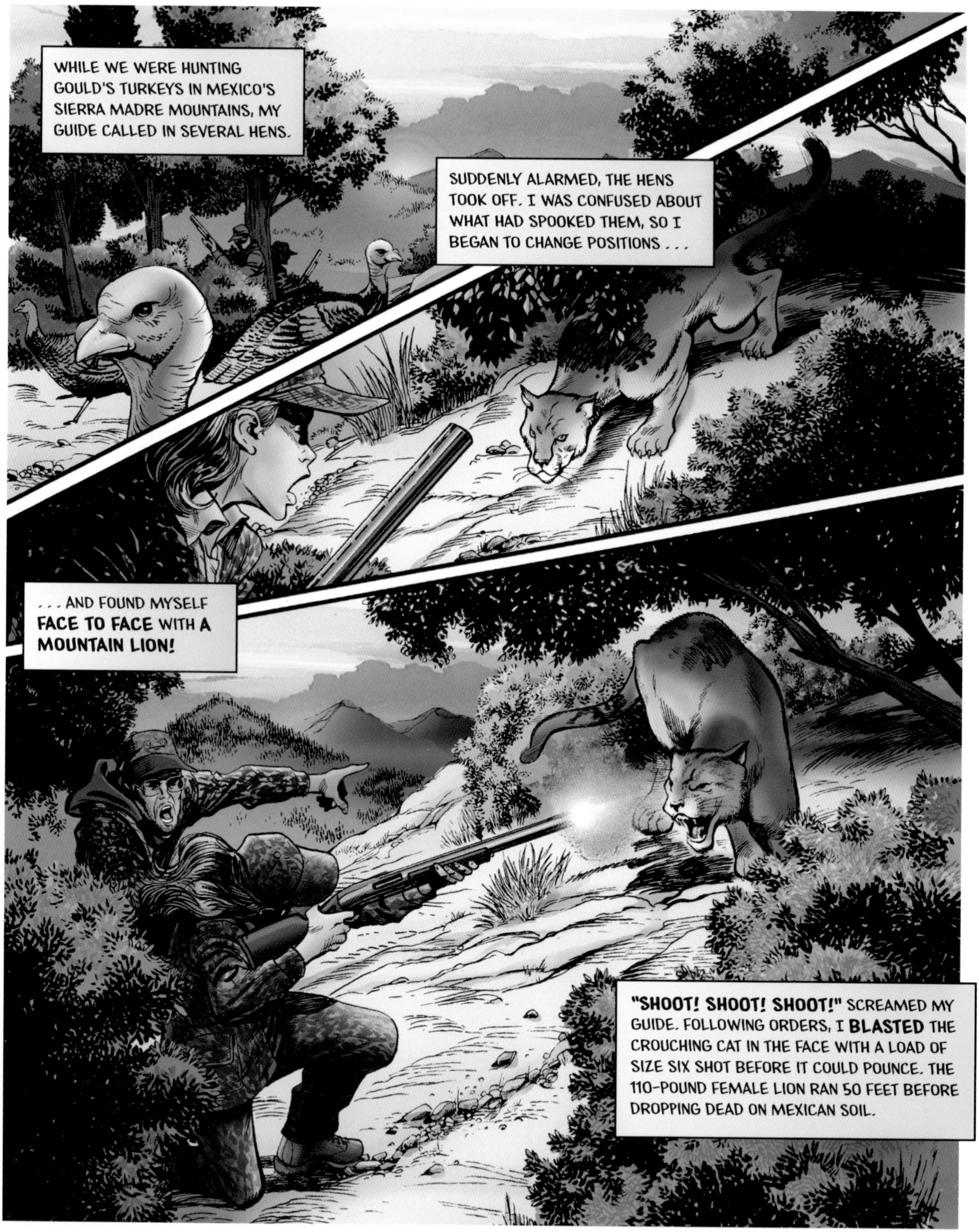
WHILE WE WERE HUNTING GOULD'S TURKEYS IN MEXICO'S SIERRA MADRE MOUNTAINS, MY GUIDE CALLED IN SEVERAL HENS.
SUDDENLY ALARMED, THE HENS TOOK OFF. I WAS CONFUSED ABOUT WHAT HAD SPOOKED THEM, SO I BEGAN TO CHANGE POSITIONS . . .
. . . AND FOUND MYSELF **FACE TO FACE** WITH **A MOUNTAIN LION!**
"SHOOT! SHOOT! SHOOT!" SCREAMED MY GUIDE. FOLLOWING ORDERS, I **BLASTED** THE CROUCHING CAT IN THE FACE WITH A LOAD OF SIZE SIX SHOT BEFORE IT COULD POUNCE. THE 110-POUND FEMALE LION RAN 50 FEET BEFORE DROPPING DEAD ON MEXICAN SOIL.

On the Bayou

KEEPING HIGH AND DRY The best way to navigate a swamp is on an airboat. Don't have one of those? Well, then—I guess you're just going to have to walk and wade.

BEWARE THE WATER Stay out of it as much as possible. If the wet route looks like your only option, observe the wildlife before wading or swimming. If the ibis won't go there, you shouldn't either. Watch for crocodiles and alligators, and don't forget serpents either: Venomous snakes and deadly constrictors live in and near water.

NAVIGATE CAREFULLY It's easy to get lost with everything looking alike, so pick the direction you believe to be toward safety, and maintain that heading, deviating only to avoid obstacles. Before going around something, check your heading and pick a fixed point on the other side to walk toward. It will be easier to get back on course quickly.

DON'T GET STUCK Swamp mud and silt can be extremely sticky and deep, and underwater root tangles can trap your feet. Quicksand likely won't kill you, but it can slow you down. Carry a long pole to check water depth and to probe the ground ahead before you take a step. Peat bogs amplify these risks, as they're deeper and contain a thick tangle of vegetation that can trap you. Simply walk around them instead.

Louisiana Gator Trap // by Aaron Artgue, Opelousas, LA

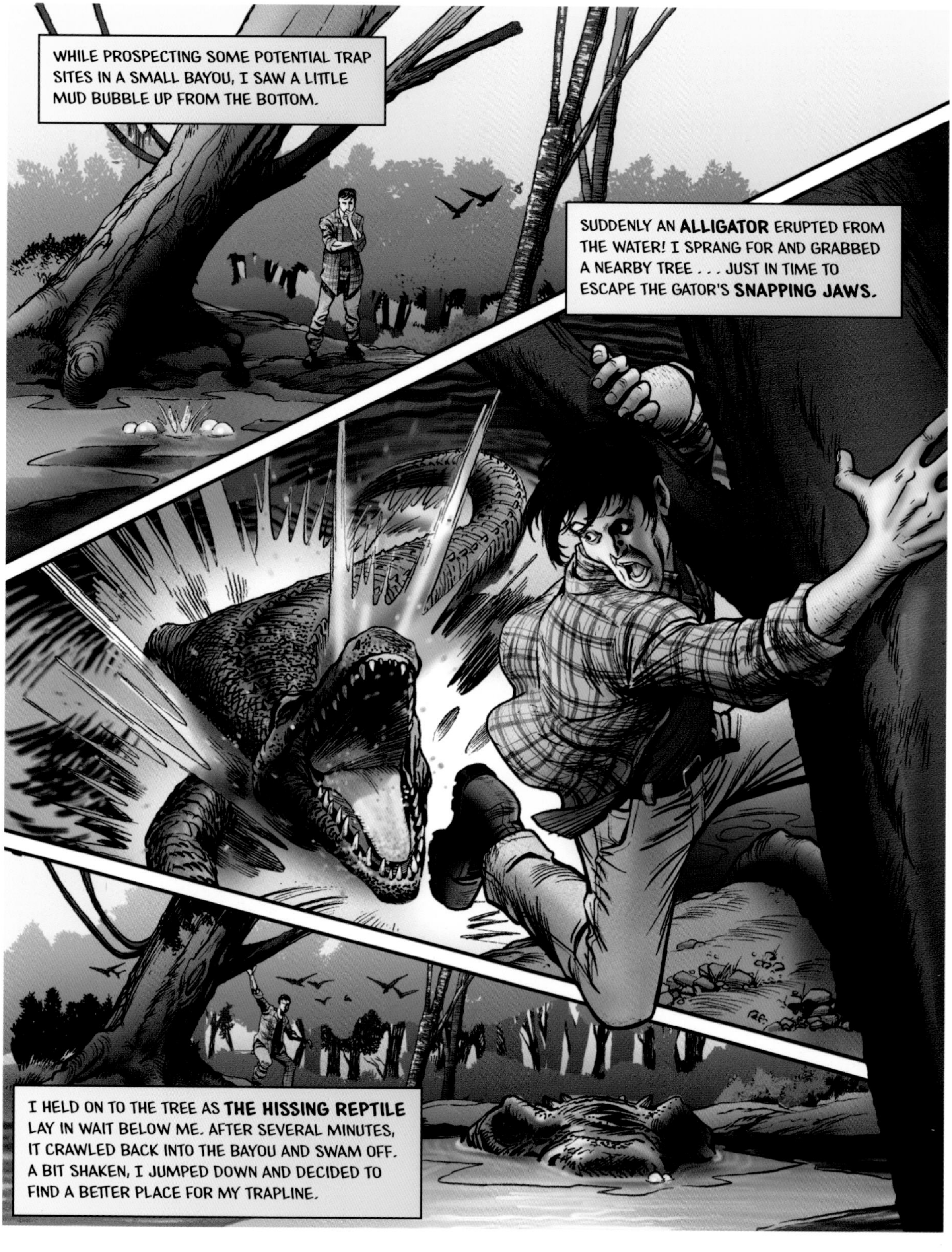
WHILE PROSPECTING SOME POTENTIAL TRAP SITES IN A SMALL BAYOU, I SAW A LITTLE MUD BUBBLE UP FROM THE BOTTOM.
SUDDENLY AN **ALLIGATOR** ERUPTED FROM THE WATER! I SPRANG FOR AND GRABBED A NEARBY TREE . . . JUST IN TIME TO ESCAPE THE GATOR'S **SNAPPING JAWS.**
I HELD ON TO THE TREE AS **THE HISSING REPTILE** LAY IN WAIT BELOW ME. AFTER SEVERAL MINUTES, IT CRAWLED BACK INTO THE BAYOU AND SWAM OFF. A BIT SHAKEN, I JUMPED DOWN AND DECIDED TO FIND A BETTER PLACE FOR MY TRAPLINE.

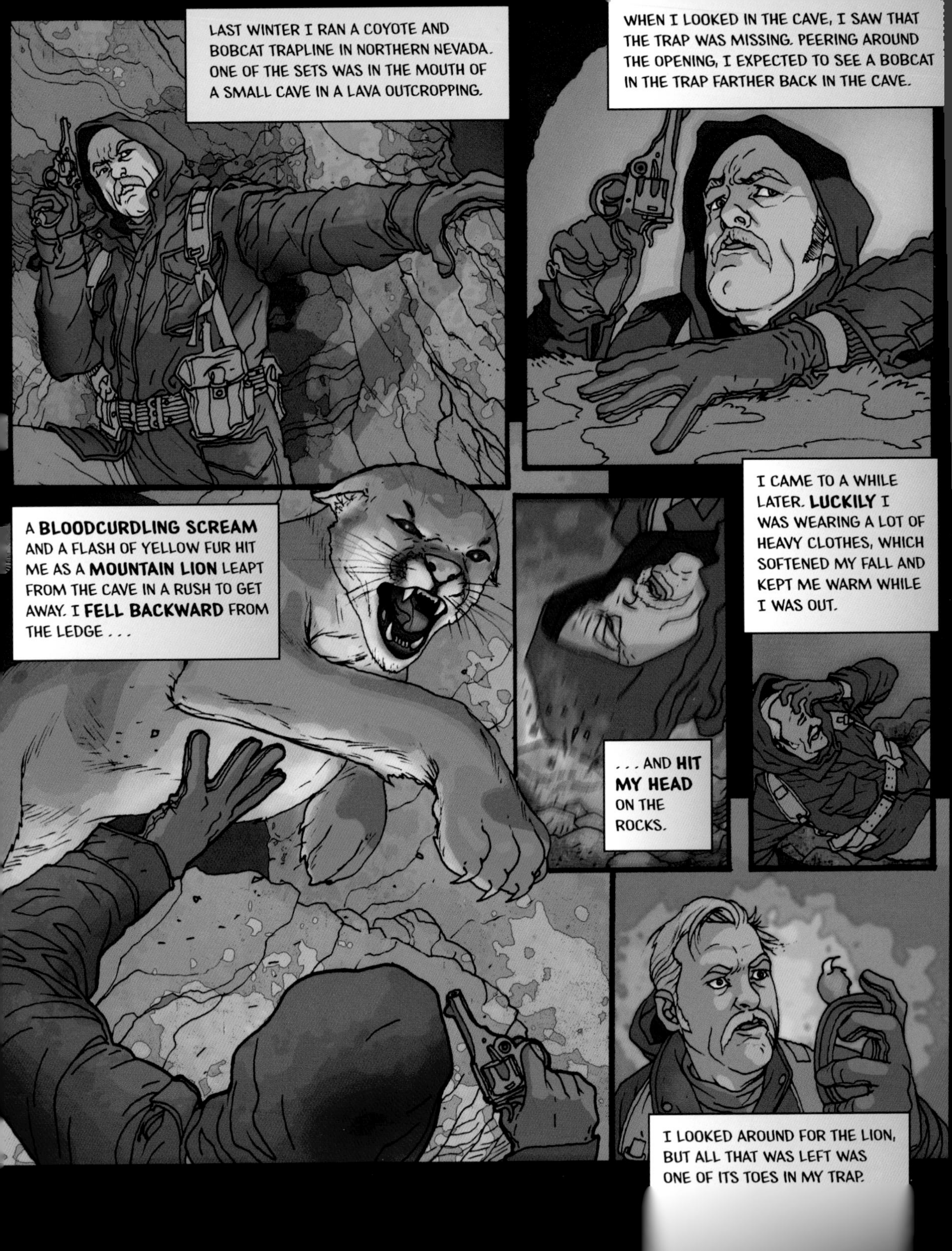
LAST WINTER I RAN A COYOTE AND BOBCAT TRAPLINE IN NORTHERN NEVADA. ONE OF THE SETS WAS IN THE MOUTH OF A SMALL CAVE IN A LAVA OUTCROPPING.
WHEN I LOOKED IN THE CAVE, I SAW THAT THE TRAP WAS MISSING. PEERING AROUND THE OPENING, I EXPECTED TO SEE A BOBCAT IN THE TRAP FARTHER BACK IN THE CAVE.
A BLOODCURDLING SCREAM AND A FLASH OF YELLOW FUR HIT ME AS A MOUNTAIN LION LEAPT FROM THE CAVE IN A RUSH TO GET AWAY. I FELL BACKWARD FROM THE LEDGE . . .
. . . AND HIT MY HEAD ON THE ROCKS.
I CAME TO A WHILE LATER. LUCKILY I WAS WEARING A LOT OF HEAVY CLOTHES, WHICH SOFTENED MY FALL AND KEPT ME WARM WHILE I WAS OUT.
I LOOKED AROUND FOR THE LION, BUT ALL THAT WAS LEFT WAS ONE OF ITS TOES IN MY TRAP.

"**Man is the only kind of varmint that sets his own trap, baits it, then steps in it.**"

—*John Steinbeck*

I Charged a Bear // by Richard G. Clark, Wasilla, AK

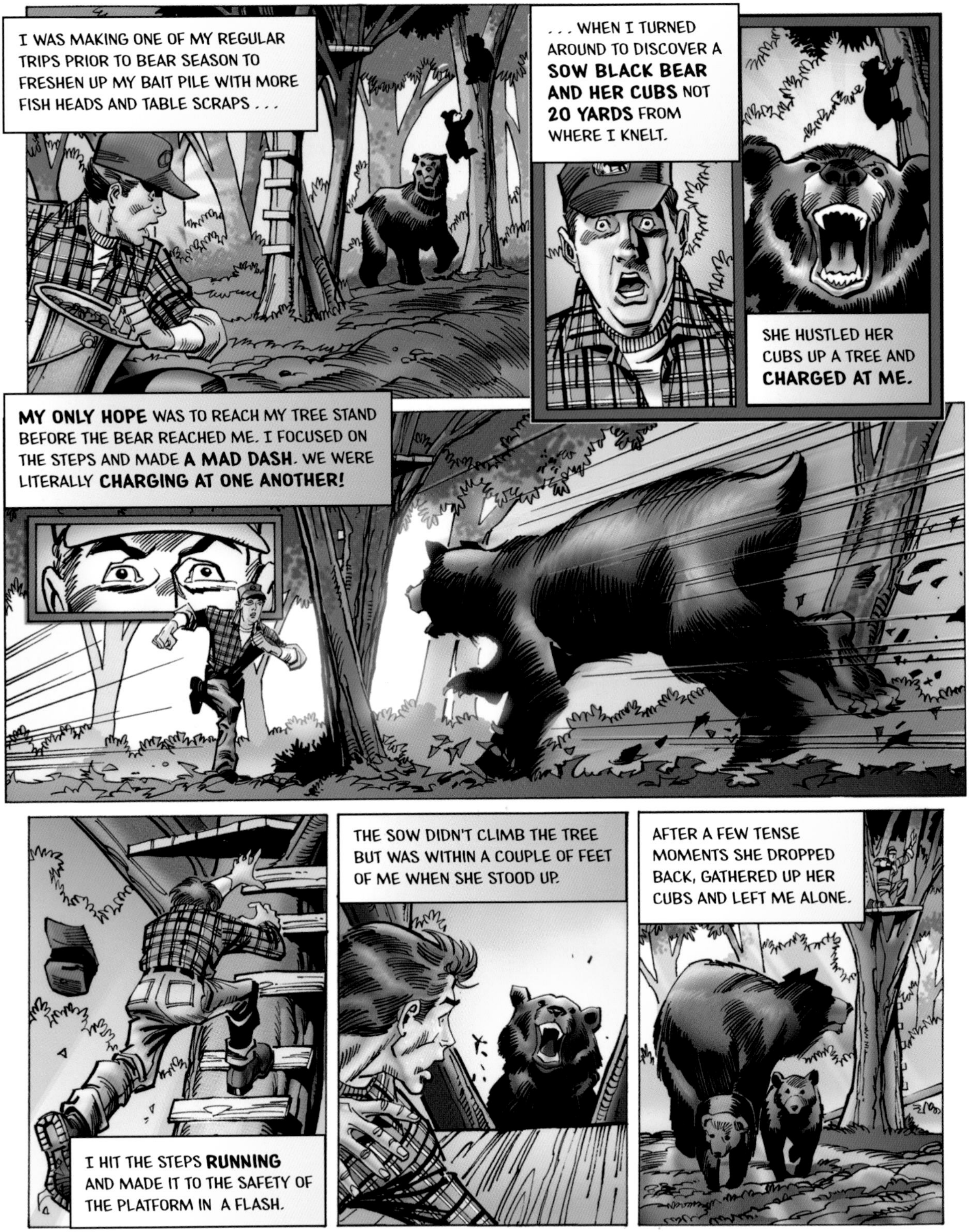
I WAS MAKING ONE OF MY REGULAR TRIPS PRIOR TO BEAR SEASON TO FRESHEN UP MY BAIT PILE WITH MORE FISH HEADS AND TABLE SCRAPS . . .
. . . WHEN I TURNED AROUND TO DISCOVER A SOW BLACK BEAR AND HER CUBS NOT 20 YARDS FROM WHERE I KNELT.
SHE HUSTLED HER CUBS UP A TREE AND CHARGED AT ME.
MY ONLY HOPE WAS TO REACH MY TREE STAND BEFORE THE BEAR REACHED ME. I FOCUSED ON THE STEPS AND MADE A MAD DASH. WE WERE LITERALLY CHARGING AT ONE ANOTHER!
I HIT THE STEPS RUNNING AND MADE IT TO THE SAFETY OF THE PLATFORM IN A FLASH.
THE SOW DIDN'T CLIMB THE TREE BUT WAS WITHIN A COUPLE OF FEET OF ME WHEN SHE STOOD UP.
AFTER A FEW TENSE MOMENTS SHE DROPPED BACK, GATHERED UP HER CUBS AND LEFT ME ALONE.

KNOW THE NUMBERS:
Black Bears

902 POUNDS Record weight of the heaviest known black bear, shot in New Brunswick in 1972.

700 PSI Biting force of a black bear's jaws.

35 MPH Top speed of a running black bear.

5 MONTHS Longest delay between mating and offspring gestation in black bears.

33% Fat content of a black bear's milk for nursing cubs.

Killer Catamount! // by Michael Eide, Logandale, NV

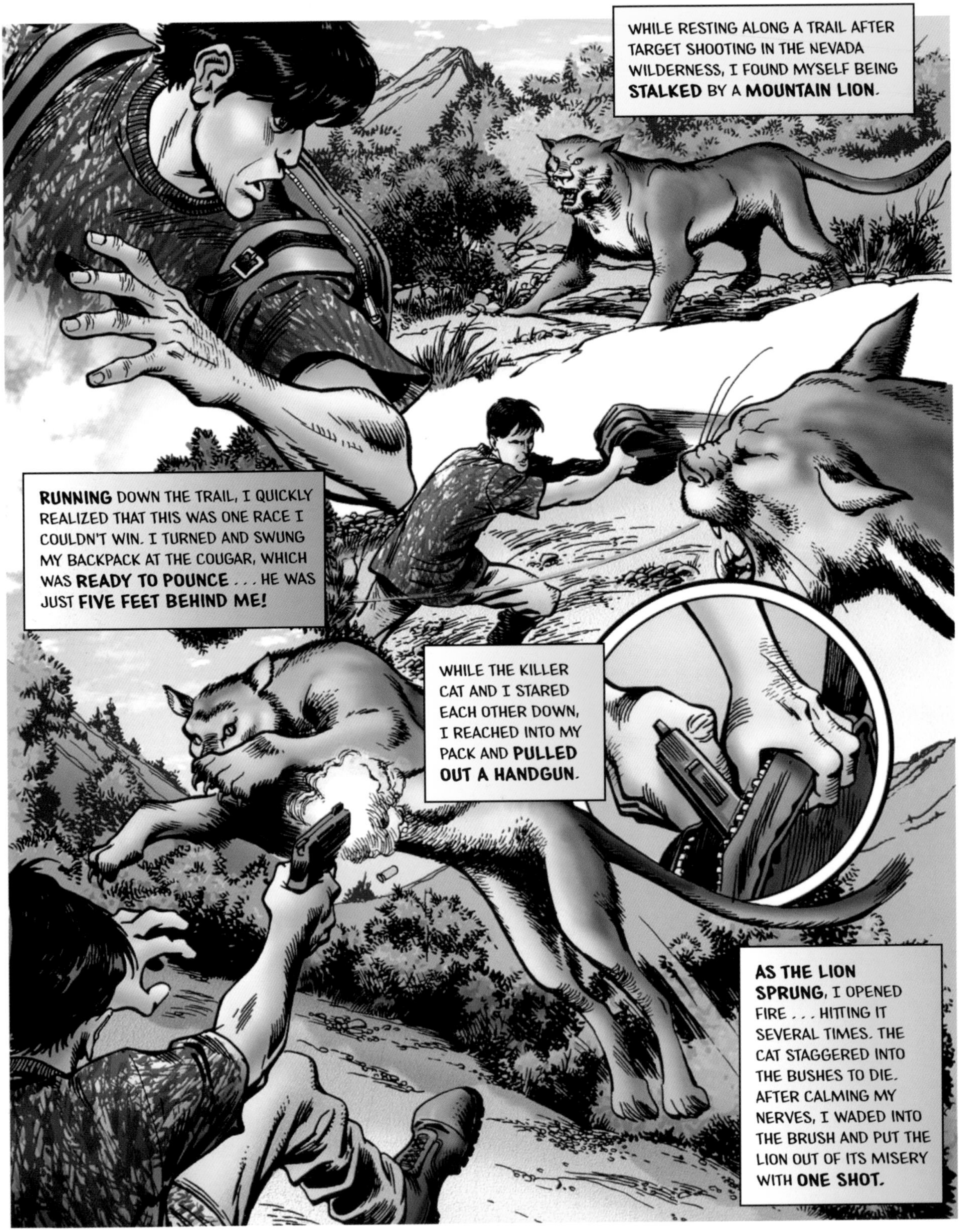
WHILE RESTING ALONG A TRAIL AFTER TARGET SHOOTING IN THE NEVADA WILDERNESS, I FOUND MYSELF BEING STALKED BY A MOUNTAIN LION.
RUNNING DOWN THE TRAIL, I QUICKLY REALIZED THAT THIS WAS ONE RACE I COULDN'T WIN. I TURNED AND SWUNG MY BACKPACK AT THE COUGAR, WHICH WAS READY TO POUNCE . . . HE WAS JUST FIVE FEET BEHIND ME!
WHILE THE KILLER CAT AND I STARED EACH OTHER DOWN, I REACHED INTO MY PACK AND PULLED OUT A HANDGUN.
AS THE LION SPRUNG, I OPENED FIRE . . . HITTING IT SEVERAL TIMES. THE CAT STAGGERED INTO THE BUSHES TO DIE. AFTER CALMING MY NERVES, I WADED INTO THE BRUSH AND PUT THE LION OUT OF ITS MISERY WITH ONE SHOT.

Later, Gator // by Terrence A. Cronin Sr., M.D., Melbourne, FL

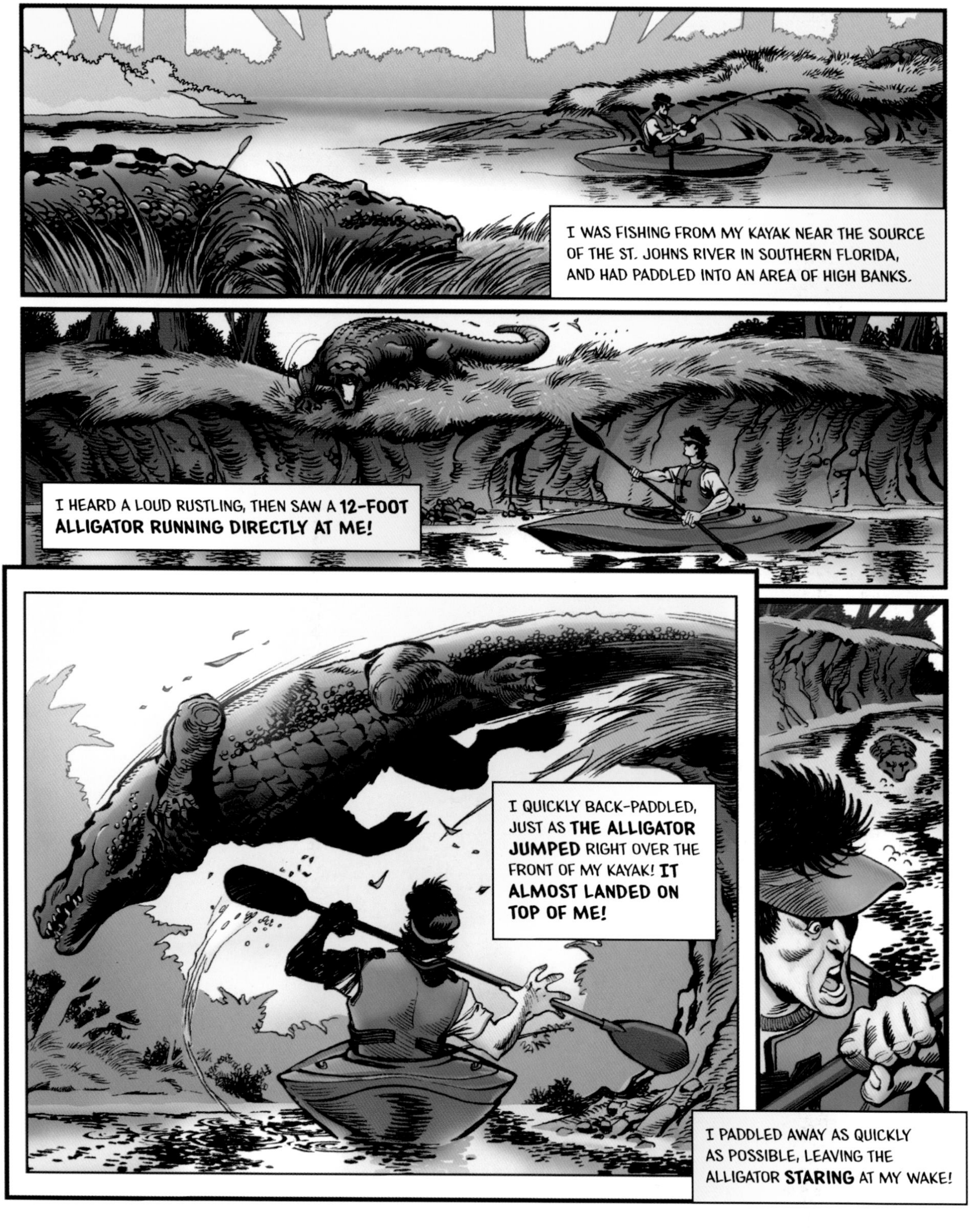

I WAS FISHING FROM MY KAYAK NEAR THE SOURCE OF THE ST. JOHNS RIVER IN SOUTHERN FLORIDA, AND HAD PADDLED INTO AN AREA OF HIGH BANKS.
I HEARD A LOUD RUSTLING, THEN SAW A **12-FOOT ALLIGATOR RUNNING DIRECTLY AT ME!**
I QUICKLY BACK-PADDLED, JUST AS **THE ALLIGATOR JUMPED** RIGHT OVER THE FRONT OF MY KAYAK! **IT ALMOST LANDED ON TOP OF ME!**
I PADDLED AWAY AS QUICKLY AS POSSIBLE, LEAVING THE ALLIGATOR **STARING** AT MY WAKE!

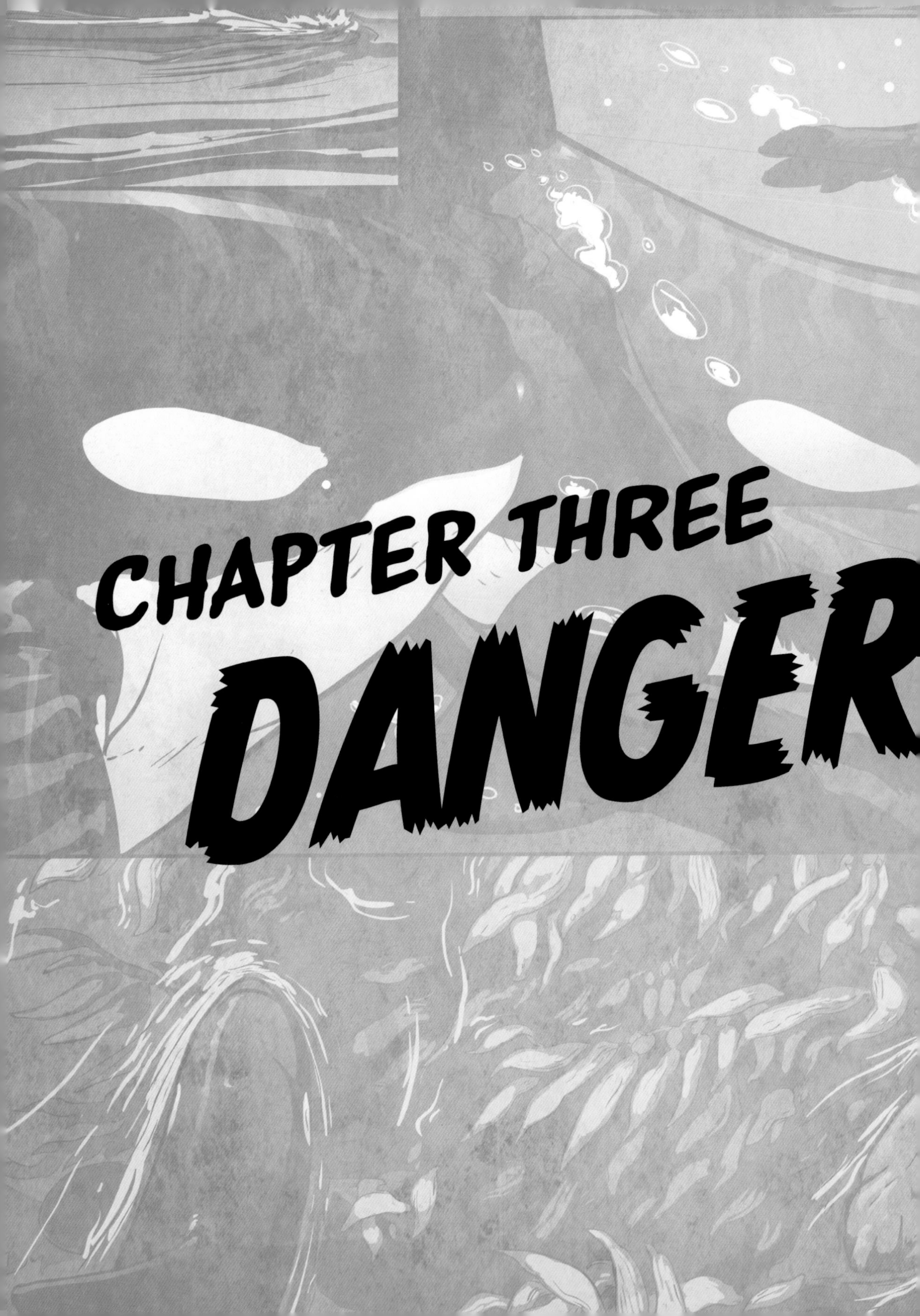
CHAPTER THREE
DANGER

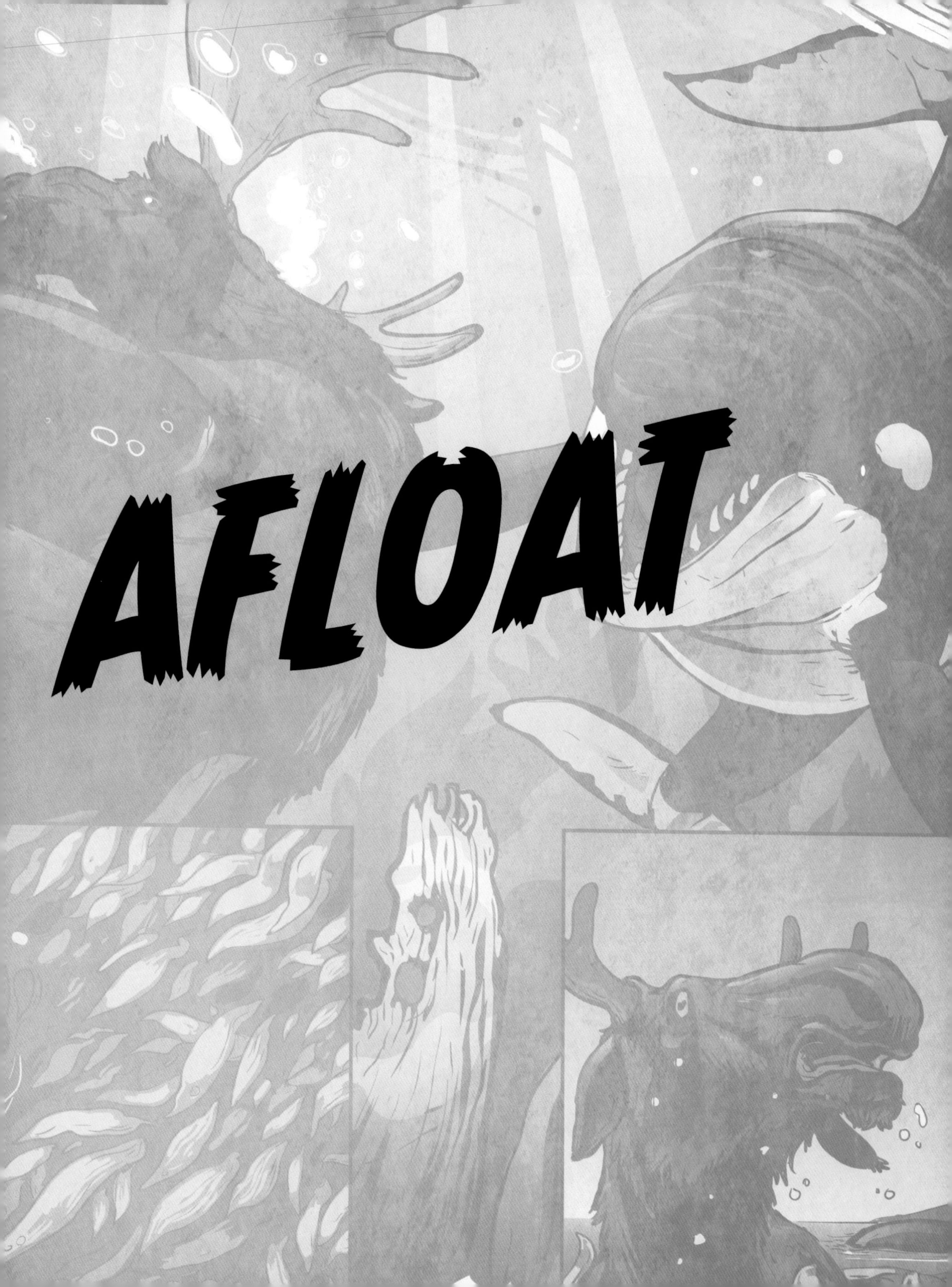
AFLOAT

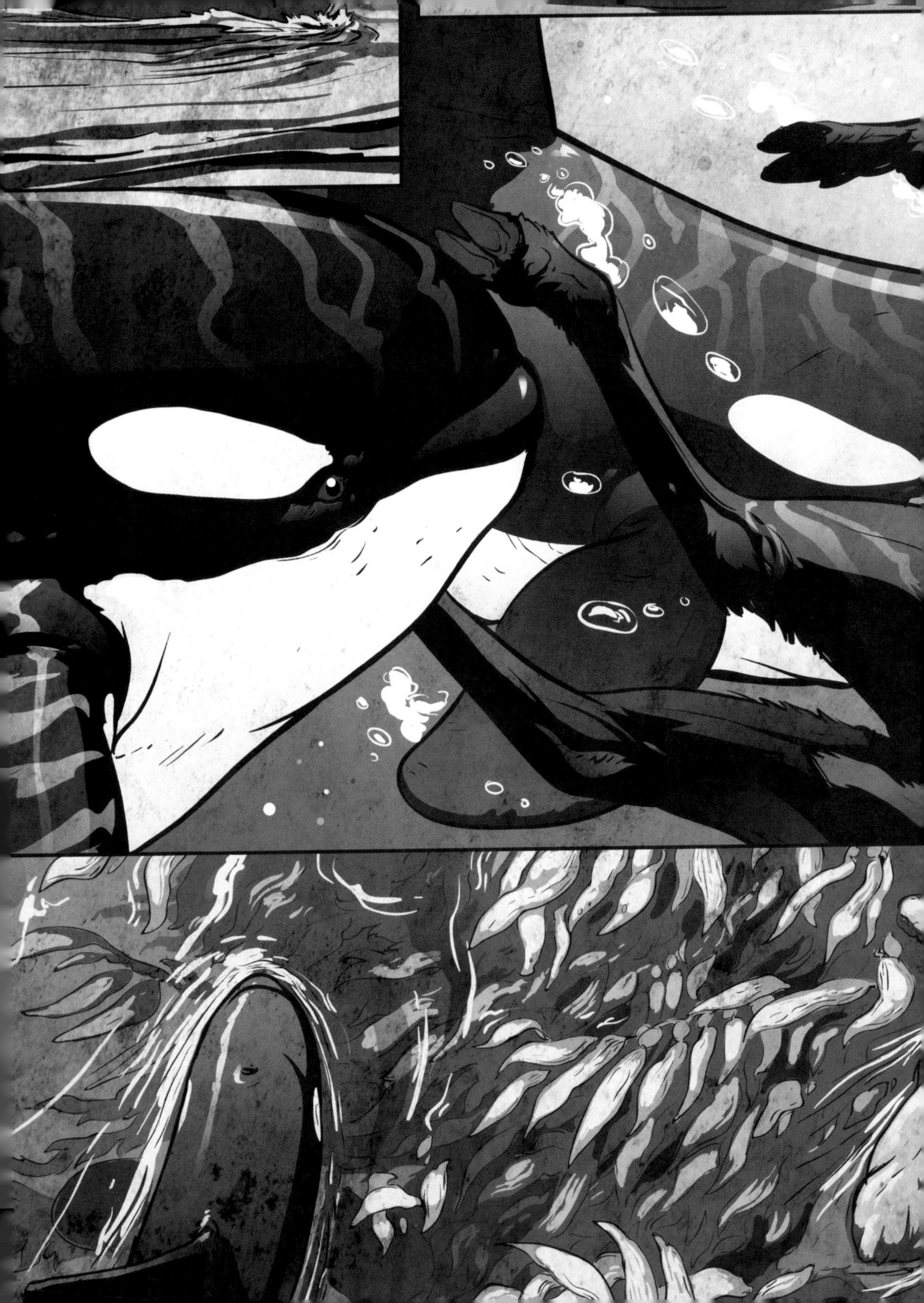

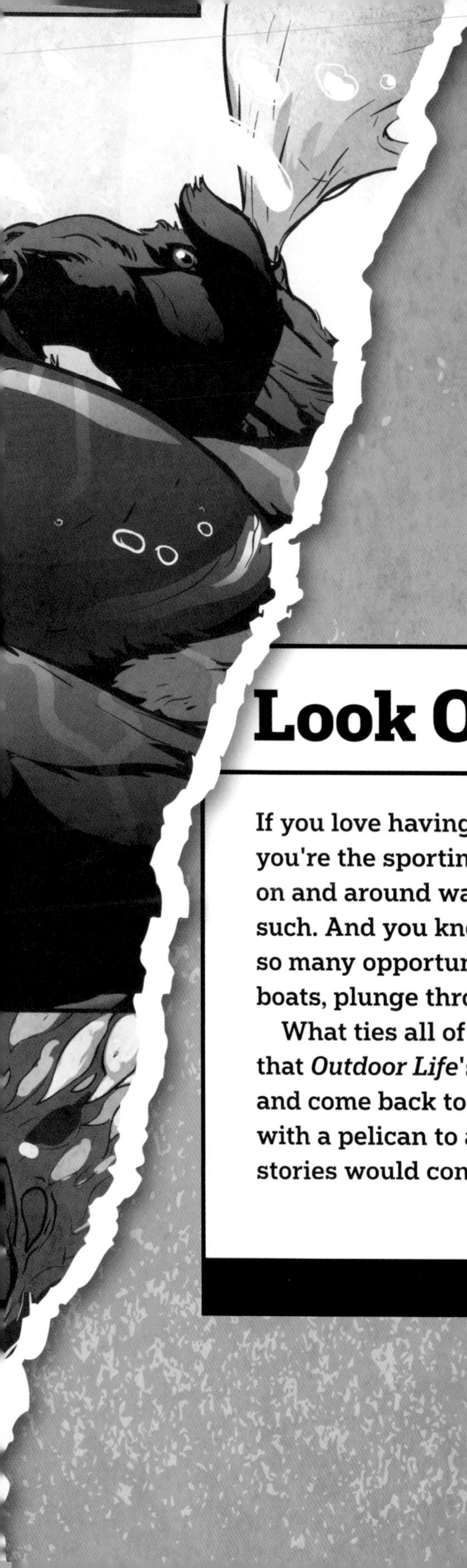

Look Out Below!

If you love having fun in the great outdoors, especially if you're the sporting type, you probably spend a lot of time on and around water . . . fishing, boating, swimming, and such. And you know what that means? It means you have so many opportunities to be bitten by sharks, fall off of boats, plunge through broken ice, or get lost in a swamp.

What ties all of these watery perils together? The fact that *Outdoor Life*'s readers have faced them, survived, and come back to tell the tale. From a comical encounter with a pelican to a terrifying tale of a tsunami, these stories would convince lesser souls to stay on dry land.

Clash of the Titans // by John F. Barry, Juneau, AK

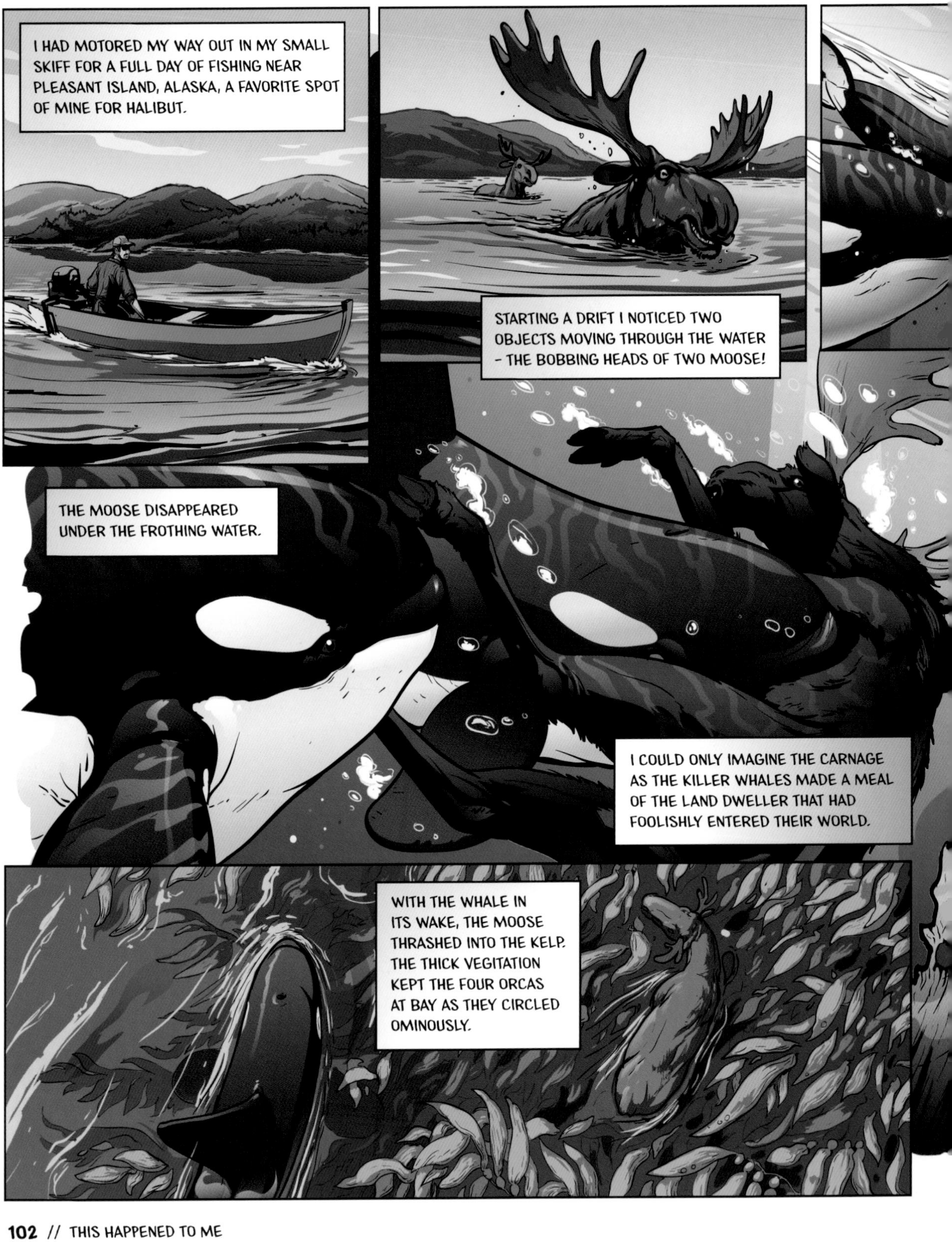

I HAD MOTORED MY WAY OUT IN MY SMALL SKIFF FOR A FULL DAY OF FISHING NEAR PLEASANT ISLAND, ALASKA, A FAVORITE SPOT OF MINE FOR HALIBUT.
STARTING A DRIFT I NOTICED TWO OBJECTS MOVING THROUGH THE WATER - THE BOBBING HEADS OF TWO MOOSE!
THE MOOSE DISAPPEARED UNDER THE FROTHING WATER.
I COULD ONLY IMAGINE THE CARNAGE AS THE KILLER WHALES MADE A MEAL OF THE LAND DWELLER THAT HAD FOOLISHLY ENTERED THEIR WORLD.
WITH THE WHALE IN ITS WAKE, THE MOOSE THRASHED INTO THE KELP. THE THICK VEGITATION KEPT THE FOUR ORCAS AT BAY AS THEY CIRCLED OMINOUSLY.

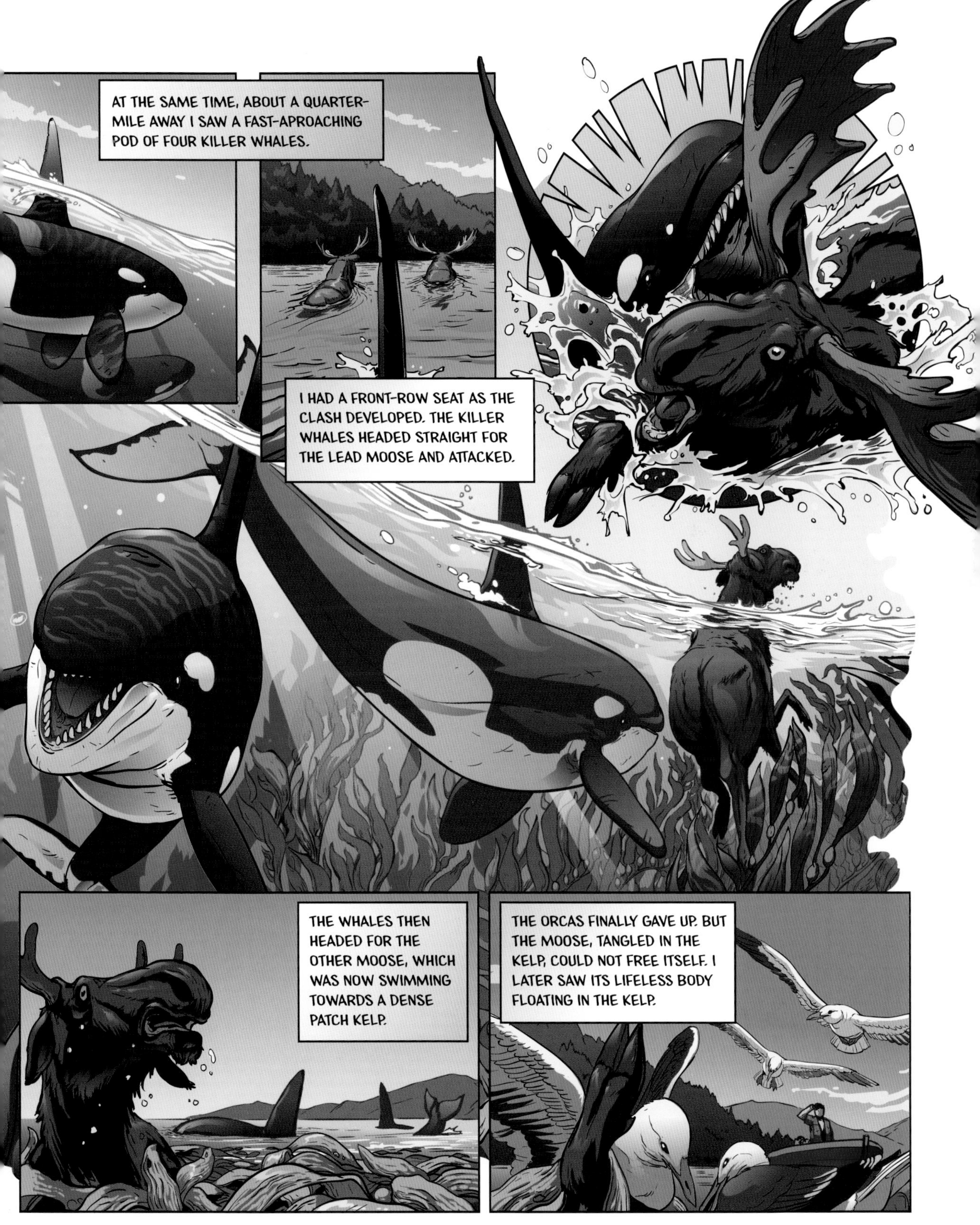
AT THE SAME TIME, ABOUT A QUARTER-MILE AWAY I SAW A FAST-APROACHING POD OF FOUR KILLER WHALES.
I HAD A FRONT-ROW SEAT AS THE CLASH DEVELOPED. THE KILLER WHALES HEADED STRAIGHT FOR THE LEAD MOOSE AND ATTACKED.
THE WHALES THEN HEADED FOR THE OTHER MOOSE, WHICH WAS NOW SWIMMING TOWARDS A DENSE PATCH KELP.
THE ORCAS FINALLY GAVE UP. BUT THE MOOSE, TANGLED IN THE KELP, COULD NOT FREE ITSELF. I LATER SAW ITS LIFELESS BODY FLOATING IN THE KELP.

The Perfect Storm // by Chris Daniels, New Bern, NC

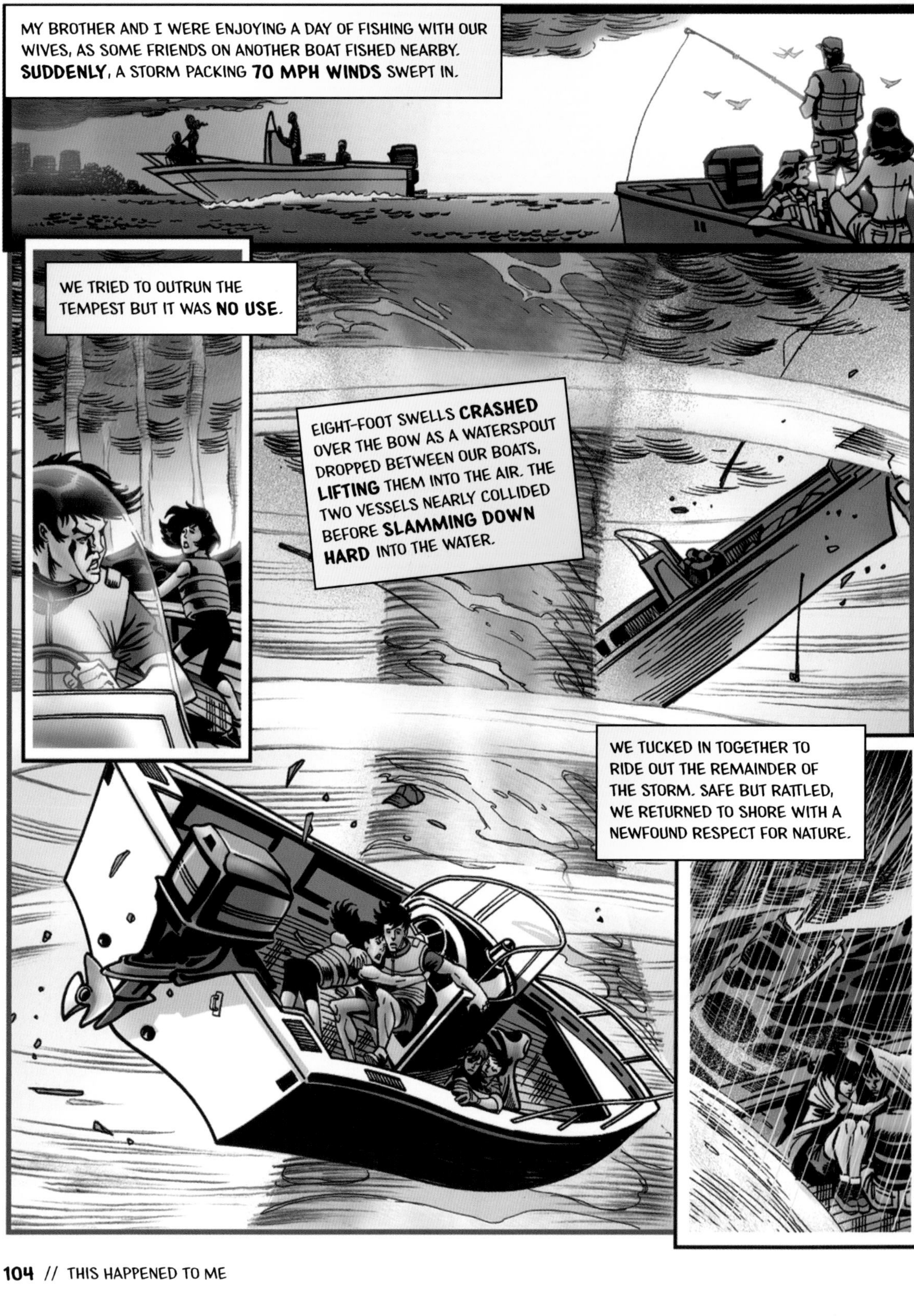
MY BROTHER AND I WERE ENJOYING A DAY OF FISHING WITH OUR WIVES, AS SOME FRIENDS ON ANOTHER BOAT FISHED NEARBY. SUDDENLY, A STORM PACKING 70 MPH WINDS SWEPT IN.
WE TRIED TO OUTRUN THE TEMPEST BUT IT WAS NO USE.
EIGHT-FOOT SWELLS CRASHED OVER THE BOW AS A WATERSPOUT DROPPED BETWEEN OUR BOATS, LIFTING THEM INTO THE AIR. THE TWO VESSELS NEARLY COLLIDED BEFORE SLAMMING DOWN HARD INTO THE WATER.
WE TUCKED IN TOGETHER TO RIDE OUT THE REMAINDER OF THE STORM. SAFE BUT RATTLED, WE RETURNED TO SHORE WITH A NEWFOUND RESPECT FOR NATURE.

Safety at Sea

SET SAIL So you're on a big boat, and someone else is at the wheel. Don't relax just yet! First note where the lifeboats and life jackets are stowed, and read the card on the back of your stateroom door to learn the location of your lifeboat-muster area. Then go find it. If there's an evacuation drill, attend and pay attention. In an emergency, the captain will sound an alarm: seven short blasts followed by one long one. If you hear this alarm, make a beeline for the muster area and board the boat as instructed by the crew.

Unless you're the captain, you definitely don't want to go down with the ship. But going over the side is no picnic, either. Still, if ordered to abandon ship, move as fast as you can. Follow these steps to make a safe exit.

STEP ONE Avoid the crowd, get to the railing and prepare to jump. If the ship is tilting, jump from the high side so you aren't crushed if it capsizes. If you're over 15 feet above water, get lower or wait for the ship to sink further.

STEP TWO Cross your arms over your chest and grab your lapels, to keep your neck and shoulders from breaking when you hit the water.

STEP THREE Look for a spot in the water that's free of debris and aim for it. It will take some courage, but when you've picked your spot, don't wait.

STEP FOUR As you jump, keep your legs together, ankles crossed, to reduce the risk of injury on impact. Take a big breath just before the splash.

STEP FIVE If you're close to a sinking ship, you risk being hit by falling debris. Swim at least 100 feet from the vessel. Conserve energy with a sidestroke or backstroke while watching for obstacles or hazards.

KNOW THE NUMBERS: Catfish

650 POUNDS Weight of the Mekong giant catfish (*Pangasianodon gigas*), the largest catfish species in the world.

100,000 Number of taste buds on a catfish. Only about one-quarter of those taste buds are in its mouth; the rest are all over its body.

4,000–100,000 Number of eggs laid by female catfish during spawning periods.

350 VOLTS Energy of the electrical charge generated by an African electric catfish.

Cattie-Wampus // by Ken Simmers, North East, MD

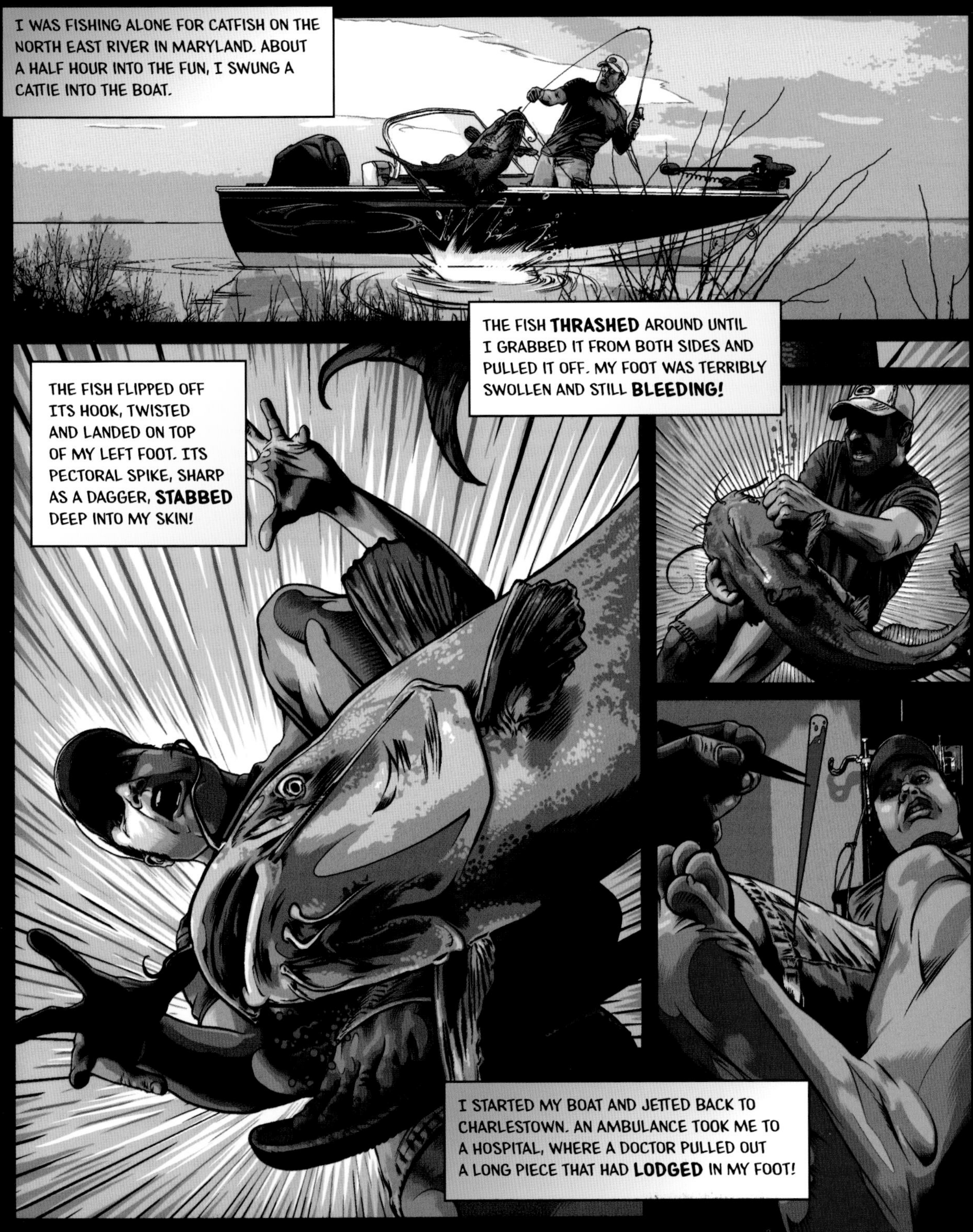

I WAS FISHING ALONE FOR CATFISH ON THE NORTH EAST RIVER IN MARYLAND. ABOUT A HALF HOUR INTO THE FUN, I SWUNG A CATTIE INTO THE BOAT.
THE FISH FLIPPED OFF ITS HOOK, TWISTED AND LANDED ON TOP OF MY LEFT FOOT. ITS PECTORAL SPIKE, SHARP AS A DAGGER, STABBED DEEP INTO MY SKIN!
THE FISH THRASHED AROUND UNTIL I GRABBED IT FROM BOTH SIDES AND PULLED IT OFF. MY FOOT WAS TERRIBLY SWOLLEN AND STILL BLEEDING!
I STARTED MY BOAT AND JETTED BACK TO CHARLESTOWN. AN AMBULANCE TOOK ME TO A HOSPITAL, WHERE A DOCTOR PULLED OUT A LONG PIECE THAT HAD LODGED IN MY FOOT!

"**Withstanding the cold develops vigor for the relaxing days of spring and summer. Besides, in this matter as in many others, it is evident that nature abhors a quitter.**"

—*Arthur C. Crandall*

Escape from an Icy Grave // by Dale Van Horn, Crosby, MN

I WAS DRIVING TO MY FISHING SPOT ACROSS MINNESOTA'S MISSION LAKE WHEN THE ICE BEGAN TO CRUMBLE.

BEHIND ME, I SAW ONLY WATER AS MY TRUCK **STARTED TO SINK!**

I TRIED TO ESCAPE, BUT THE RUNNING BOARD BENT AROUND MY FOOT . . . **I WAS TRAPPED!**

THE CAB FILLED WITH WATER AND ICE. I GULPED A LAST BREATH BEFORE BEING PULLED INTO THE **FRIGID DEPTHS.**

THIRTY FEET DOWN, THE TRUCK FINALLY CAME TO REST ON THE BOTTOM OF THE LAKE.

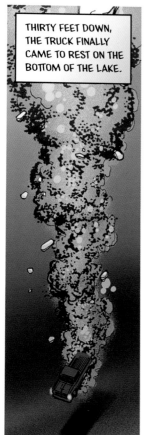

I JERKED MY FOOT FROM THE TRAPPED BOOT AND **SWAM FOR MY LIFE.**

UPON REACHING THE SURFACE, I HIT A WALL OF **SOLID ICE.** **TERROR** FILLED ME...

WITH LUNGS **BURSTING,** I FRANTICALLY SEARCHED FOR, AND FOUND, AN OPENING. FLOATING IN THE HOLE WAS A BAG OF GARBAGE FROM MY TRUCK'S BED. I USED IT TO STRUGGLE TO SAFETY . . . ESCAPING MY **ICY GRAVE.**

When Pelicans Attack // by John Slimp, West Magic, ID

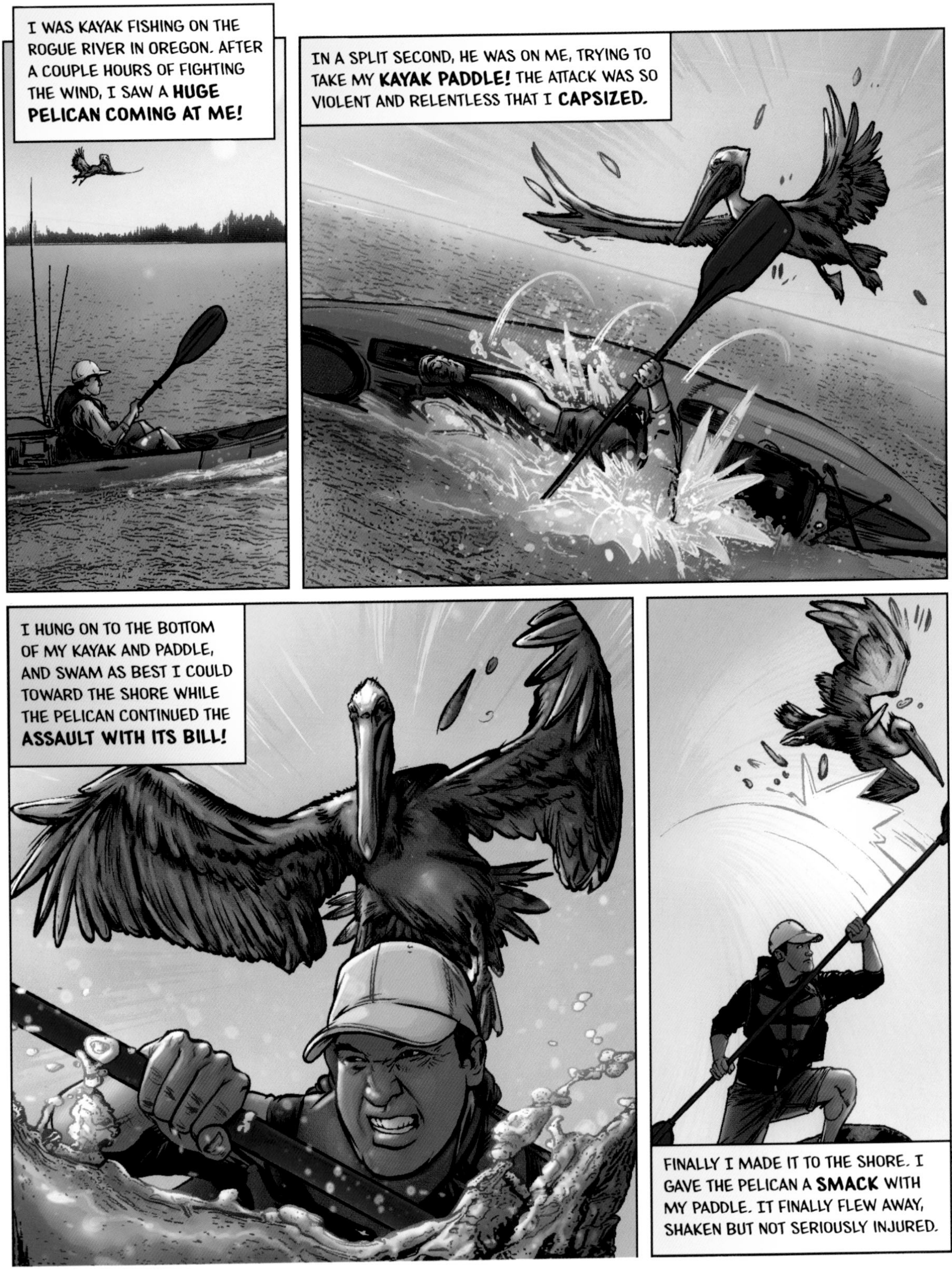
I WAS KAYAK FISHING ON THE ROGUE RIVER IN OREGON. AFTER A COUPLE HOURS OF FIGHTING THE WIND, I SAW A **HUGE PELICAN COMING AT ME!**
IN A SPLIT SECOND, HE WAS ON ME, TRYING TO TAKE MY **KAYAK PADDLE!** THE ATTACK WAS SO VIOLENT AND RELENTLESS THAT I **CAPSIZED.**
I HUNG ON TO THE BOTTOM OF MY KAYAK AND PADDLE, AND SWAM AS BEST I COULD TOWARD THE SHORE WHILE THE PELICAN CONTINUED THE **ASSAULT WITH ITS BILL!**
FINALLY I MADE IT TO THE SHORE. I GAVE THE PELICAN A **SMACK** WITH MY PADDLE. IT FINALLY FLEW AWAY, SHAKEN BUT NOT SERIOUSLY INJURED.

Swamped by a Sub // by Barry Downer, Dillwyn, VA

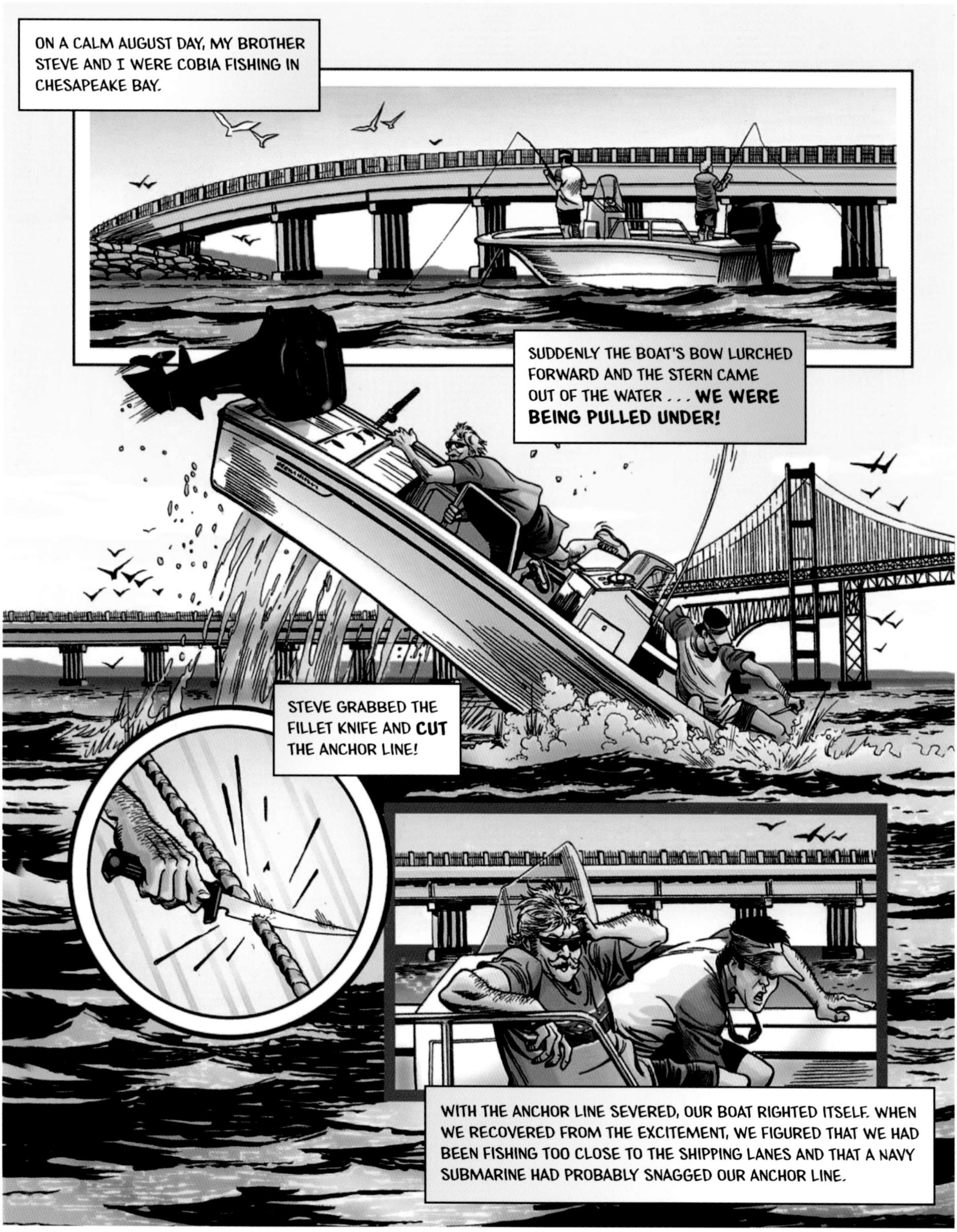
ON A CALM AUGUST DAY, MY BROTHER STEVE AND I WERE COBIA FISHING IN CHESAPEAKE BAY.
SUDDENLY THE BOAT'S BOW LURCHED FORWARD AND THE STERN CAME OUT OF THE WATER . . . WE WERE BEING PULLED UNDER!
STEVE GRABBED THE FILLET KNIFE AND CUT THE ANCHOR LINE!
WITH THE ANCHOR LINE SEVERED, OUR BOAT RIGHTED ITSELF. WHEN WE RECOVERED FROM THE EXCITEMENT, WE FIGURED THAT WE HAD BEEN FISHING TOO CLOSE TO THE SHIPPING LANES AND THAT A NAVY SUBMARINE HAD PROBABLY SNAGGED OUR ANCHOR LINE.

Tsunami Race // by Jolene Cardigan, Ocean City, NJ

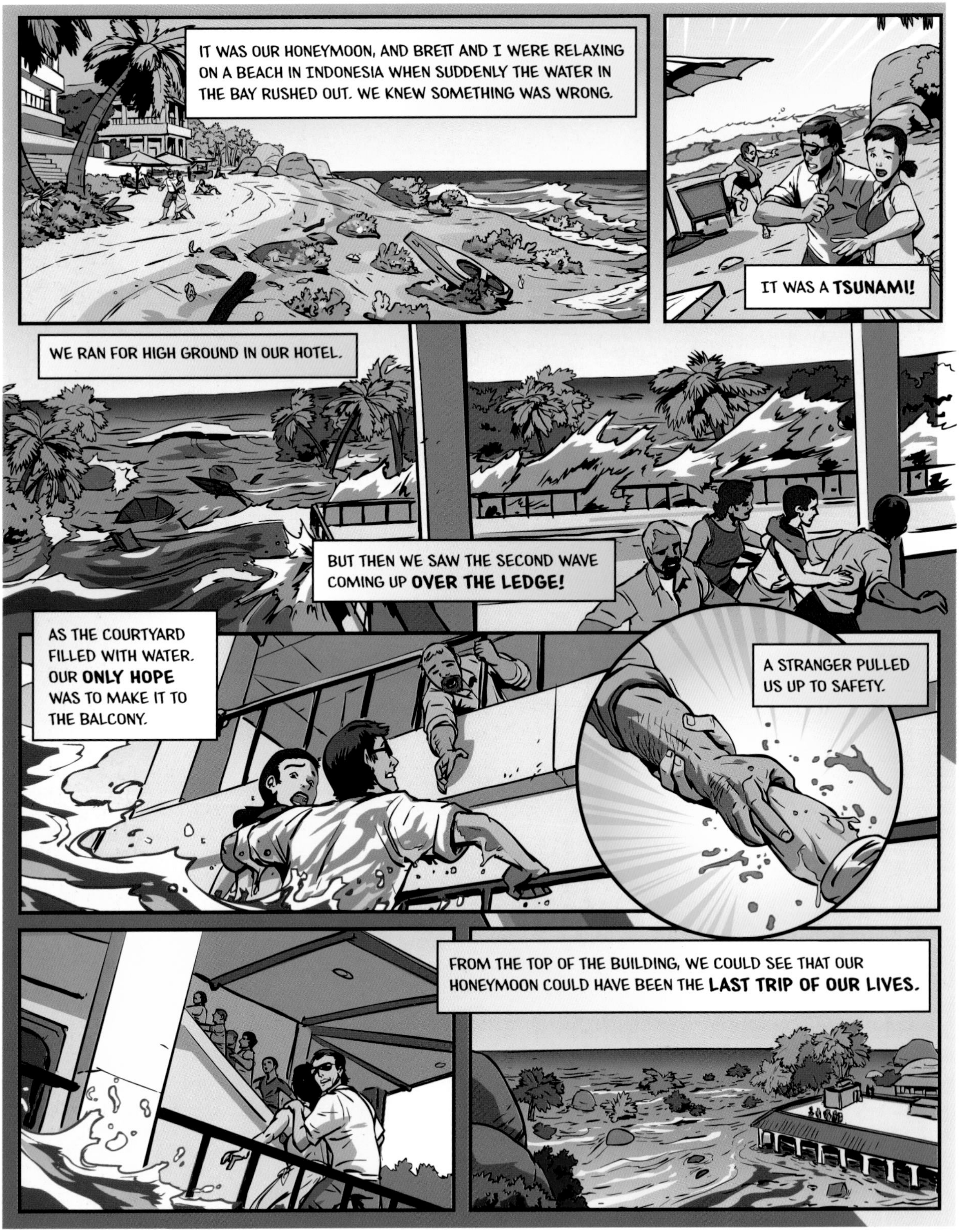
IT WAS OUR HONEYMOON, AND BRETT AND I WERE RELAXING ON A BEACH IN INDONESIA WHEN SUDDENLY THE WATER IN THE BAY RUSHED OUT. WE KNEW SOMETHING WAS WRONG.
IT WAS A TSUNAMI!
WE RAN FOR HIGH GROUND IN OUR HOTEL.
BUT THEN WE SAW THE SECOND WAVE COMING UP OVER THE LEDGE!
AS THE COURTYARD FILLED WITH WATER, OUR ONLY HOPE WAS TO MAKE IT TO THE BALCONY.
A STRANGER PULLED US UP TO SAFETY.
FROM THE TOP OF THE BUILDING, WE COULD SEE THAT OUR HONEYMOON COULD HAVE BEEN THE LAST TRIP OF OUR LIVES.

Crashing Wave

BAD TIDINGS A tsunami can travel through deep water at more than 600 miles per hour, crossing an ocean in less than a day. And it won't slow down when it hits shore—shallower water actually channels the wave's energy and speeds it up. Here's how to tell if a big wave is coming, and what to do.

A MAJOR SHAKE-UP An earthquake in a coastal region is an obvious warning sign. If you live near the earthquake, seek out high ground. Even if the earthquake is across the ocean, monitor broadcasts for warnings—tsunamis can travel long distances. It's not just earthquakes that cause tsunamis. Volcanic activity, landslides, or impact from space objects can all set one off. And since the biggest tsunamis are as tall as 100 feet, you'll want to get at least that high above sea level. Anytime you're in a coastal area, think about where you would go in a big-wave emergency.

ANTSY ANIMALS Look out for changes in animal behavior. Scientists believe critters pick up on the earth's vibrations before we do, so if they're nervous, it may be for good reason.

RECEDING WATER The first part of a tsunami to reach land is the drawback trough, which causes coastal waters to recede, exposing normally submerged areas. If you spot a drawback, don't stick around: You've got about five minutes before the big wave hits.

PLOT YOUR ESCAPE Do a little recon to identify escape routes to high ground. Plan on following designated tsunami evacuation routes (if they're established in your area) or simply heading inland and uphill as quickly as possible.

STAY TUNED Keep your ear tuned to the radio and TV for warnings. Evacuate immediately upon receiving notice of an impending tsunami.

GET THE HECK OUT Unless you have a death wish, don't go to the beach to watch the waves come ashore. Immediately meet up with your loved ones and head for high ground—and then keep going, just in case.

That Dam Pipe // by Rick Petrekovic, Prior Lake, MN

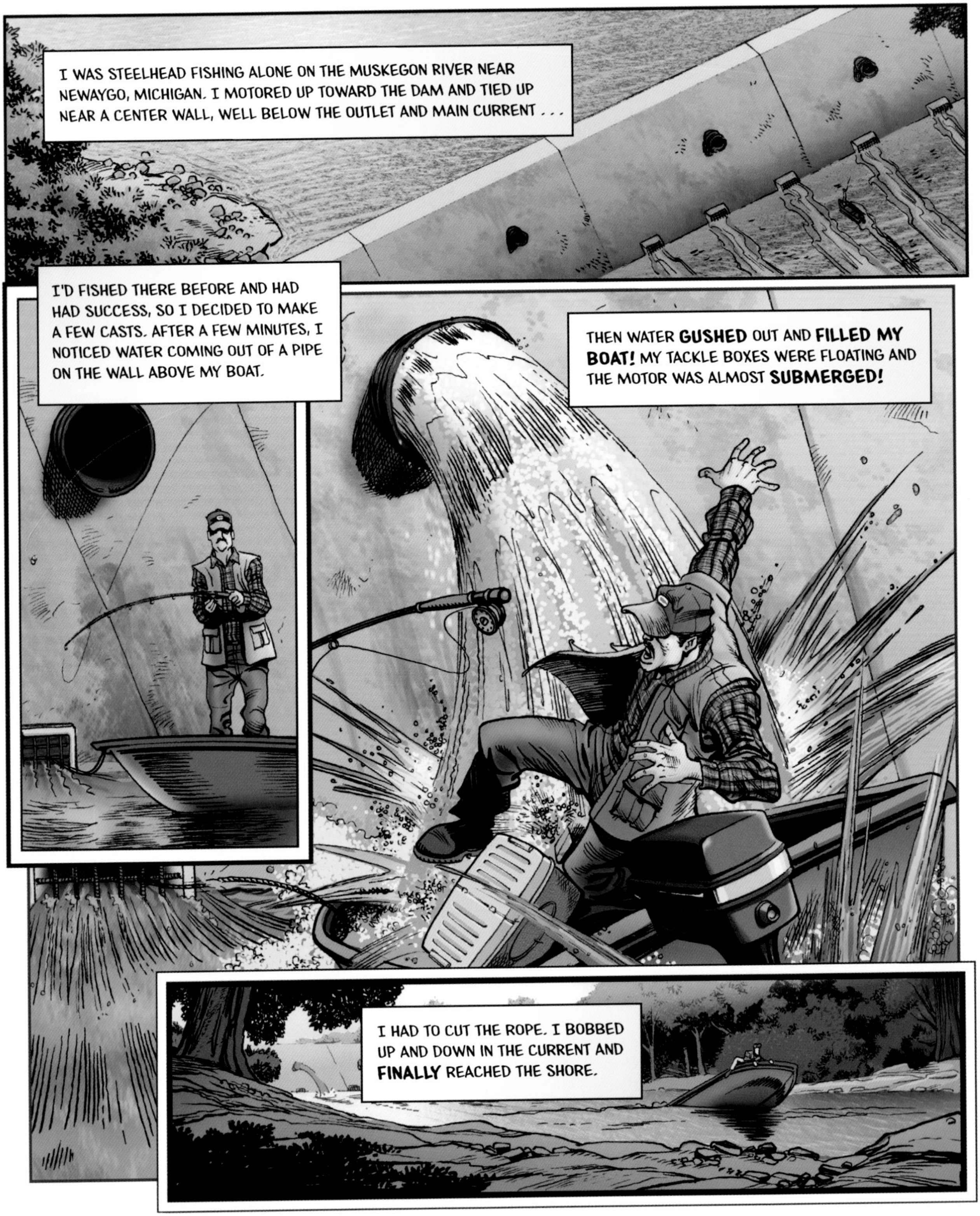
I WAS STEELHEAD FISHING ALONE ON THE MUSKEGON RIVER NEAR NEWAYGO, MICHIGAN. I MOTORED UP TOWARD THE DAM AND TIED UP NEAR A CENTER WALL, WELL BELOW THE OUTLET AND MAIN CURRENT . . .
I'D FISHED THERE BEFORE AND HAD HAD SUCCESS, SO I DECIDED TO MAKE A FEW CASTS. AFTER A FEW MINUTES, I NOTICED WATER COMING OUT OF A PIPE ON THE WALL ABOVE MY BOAT.
THEN WATER **GUSHED** OUT AND **FILLED MY BOAT!** MY TACKLE BOXES WERE FLOATING AND THE MOTOR WAS ALMOST **SUBMERGED!**
I HAD TO CUT THE ROPE. I BOBBED UP AND DOWN IN THE CURRENT AND **FINALLY** REACHED THE SHORE.

KNOW THE NUMBERS:
Dams

984 FEET Height of the Nurek Dam, the tallest man-made dam in the world, located on the Vakhsh River in Tajikistan.

362,000 GALLONS Maximum amount of water taken in every second by the "Glory Hole" spillway at the Monticello Dam in Napa County, California.

171,000 Estimated number of people lost in the 1975 Banqiao Dam collapse in China (reports vary between 90,000 and 230,000).

706 MILLION CUBIC YARDS Volume of the largest dam built, the Syncrude Tailings Dam in Canada.

94.7 TERAWATT-HOURS Most power generated annually, by the Itaipu Dam on the Parana River, at the Brazil-Paraguay border.

A Life on the Line // by Gene Horowitz, Allegheny, PA

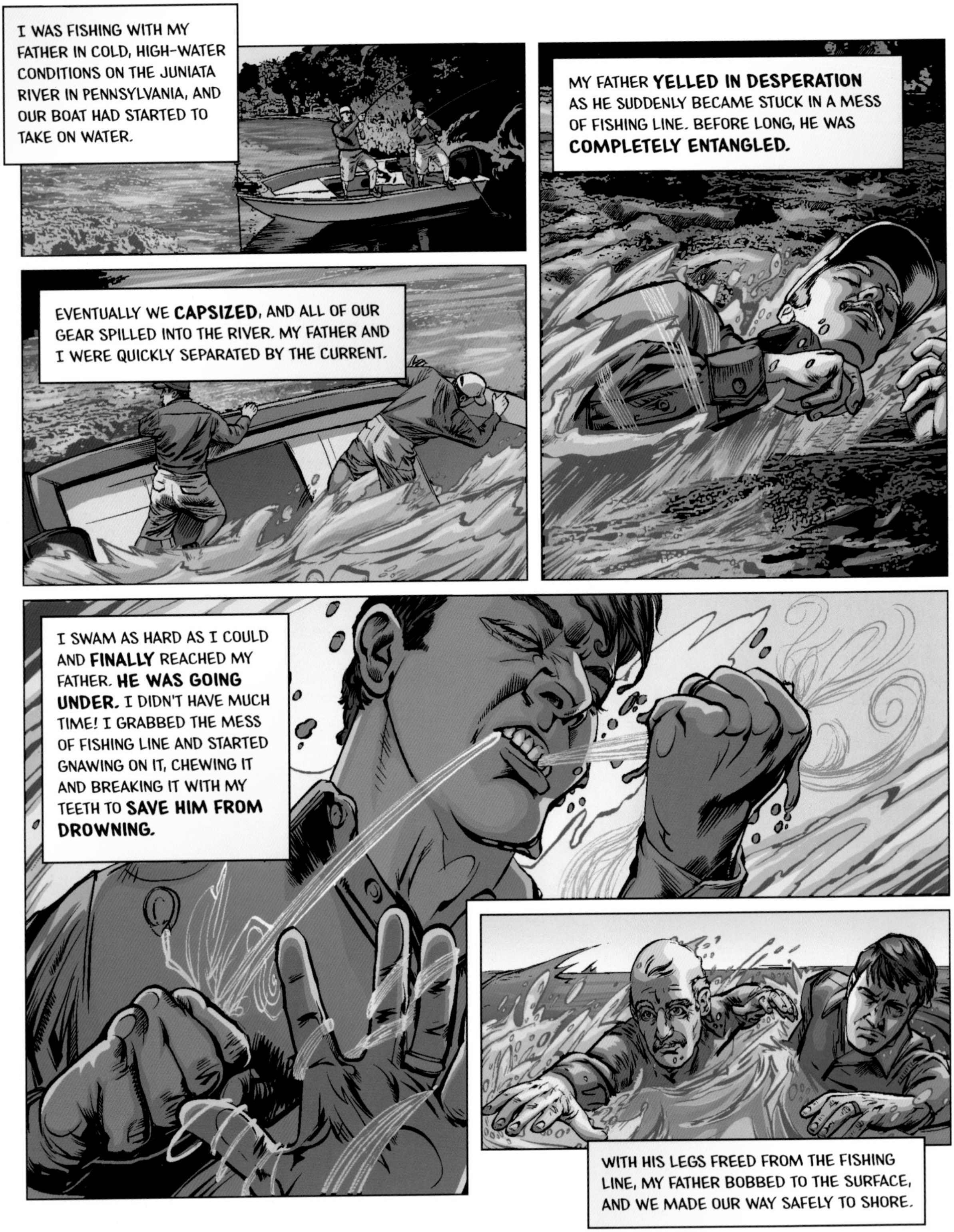
I WAS FISHING WITH MY FATHER IN COLD, HIGH-WATER CONDITIONS ON THE JUNIATA RIVER IN PENNSYLVANIA, AND OUR BOAT HAD STARTED TO TAKE ON WATER.
EVENTUALLY WE **CAPSIZED**, AND ALL OF OUR GEAR SPILLED INTO THE RIVER. MY FATHER AND I WERE QUICKLY SEPARATED BY THE CURRENT.
MY FATHER **YELLED IN DESPERATION** AS HE SUDDENLY BECAME STUCK IN A MESS OF FISHING LINE. BEFORE LONG, HE WAS **COMPLETELY ENTANGLED.**
I SWAM AS HARD AS I COULD AND **FINALLY** REACHED MY FATHER. **HE WAS GOING UNDER.** I DIDN'T HAVE MUCH TIME! I GRABBED THE MESS OF FISHING LINE AND STARTED GNAWING ON IT, CHEWING IT AND BREAKING IT WITH MY TEETH TO **SAVE HIM FROM DROWNING.**
WITH HIS LEGS FREED FROM THE FISHING LINE, MY FATHER BOBBED TO THE SURFACE, AND WE MADE OUR WAY SAFELY TO SHORE.

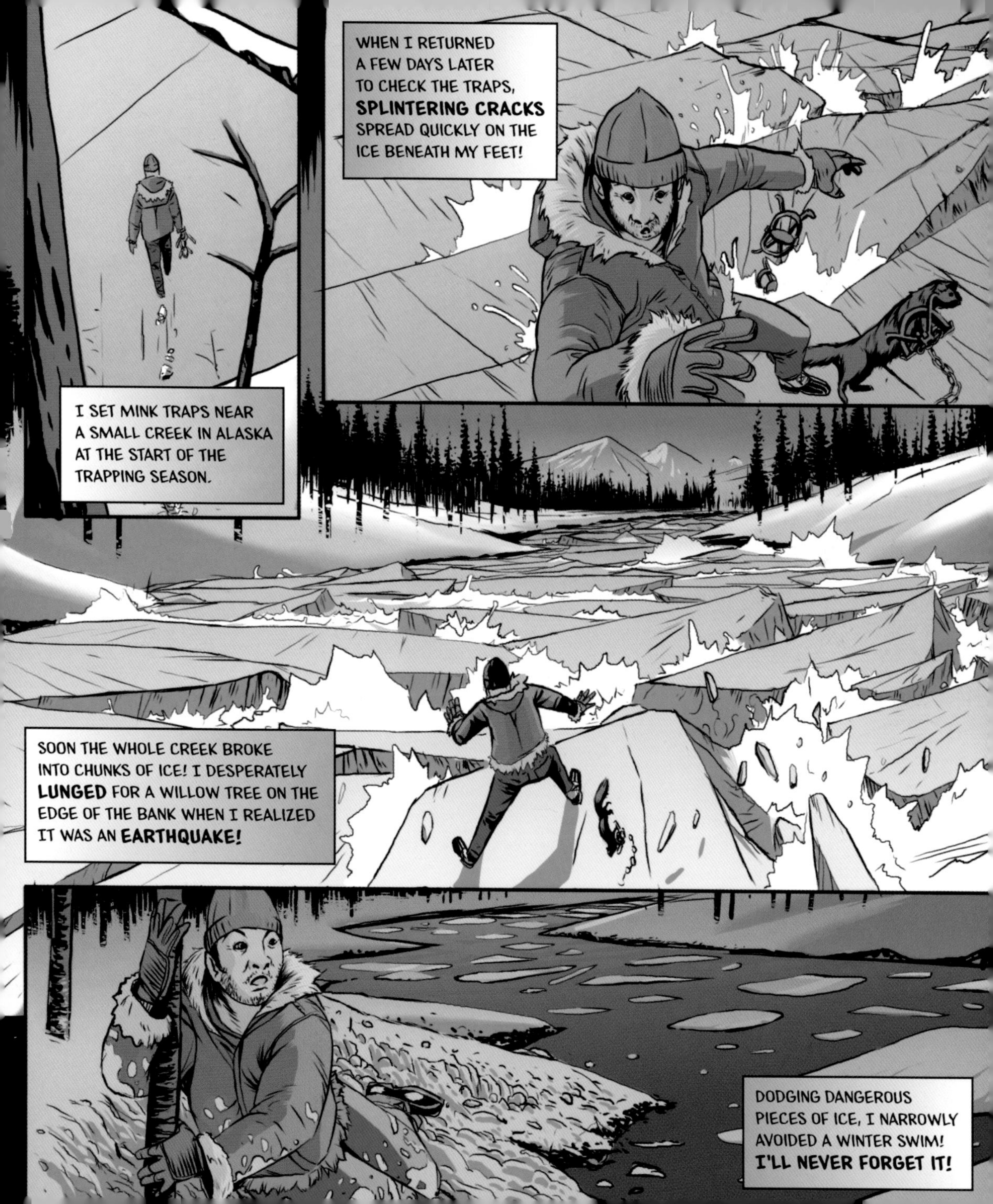
I SET MINK TRAPS NEAR A SMALL CREEK IN ALASKA AT THE START OF THE TRAPPING SEASON.
WHEN I RETURNED A FEW DAYS LATER TO CHECK THE TRAPS, **SPLINTERING CRACKS** SPREAD QUICKLY ON THE ICE BENEATH MY FEET!
SOON THE WHOLE CREEK BROKE INTO CHUNKS OF ICE! I DESPERATELY **LUNGED** FOR A WILLOW TREE ON THE EDGE OF THE BANK WHEN I REALIZED IT WAS AN **EARTHQUAKE!**
DODGING DANGEROUS PIECES OF ICE, I NARROWLY AVOIDED A WINTER SWIM! **I'LL NEVER FORGET IT!**

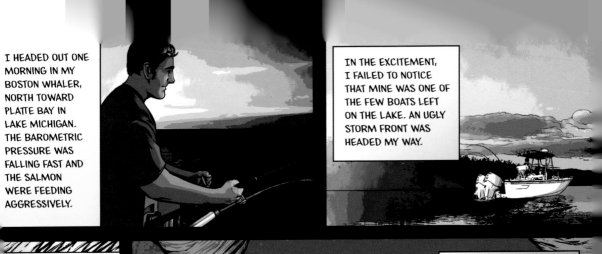

I HEADED OUT ONE MORNING IN MY BOSTON WHALER, NORTH TOWARD PLATTE BAY IN LAKE MICHIGAN. THE BAROMETRIC PRESSURE WAS FALLING FAST AND THE SALMON WERE FEEDING AGGRESSIVELY.

IN THE EXCITEMENT, I FAILED TO NOTICE THAT MINE WAS ONE OF THE FEW BOATS LEFT ON THE LAKE. AN UGLY STORM FRONT WAS HEADED MY WAY.

SUDDENLY A SERIES OF **WATERSPOUTS** APPEARED ON THE SURFACE OF THE LAKE AND WERE **COMING STRAIGHT AT ME!**

SOMEHOW I MANAGED TO KEEP THE BOAT HEADED DIRECTLY INTO THE WAVES, WHICH WERE **BREAKING ABOVE MY HEAD!**

I MADE IT IN TO PORT. THE LIGHTHOUSE ON THE END OF THE NORTH PIER NEVER LOOKED SO GOOD. I KISSED THE GROUND AS SOON AS I GOT OFF THE BOAT.

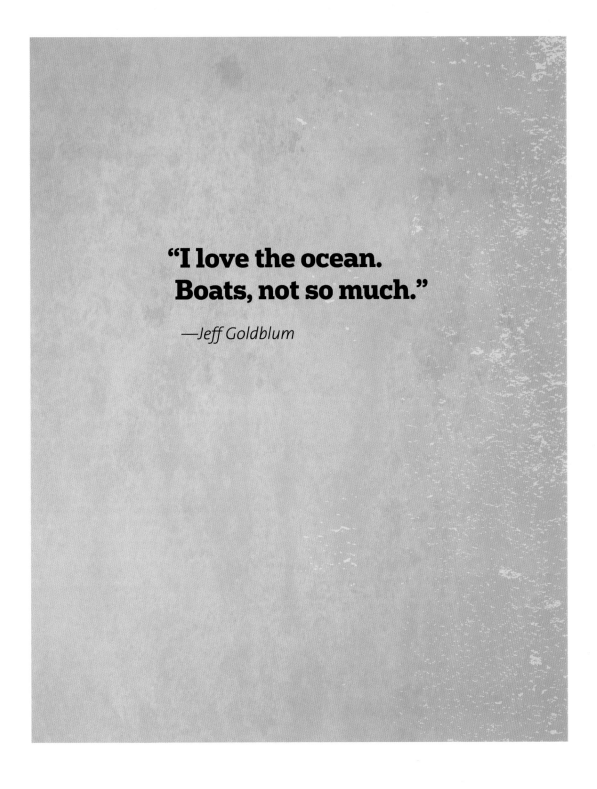

"I love the ocean.
Boats, not so much."

—*Jeff Goldblum*

Shark Bait // by David Carter, Ventura, CA

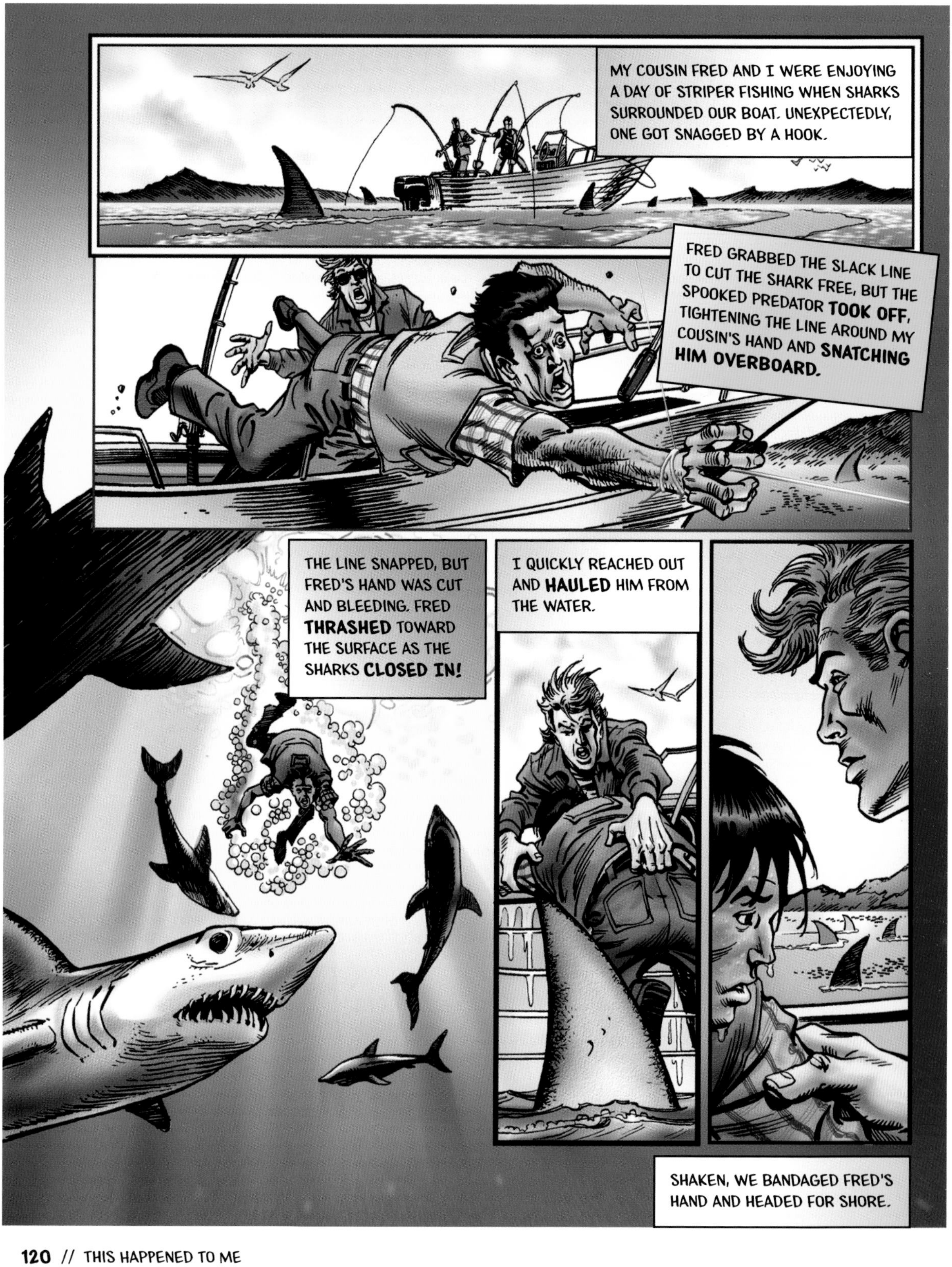
MY COUSIN FRED AND I WERE ENJOYING A DAY OF STRIPER FISHING WHEN SHARKS SURROUNDED OUR BOAT. UNEXPECTEDLY, ONE GOT SNAGGED BY A HOOK.
FRED GRABBED THE SLACK LINE TO CUT THE SHARK FREE, BUT THE SPOOKED PREDATOR TOOK OFF, TIGHTENING THE LINE AROUND MY COUSIN'S HAND AND SNATCHING HIM OVERBOARD.
THE LINE SNAPPED, BUT FRED'S HAND WAS CUT AND BLEEDING. FRED THRASHED TOWARD THE SURFACE AS THE SHARKS CLOSED IN!
I QUICKLY REACHED OUT AND HAULED HIM FROM THE WATER.
SHAKEN, WE BANDAGED FRED'S HAND AND HEADED FOR SHORE.

Ancient Predators

Efficient, powerful hunters, over 400 species of shark have successfully survived throughout Earth's oceans for hundreds of millions of years. Despite of their reputation as savage, bloodthirsty killers, just a few of those species have been known to attack humans, and then only rarely.

Sharks can:
- Bite with a strength of up to 40,000 psi
- Shed and replace 30,000 teeth throughout their lifetime
- Detect one drop of blood in an Olympic-sized swimming pool
- Find prey by detecting electrical impulses from their bodies

TOOTHY TERROR Sharks don't usually hunt people as a food source, which is why most shark bites stop there: Once the shark realizes you're not a seal, it leaves you alone. Unfortunately, that little "mistake" can do real and permanent damage to the human who is mistaken for a meal.

Most shark threats are in the shallows and near food sources. Coral reefs are popular hangouts— and happen to be desirable dive sites, too. If you're diving in these areas, be aware of the shark risk before you enter the water. Swim with at least one partner; sharks are less likely to mess with a group.

If you do suddenly find yourself in close quarters with one of these beasts, your best bet is to get out of the water, swimming away with smooth, even strokes that won't attract its attention.

When a shark wants to eat you, it will hunch its back, lower its fins, and rush at you in a zigzag. Thrust your spear gun, knife, or whatever else you've got to discourage it, punch its sensitive nose, or stab at its eyes or gills.

Some divers have reported successful evasion by descending to the seafloor and waiting for the sharks to leave. But that only works if you've got an air tank.

Boat Launched // by Bill W. Hippel, Houston, TX

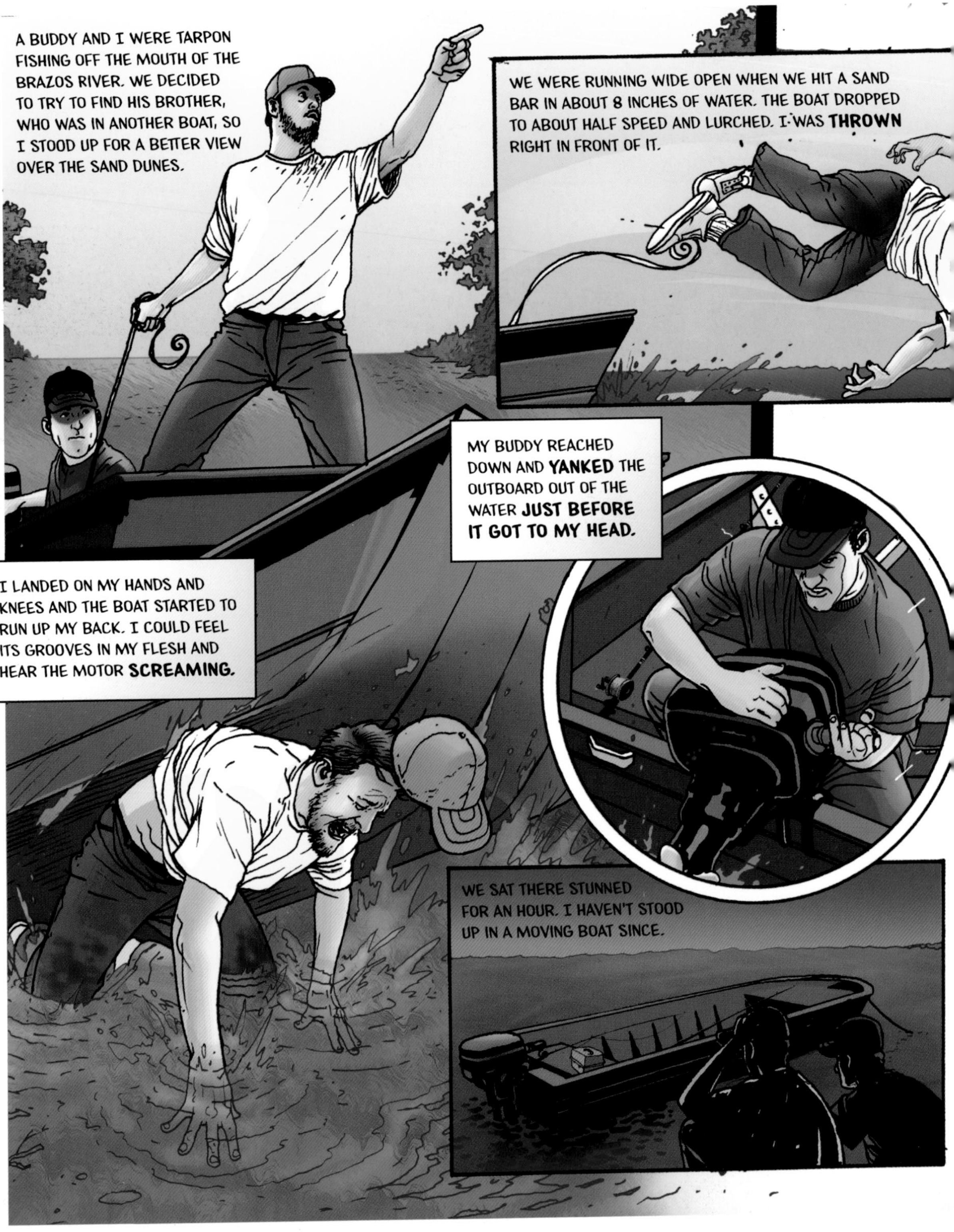
A BUDDY AND I WERE TARPON FISHING OFF THE MOUTH OF THE BRAZOS RIVER. WE DECIDED TO TRY TO FIND HIS BROTHER, WHO WAS IN ANOTHER BOAT, SO I STOOD UP FOR A BETTER VIEW OVER THE SAND DUNES.
WE WERE RUNNING WIDE OPEN WHEN WE HIT A SAND BAR IN ABOUT 8 INCHES OF WATER. THE BOAT DROPPED TO ABOUT HALF SPEED AND LURCHED. I WAS THROWN RIGHT IN FRONT OF IT.
I LANDED ON MY HANDS AND KNEES AND THE BOAT STARTED TO RUN UP MY BACK. I COULD FEEL ITS GROOVES IN MY FLESH AND HEAR THE MOTOR SCREAMING.
MY BUDDY REACHED DOWN AND YANKED THE OUTBOARD OUT OF THE WATER JUST BEFORE IT GOT TO MY HEAD.
WE SAT THERE STUNNED FOR AN HOUR. I HAVEN'T STOOD UP IN A MOVING BOAT SINCE.

Barging In // by Bill Correll, Asotin, WA

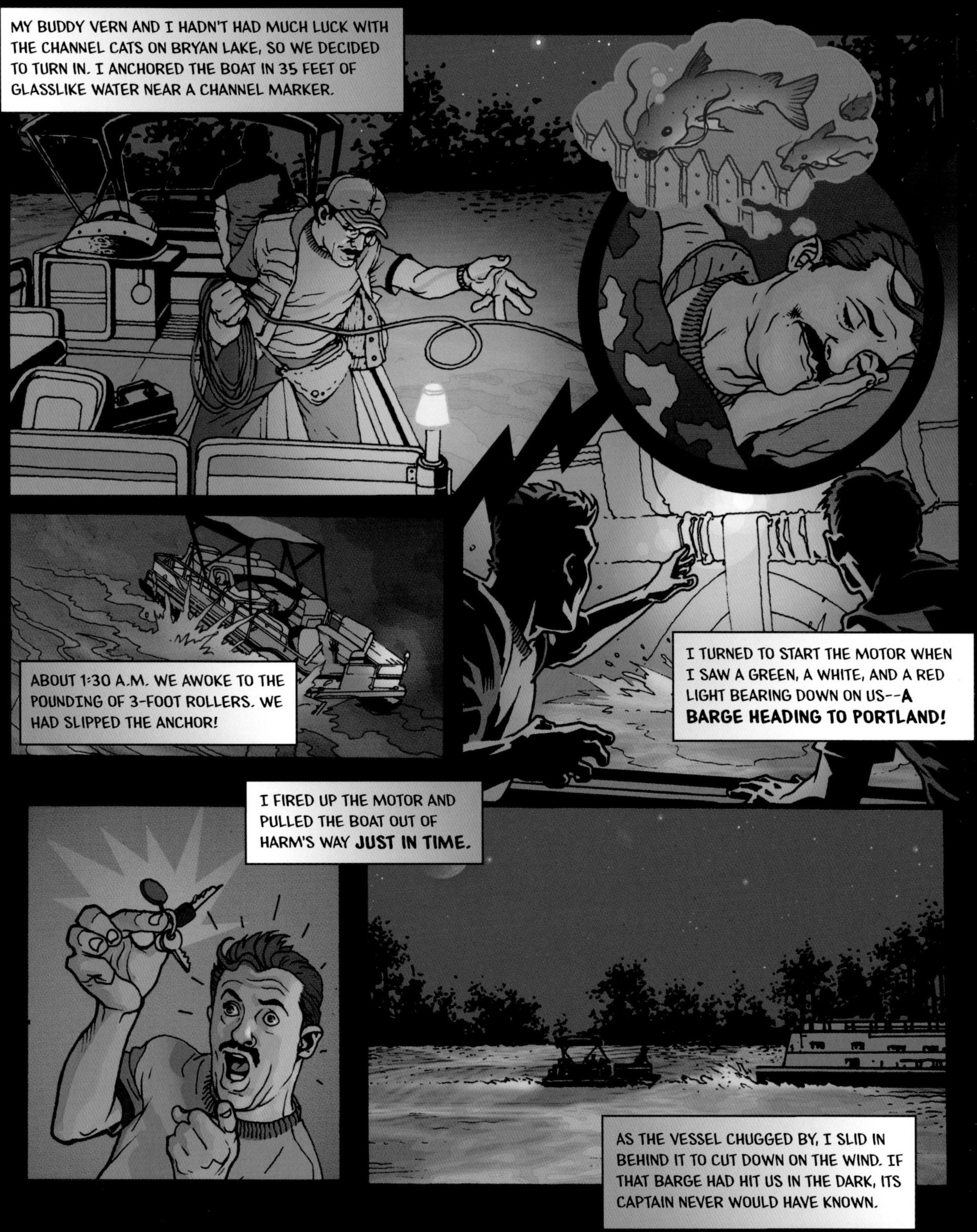
MY BUDDY VERN AND I HADN'T HAD MUCH LUCK WITH THE CHANNEL CATS ON BRYAN LAKE, SO WE DECIDED TO TURN IN. I ANCHORED THE BOAT IN 35 FEET OF GLASSLIKE WATER NEAR A CHANNEL MARKER.
ABOUT 1:30 A.M. WE AWOKE TO THE POUNDING OF 3-FOOT ROLLERS. WE HAD SLIPPED THE ANCHOR!
I TURNED TO START THE MOTOR WHEN I SAW A GREEN, A WHITE, AND A RED LIGHT BEARING DOWN ON US--A BARGE HEADING TO PORTLAND!
I FIRED UP THE MOTOR AND PULLED THE BOAT OUT OF HARM'S WAY JUST IN TIME.
AS THE VESSEL CHUGGED BY, I SLID IN BEHIND IT TO CUT DOWN ON THE WIND. IF THAT BARGE HAD HIT US IN THE DARK, ITS CAPTAIN NEVER WOULD HAVE KNOWN.

KNOW THE NUMBERS:
Thin Ice

4 INCHES Minimum ice thickness that can support a person.

689 Number of hypothermia-related fatalities ocurring each year in the United States.

10 TO 60 SECONDS Time you have to escape an automobile before it sinks after crashing through the ice.

1 TO 3 HOURS Time that someone with a flotation device can stay alive in 40°F water.

187 FEET Record distance for an under-ice swim, set by Wim Hof in 2000 at the Finnish village of Kolari.

15 TO 45 MINUTES Amount of time a person will likely remain alive in the water after falling through ice, provided he or she gets immediate medical attention after rescue.

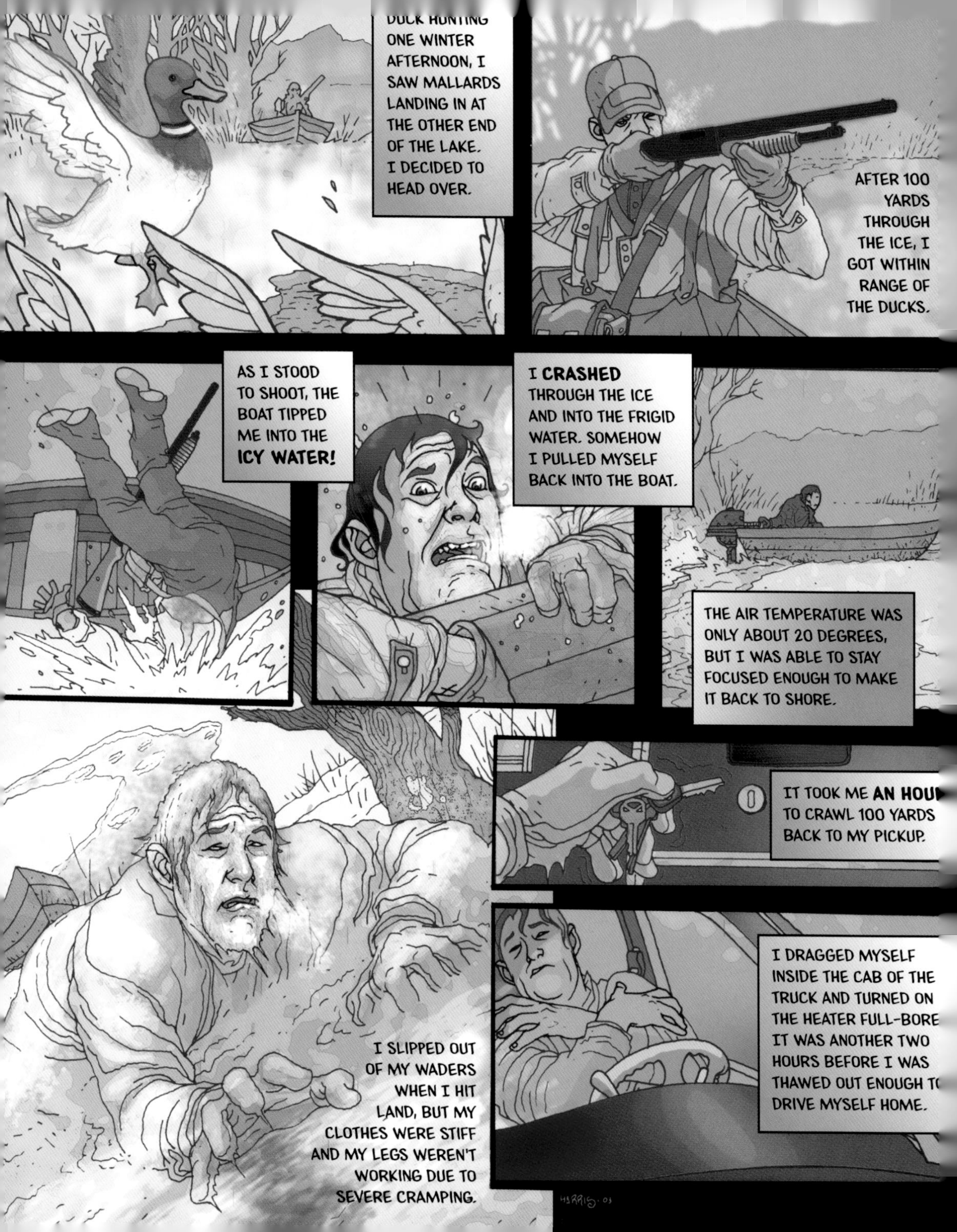
DUCK HUNTING ONE WINTER AFTERNOON, I SAW MALLARDS LANDING IN AT THE OTHER END OF THE LAKE. I DECIDED TO HEAD OVER.
AFTER 100 YARDS THROUGH THE ICE, I GOT WITHIN RANGE OF THE DUCKS.
AS I STOOD TO SHOOT, THE BOAT TIPPED ME INTO THE **ICY WATER!**
I **CRASHED** THROUGH THE ICE AND INTO THE FRIGID WATER. SOMEHOW I PULLED MYSELF BACK INTO THE BOAT.
THE AIR TEMPERATURE WAS ONLY ABOUT 20 DEGREES, BUT I WAS ABLE TO STAY FOCUSED ENOUGH TO MAKE IT BACK TO SHORE.
I SLIPPED OUT OF MY WADERS WHEN I HIT LAND, BUT MY CLOTHES WERE STIFF AND MY LEGS WEREN'T WORKING DUE TO SEVERE CRAMPING.
IT TOOK ME **AN HOU** TO CRAWL 100 YARDS BACK TO MY PICKUP.
I DRAGGED MYSELF INSIDE THE CAB OF THE TRUCK AND TURNED ON THE HEATER FULL-BORE IT WAS ANOTHER TWO HOURS BEFORE I WAS THAWED OUT ENOUGH T DRIVE MYSELF HOME.

"The two best days of owning a boat are the day you buy it and the day you sell it."

—*Howie Carr*

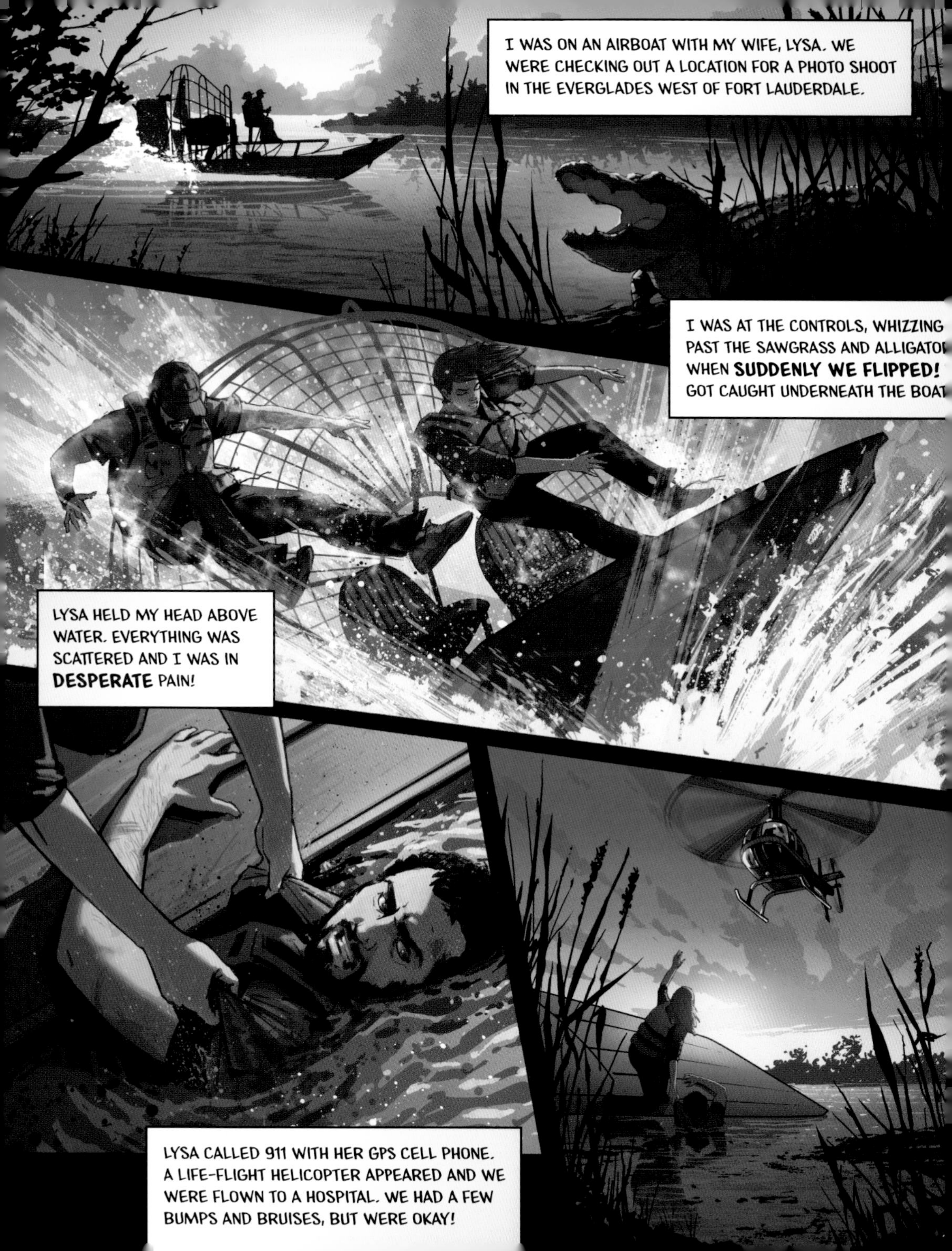
I WAS ON AN AIRBOAT WITH MY WIFE, LYSA. WE WERE CHECKING OUT A LOCATION FOR A PHOTO SHOOT IN THE EVERGLADES WEST OF FORT LAUDERDALE.
I WAS AT THE CONTROLS, WHIZZING PAST THE SAWGRASS AND ALLIGATO WHEN **SUDDENLY WE FLIPPED!** GOT CAUGHT UNDERNEATH THE BOA
LYSA HELD MY HEAD ABOVE WATER. EVERYTHING WAS SCATTERED AND I WAS IN **DESPERATE** PAIN!
LYSA CALLED 911 WITH HER GPS CELL PHONE. A LIFE-FLIGHT HELICOPTER APPEARED AND WE WERE FLOWN TO A HOSPITAL. WE HAD A FEW BUMPS AND BRUISES, BUT WERE OKAY!

Tethered to Death by Robert F. Slatzer, Hollywood, CA

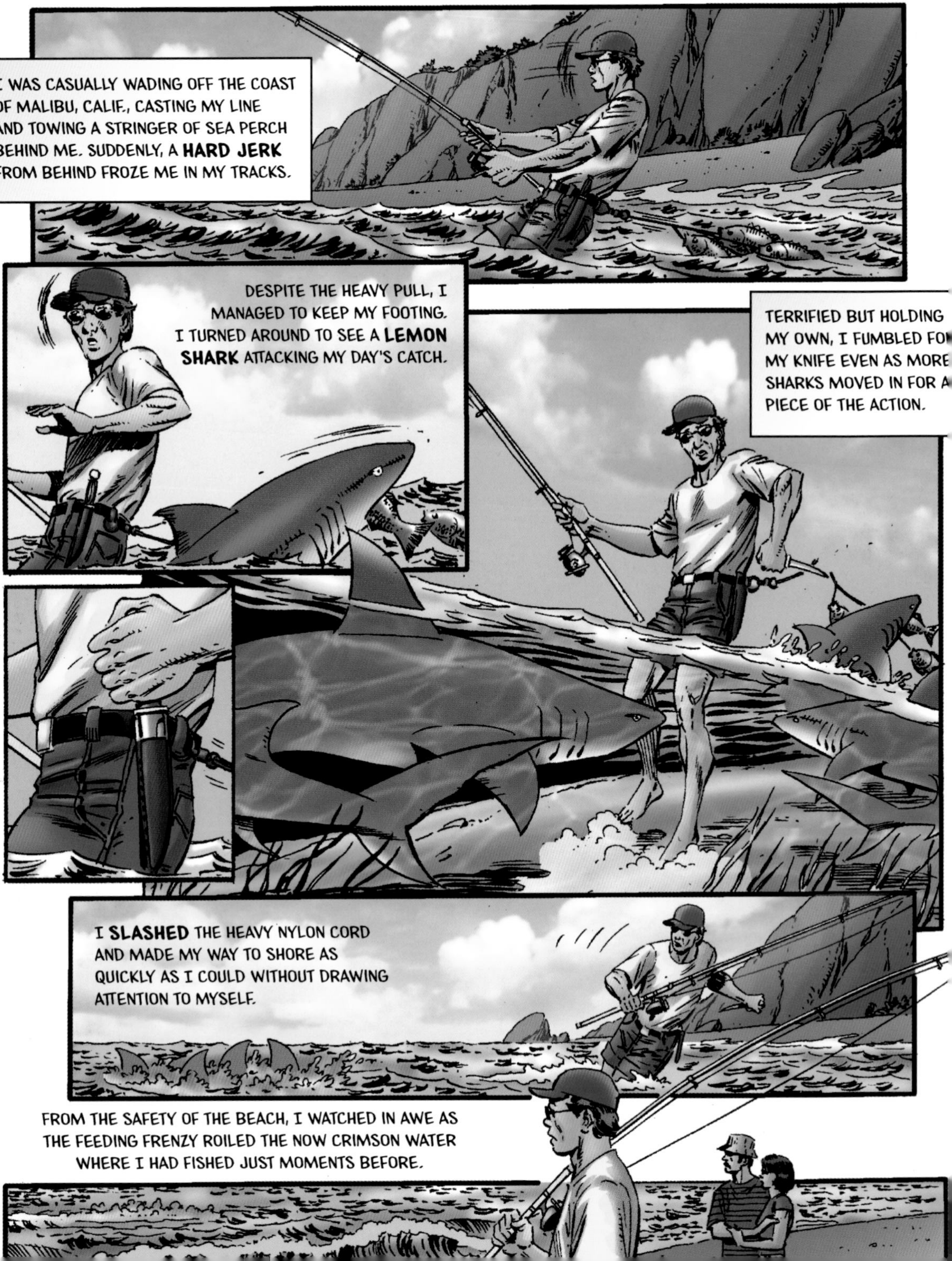

I WAS CASUALLY WADING OFF THE COAST OF MALIBU, CALIF., CASTING MY LINE AND TOWING A STRINGER OF SEA PERCH BEHIND ME. SUDDENLY, A **HARD JERK** FROM BEHIND FROZE ME IN MY TRACKS.
DESPITE THE HEAVY PULL, I MANAGED TO KEEP MY FOOTING. I TURNED AROUND TO SEE A **LEMON SHARK** ATTACKING MY DAY'S CATCH.
TERRIFIED BUT HOLDING MY OWN, I FUMBLED FOR MY KNIFE EVEN AS MORE SHARKS MOVED IN FOR A PIECE OF THE ACTION.
I **SLASHED** THE HEAVY NYLON CORD AND MADE MY WAY TO SHORE AS QUICKLY AS I COULD WITHOUT DRAWING ATTENTION TO MYSELF.
FROM THE SAFETY OF THE BEACH, I WATCHED IN AWE AS THE FEEDING FRENZY ROILED THE NOW CRIMSON WATER WHERE I HAD FISHED JUST MOMENTS BEFORE.

All Washed Up // by Fred Hornshuh, Manning, OR

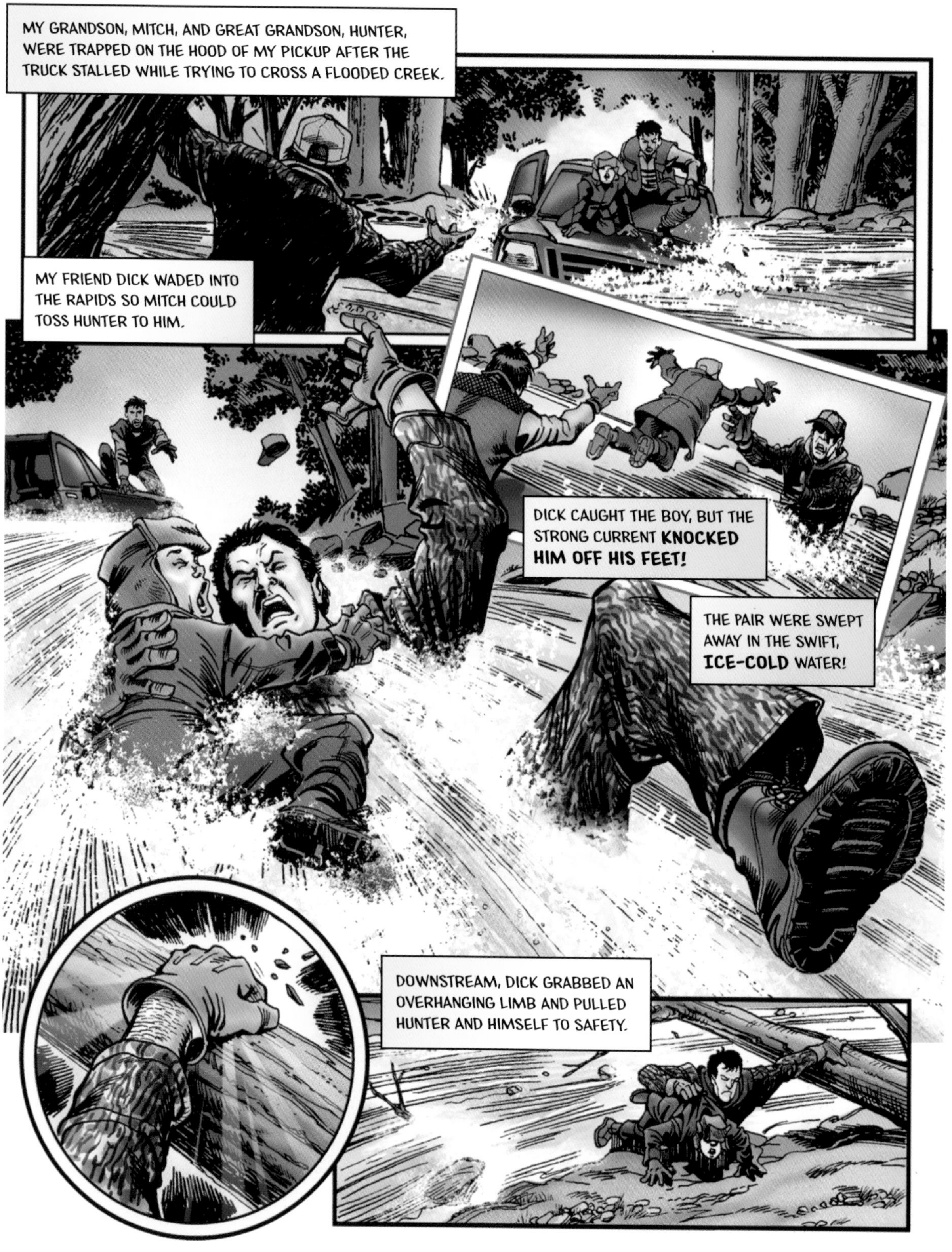
MY GRANDSON, MITCH, AND GREAT GRANDSON, HUNTER, WERE TRAPPED ON THE HOOD OF MY PICKUP AFTER THE TRUCK STALLED WHILE TRYING TO CROSS A FLOODED CREEK.
MY FRIEND DICK WADED INTO THE RAPIDS SO MITCH COULD TOSS HUNTER TO HIM.
DICK CAUGHT THE BOY, BUT THE STRONG CURRENT KNOCKED HIM OFF HIS FEET!
THE PAIR WERE SWEPT AWAY IN THE SWIFT, ICE-COLD WATER!
DOWNSTREAM, DICK GRABBED AN OVERHANGING LIMB AND PULLED HUNTER AND HIMSELF TO SAFETY.

Gar Chase! // by Brad Phillips, La Vernia, TX

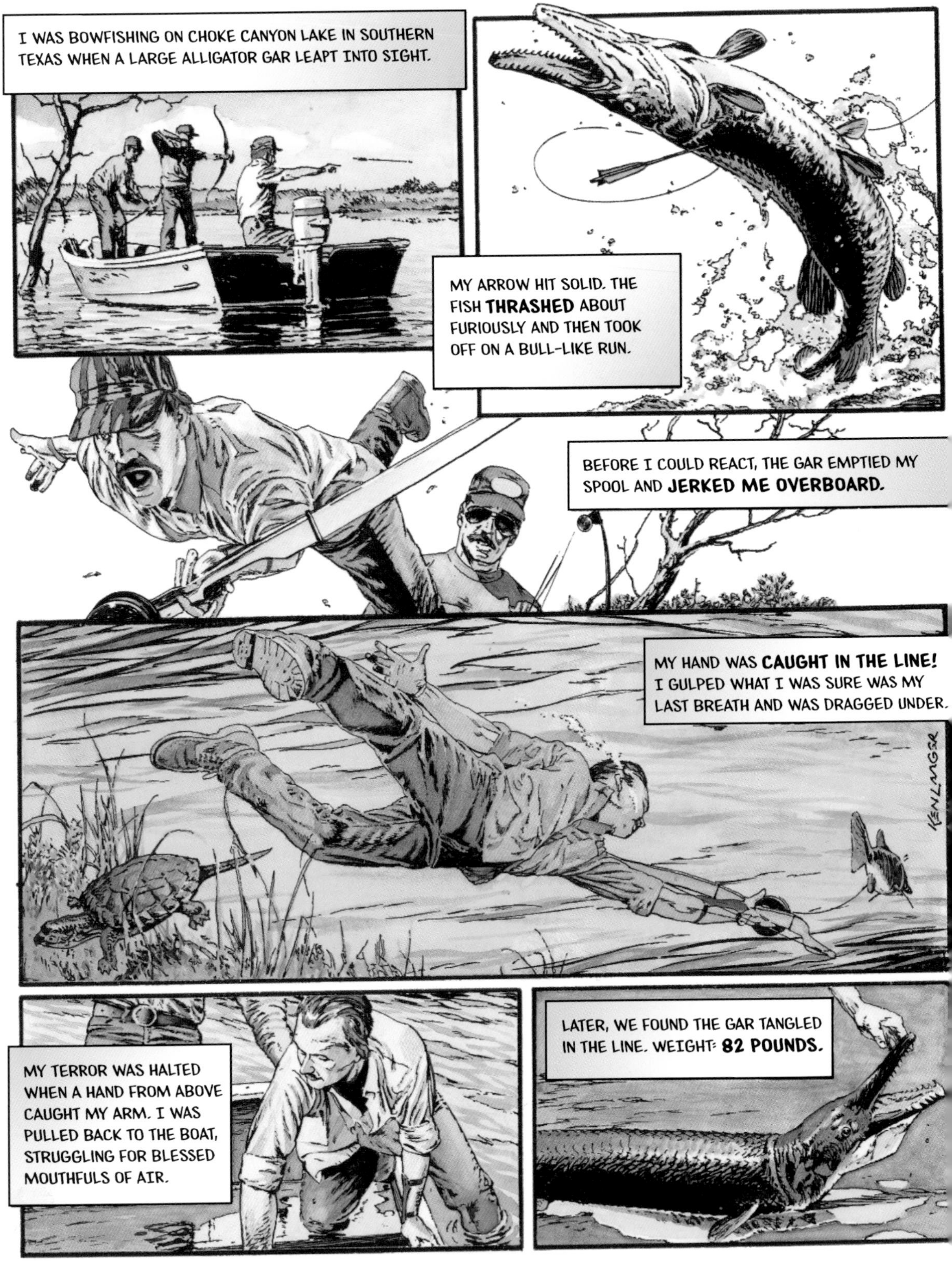

I WAS BOWFISHING ON CHOKE CANYON LAKE IN SOUTHERN TEXAS WHEN A LARGE ALLIGATOR GAR LEAPT INTO SIGHT.
MY ARROW HIT SOLID. THE FISH THRASHED ABOUT FURIOUSLY AND THEN TOOK OFF ON A BULL-LIKE RUN.
BEFORE I COULD REACT, THE GAR EMPTIED MY SPOOL AND JERKED ME OVERBOARD.
MY HAND WAS CAUGHT IN THE LINE! I GULPED WHAT I WAS SURE WAS MY LAST BREATH AND WAS DRAGGED UNDER.
KEN LAAGER
MY TERROR WAS HALTED WHEN A HAND FROM ABOVE CAUGHT MY ARM. I WAS PULLED BACK TO THE BOAT, STRUGGLING FOR BLESSED MOUTHFULS OF AIR.
LATER, WE FOUND THE GAR TANGLED IN THE LINE. WEIGHT: 82 POUNDS.

Fierce Fish

The fish known as gar or garpike are part of a family of large, toothed fish that live in waters across eastern North America, Central America, and throughout the Caribbean. Numbering seven total species, these fish range in size from 2 to 10 feet for the largest specimens of alligator gar. Their size means they have very few predators, and are generally only killed by humans and alligators.

Garpike can:
- Weigh up to 365 pounds
- Survive up to two hours out of the water
- Lay over 35,000 eggs while spawning.
- Gulp air to survive in waters with little to no oxygen content.

A REEL CHALLENGE Fishing for gar may be an interesting and challenging pastime, but avoid their eggs, as they're toxic. Despite their double rows of pointy teeth and their impressive size, even the largest alligator gar has never been known to directly attack a human, but if you're going to go fishing for one of these big beasties, especially bowfishing, follow the safety information for your equipment, and consider bringing friends (for help as well as to share the fun) and a first-aid kit along with you just in case.

One Last Breath // by Kurt Anderson, Brookston, MN

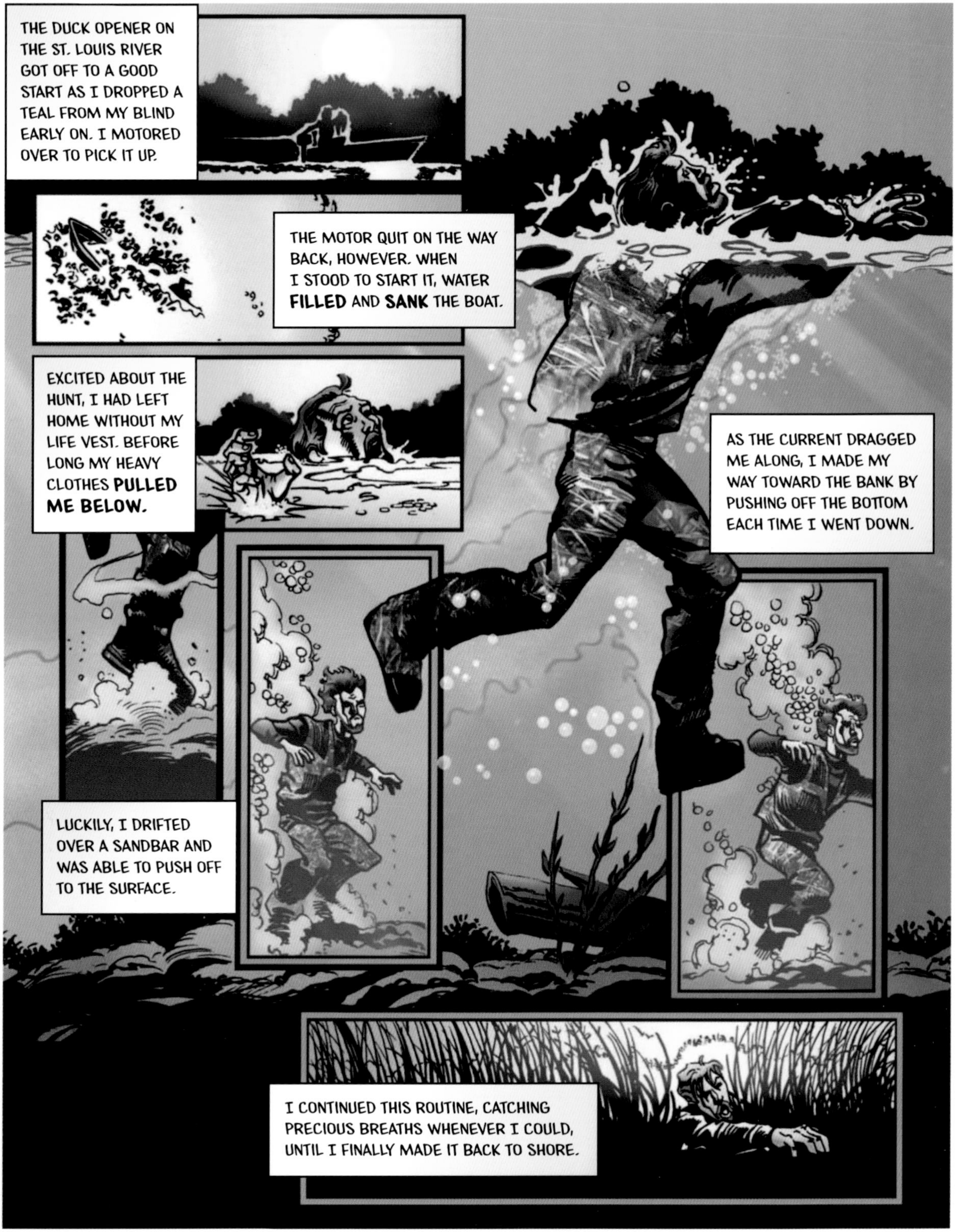

THE DUCK OPENER ON THE ST. LOUIS RIVER GOT OFF TO A GOOD START AS I DROPPED A TEAL FROM MY BLIND EARLY ON. I MOTORED OVER TO PICK IT UP.
THE MOTOR QUIT ON THE WAY BACK, HOWEVER. WHEN I STOOD TO START IT, WATER FILLED AND SANK THE BOAT.
EXCITED ABOUT THE HUNT, I HAD LEFT HOME WITHOUT MY LIFE VEST. BEFORE LONG MY HEAVY CLOTHES PULLED ME BELOW.
AS THE CURRENT DRAGGED ME ALONG, I MADE MY WAY TOWARD THE BANK BY PUSHING OFF THE BOTTOM EACH TIME I WENT DOWN.
LUCKILY, I DRIFTED OVER A SANDBAR AND WAS ABLE TO PUSH OFF TO THE SURFACE.
I CONTINUED THIS ROUTINE, CATCHING PRECIOUS BREATHS WHENEVER I COULD, UNTIL I FINALLY MADE IT BACK TO SHORE.

KNOW THE NUMBERS:
Drowning

4 OUT OF 5 Proportion of drowning victims who are male

88% Percentage of drowning victims not wearing life vests during the incident.

3,500 Average number of drowning deaths per year in the United States.

545 Number of commercial fishermen who died after falling overboard between 2000 and 2010.

0 Number of those fishermen who were wearing life vests or other personal flotation devices.

1623 Last year in which drowning was used as a form of capital punishment in England.

22 MINUTES, 22 SECONDS Longest time for a single breath held underwater by record-holder Tom Sietas of Germany.

"Give a man a fish, and you'll feed him for a day. Teach a man to fish, and he'll buy a funny hat."

—*Scott Adams*

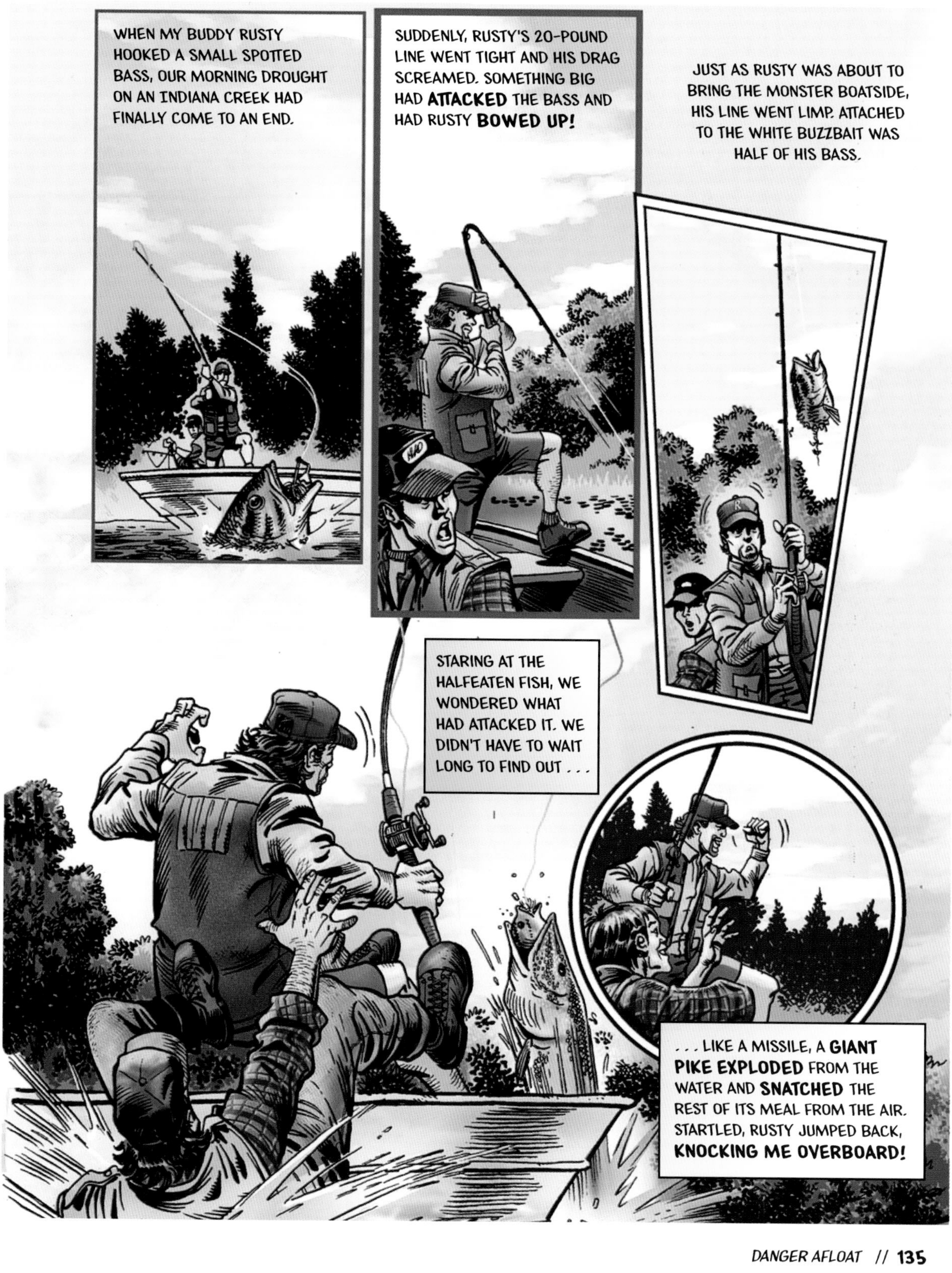
WHEN MY BUDDY RUSTY HOOKED A SMALL SPOTTED BASS, OUR MORNING DROUGHT ON AN INDIANA CREEK HAD FINALLY COME TO AN END.
SUDDENLY, RUSTY'S 20-POUND LINE WENT TIGHT AND HIS DRAG SCREAMED. SOMETHING BIG HAD **ATTACKED** THE BASS AND HAD RUSTY **BOWED UP!**
JUST AS RUSTY WAS ABOUT TO BRING THE MONSTER BOATSIDE, HIS LINE WENT LIMP. ATTACHED TO THE WHITE BUZZBAIT WAS HALF OF HIS BASS.
STARING AT THE HALFEATEN FISH, WE WONDERED WHAT HAD ATTACKED IT. WE DIDN'T HAVE TO WAIT LONG TO FIND OUT . . .
. . . LIKE A MISSILE, A **GIANT PIKE EXPLODED** FROM THE WATER AND **SNATCHED** THE REST OF ITS MEAL FROM THE AIR. STARTLED, RUSTY JUMPED BACK, **KNOCKING ME OVERBOARD!**

Battle in the Swamp // by Chris D'Zamko, Jacksonville, FL

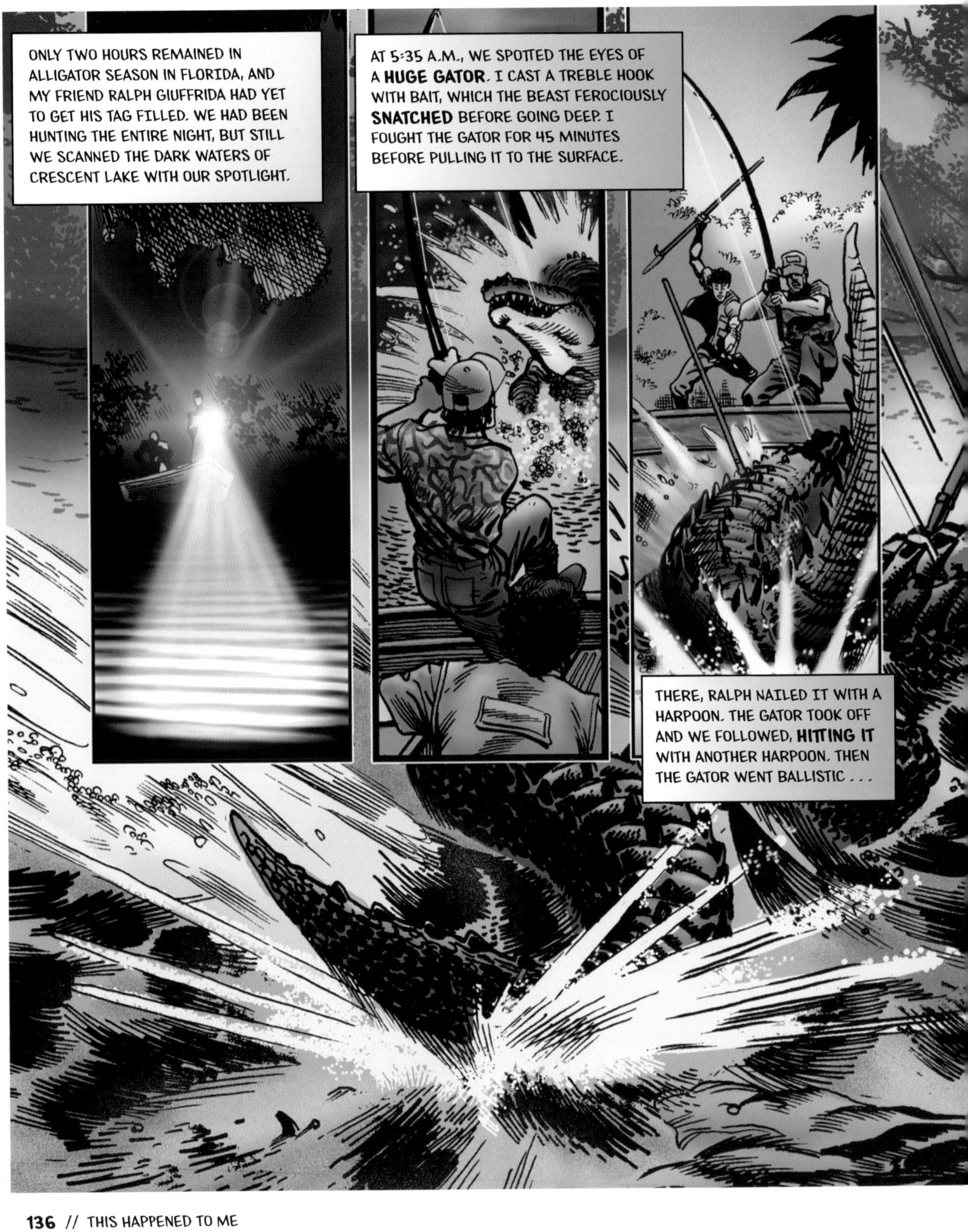
ONLY TWO HOURS REMAINED IN ALLIGATOR SEASON IN FLORIDA, AND MY FRIEND RALPH GIUFFRIDA HAD YET TO GET HIS TAG FILLED. WE HAD BEEN HUNTING THE ENTIRE NIGHT, BUT STILL WE SCANNED THE DARK WATERS OF CRESCENT LAKE WITH OUR SPOTLIGHT.
AT 5:35 A.M., WE SPOTTED THE EYES OF A **HUGE GATOR**. I CAST A TREBLE HOOK WITH BAIT, WHICH THE BEAST FEROCIOUSLY **SNATCHED** BEFORE GOING DEEP. I FOUGHT THE GATOR FOR 45 MINUTES BEFORE PULLING IT TO THE SURFACE.
THERE, RALPH NAILED IT WITH A HARPOON. THE GATOR TOOK OFF AND WE FOLLOWED, **HITTING IT** WITH ANOTHER HARPOON. THEN THE GATOR WENT BALLISTIC . . .

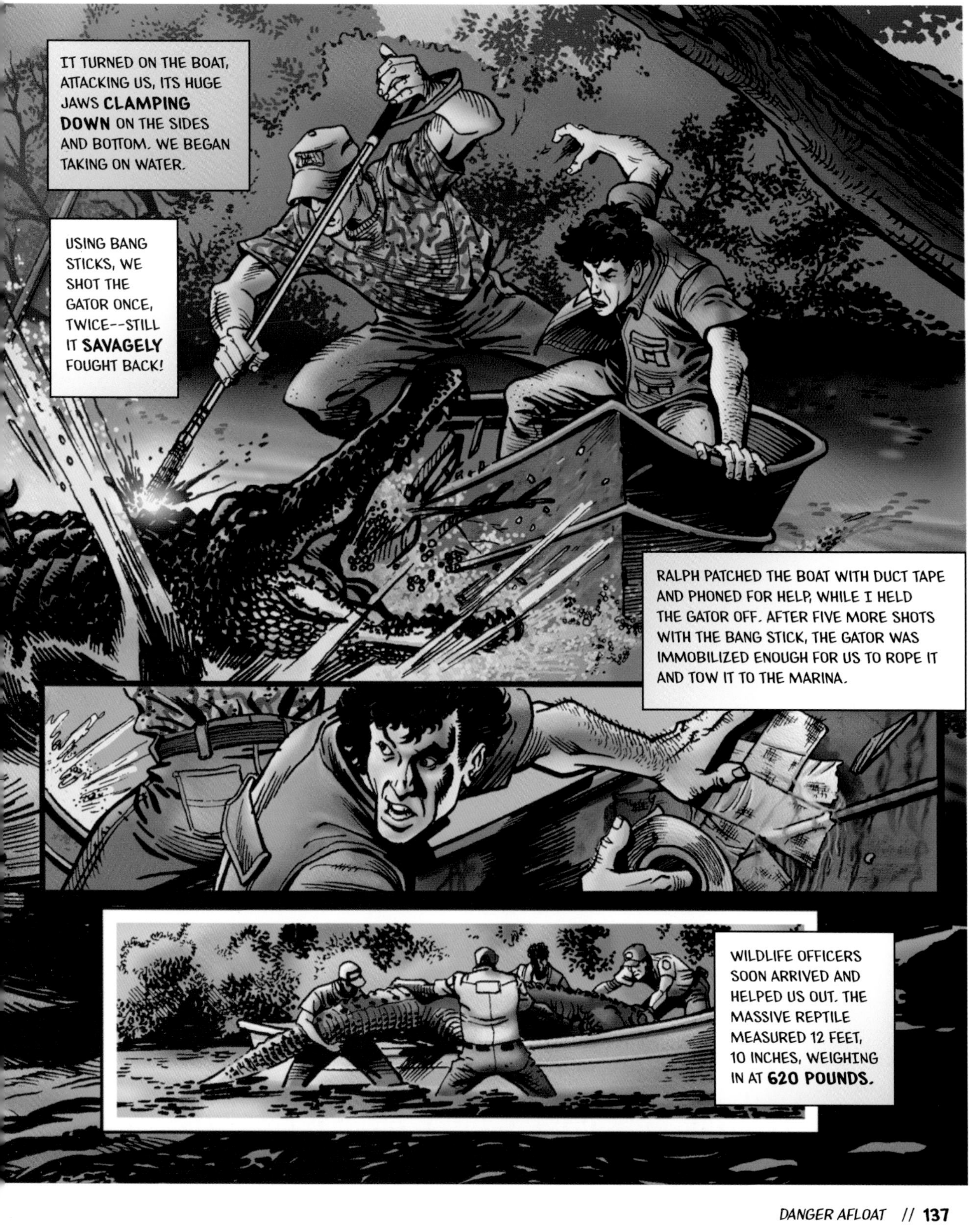
IT TURNED ON THE BOAT, ATTACKING US, ITS HUGE JAWS **CLAMPING DOWN** ON THE SIDES AND BOTTOM. WE BEGAN TAKING ON WATER.
USING BANG STICKS, WE SHOT THE GATOR ONCE, TWICE--STILL IT **SAVAGELY** FOUGHT BACK!
RALPH PATCHED THE BOAT WITH DUCT TAPE AND PHONED FOR HELP, WHILE I HELD THE GATOR OFF. AFTER FIVE MORE SHOTS WITH THE BANG STICK, THE GATOR WAS IMMOBILIZED ENOUGH FOR US TO ROPE IT AND TOW IT TO THE MARINA.
WILDLIFE OFFICERS SOON ARRIVED AND HELPED US OUT. THE MASSIVE REPTILE MEASURED 12 FEET, 10 INCHES, WEIGHING IN AT **620 POUNDS.**

Fishing for Stitches // by Harold Lincoln, Newcastle, WY

MY SON AND I WERE FLOAT-FISHING THE MULCHATNA RIVER IN ALASKA WHEN A TREE **SUDDENLY FELL** DIRECTLY ACROSS THE NARROW CHANNEL WE WERE NAVIGATING.

AFTER HITTING ME ON THE SIDE OF THE HEAD AND ALMOST **RIPPING MY EAR OFF**, THE TREE LANDED ON THE BOW OF OUR BOAT . . . AND **NEARLY SWAMPED US!**

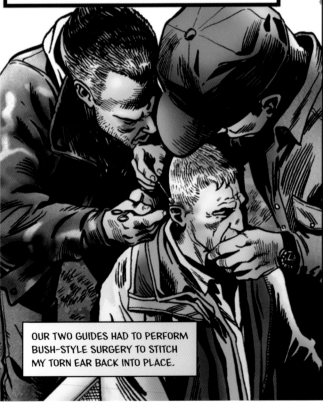

OUR TWO GUIDES HAD TO PERFORM BUSH-STYLE SURGERY TO STITCH MY TORN EAR BACK INTO PLACE.

THREE DAYS OF SUCCESSFUL FISHING LATER, A BUSH PLANE PICKED US UP AND TOOK US BACK TO ANCHORAGE, WHERE DOCTORS WERE IMPRESSED WITH MY SUTURES.

Lemon-Aid // by Rebecca Burg, Key West, FL

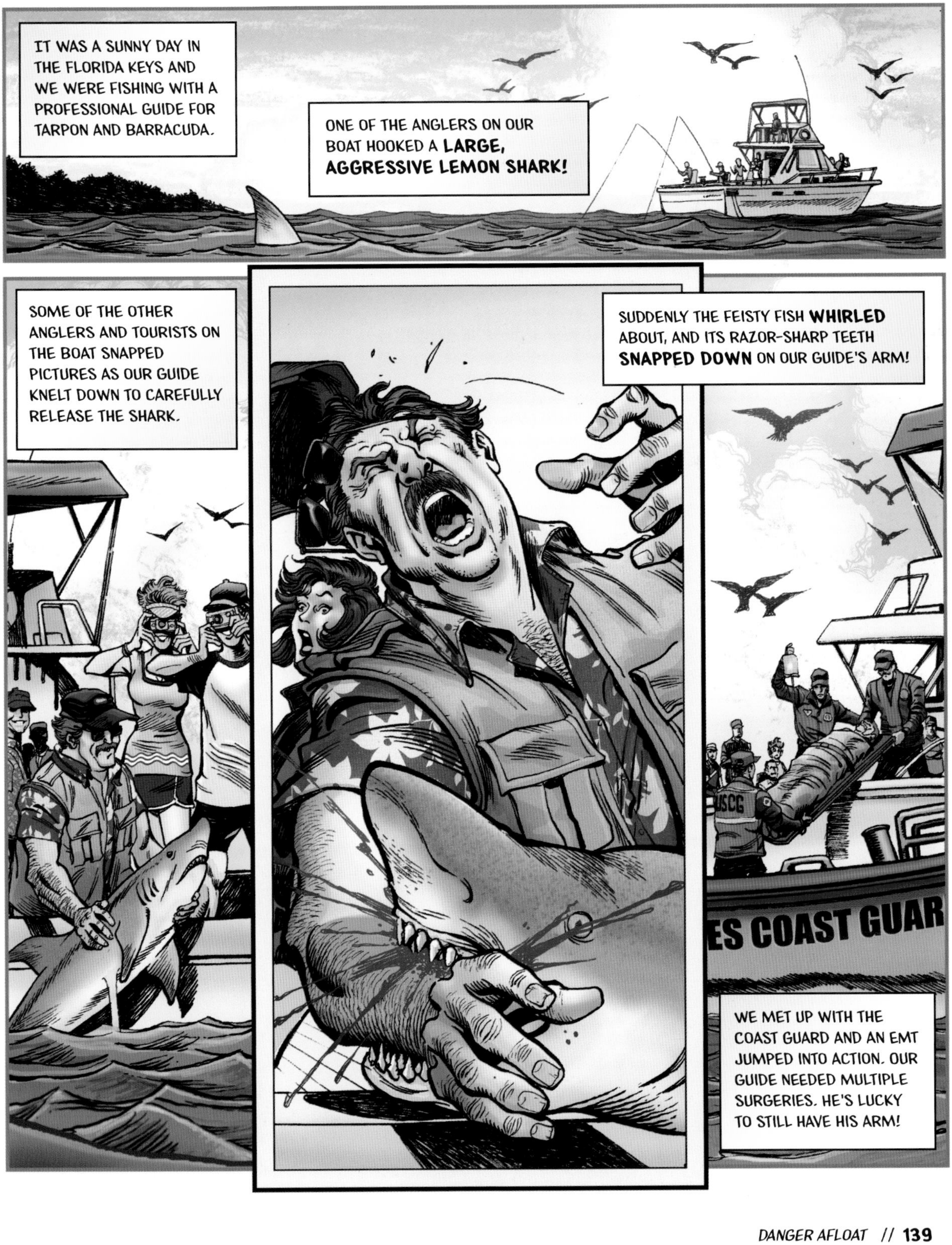
IT WAS A SUNNY DAY IN THE FLORIDA KEYS AND WE WERE FISHING WITH A PROFESSIONAL GUIDE FOR TARPON AND BARRACUDA.
ONE OF THE ANGLERS ON OUR BOAT HOOKED A **LARGE, AGGRESSIVE LEMON SHARK!**
SOME OF THE OTHER ANGLERS AND TOURISTS ON THE BOAT SNAPPED PICTURES AS OUR GUIDE KNELT DOWN TO CAREFULLY RELEASE THE SHARK.
SUDDENLY THE FEISTY FISH **WHIRLED** ABOUT, AND ITS RAZOR-SHARP TEETH **SNAPPED DOWN** ON OUR GUIDE'S ARM!
USCG
ES COAST GUAR
WE MET UP WITH THE COAST GUARD AND AN EMT JUMPED INTO ACTION. OUR GUIDE NEEDED MULTIPLE SURGERIES. HE'S LUCKY TO STILL HAVE HIS ARM!

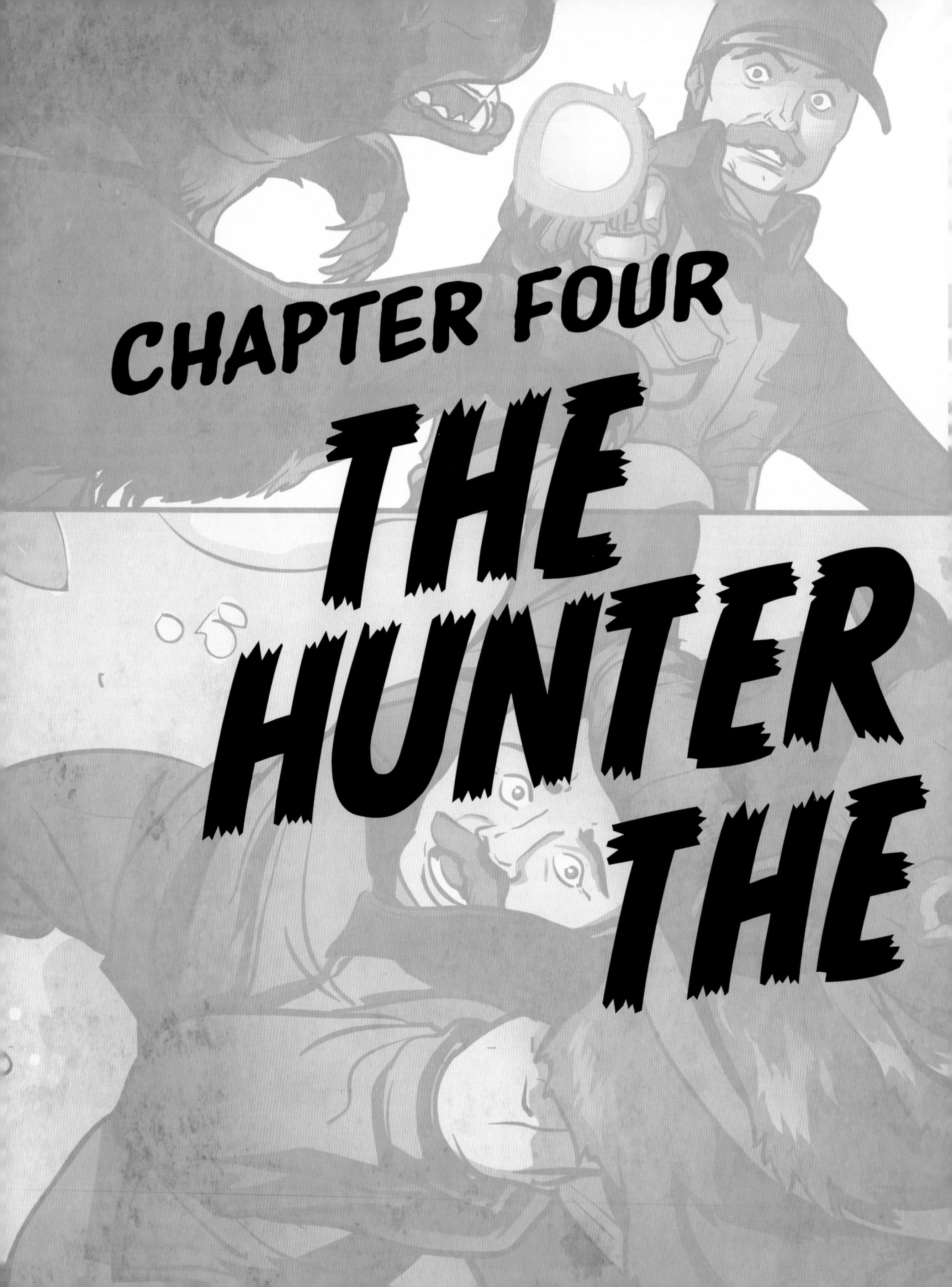

CHAPTER FOUR

THE HUNTER THE

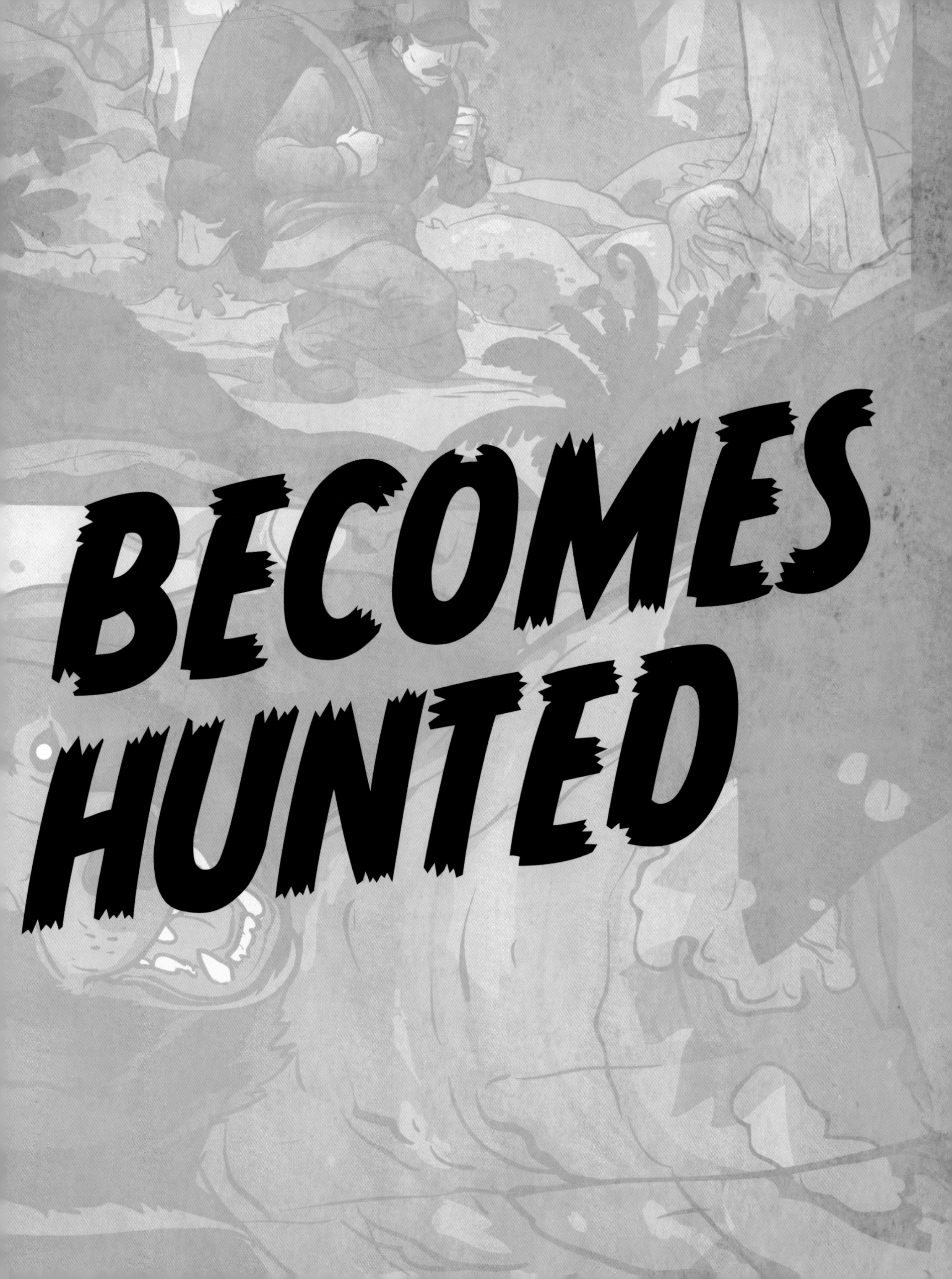
BECOMES
HUNTED

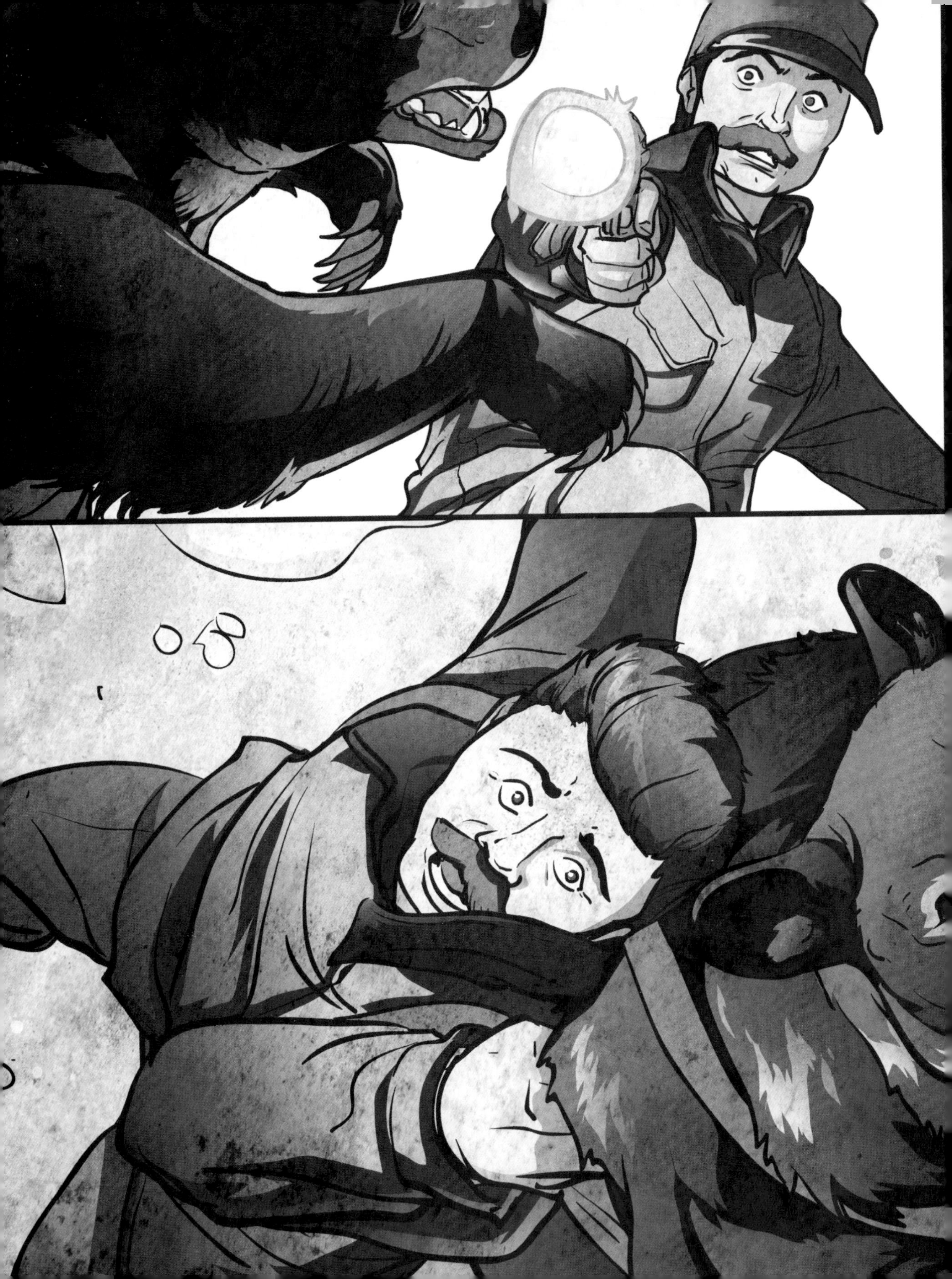

Don't Blink!

Every hunter has at least imagined one of these scary moments . . . that instant where the gun jams, the bear charges, the wounded elk lowers its massive antlers and looks you straight in the eye. Every time you head out to match wits with Mother Nature, there's a chance she just might come out on top.

In the bone-chilling tales that follow, hunters face terrors both common (an enraged Cape buffalo or an angry mama bear) and just plain bizarre (it's amazing how many people get injured by animals they've already killed!). These folks came home with something even better than dinner—a great story. And maybe a new scar.

The Bearest Escape // by Jim Devorak, Billings, MT

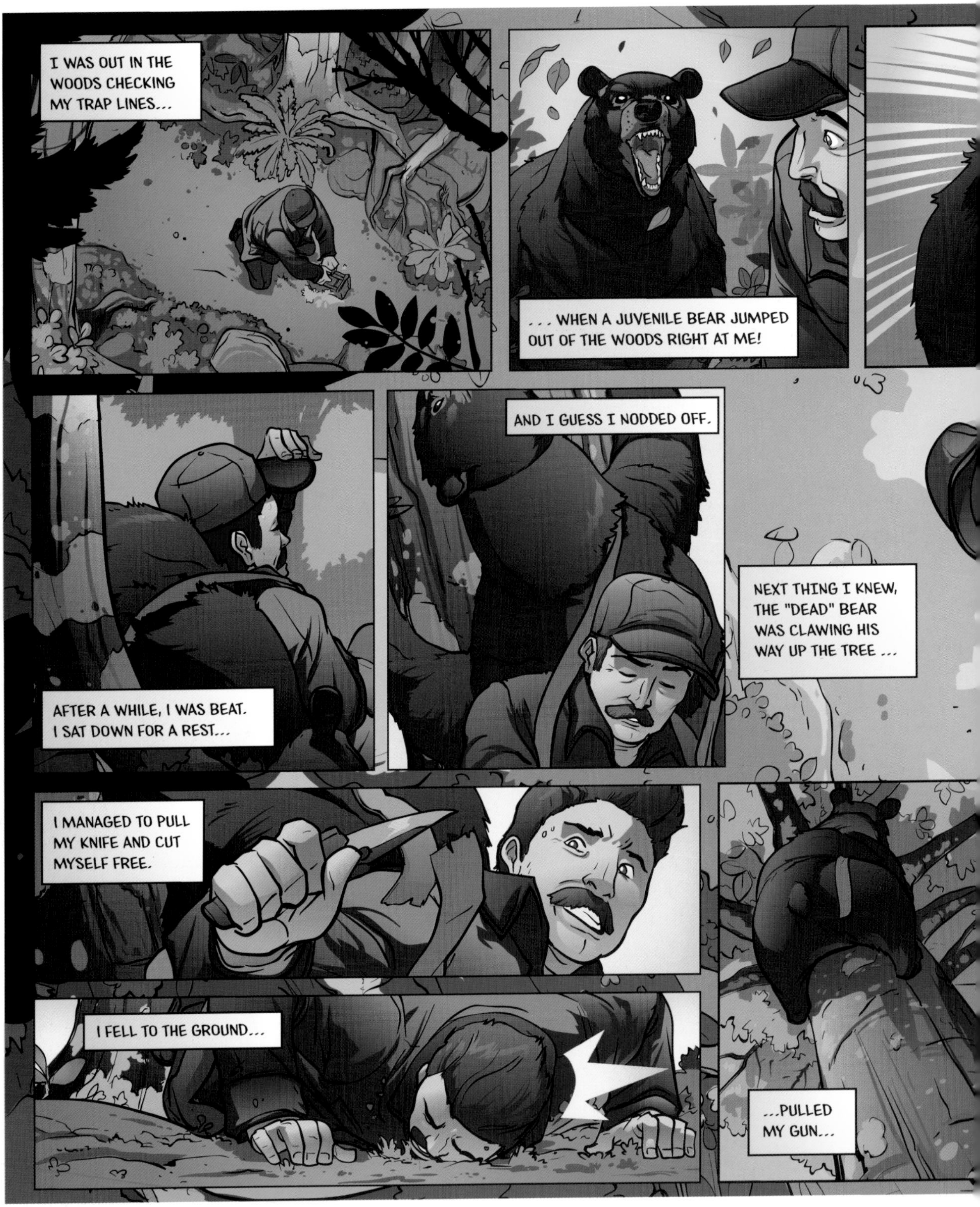
I WAS OUT IN THE WOODS CHECKING MY TRAP LINES...
... WHEN A JUVENILE BEAR JUMPED OUT OF THE WOODS RIGHT AT ME!
AFTER A WHILE, I WAS BEAT. I SAT DOWN FOR A REST...
AND I GUESS I NODDED OFF.
NEXT THING I KNEW, THE "DEAD" BEAR WAS CLAWING HIS WAY UP THE TREE ...
I MANAGED TO PULL MY KNIFE AND CUT MYSELF FREE.
I FELL TO THE GROUND...
...PULLED MY GUN...

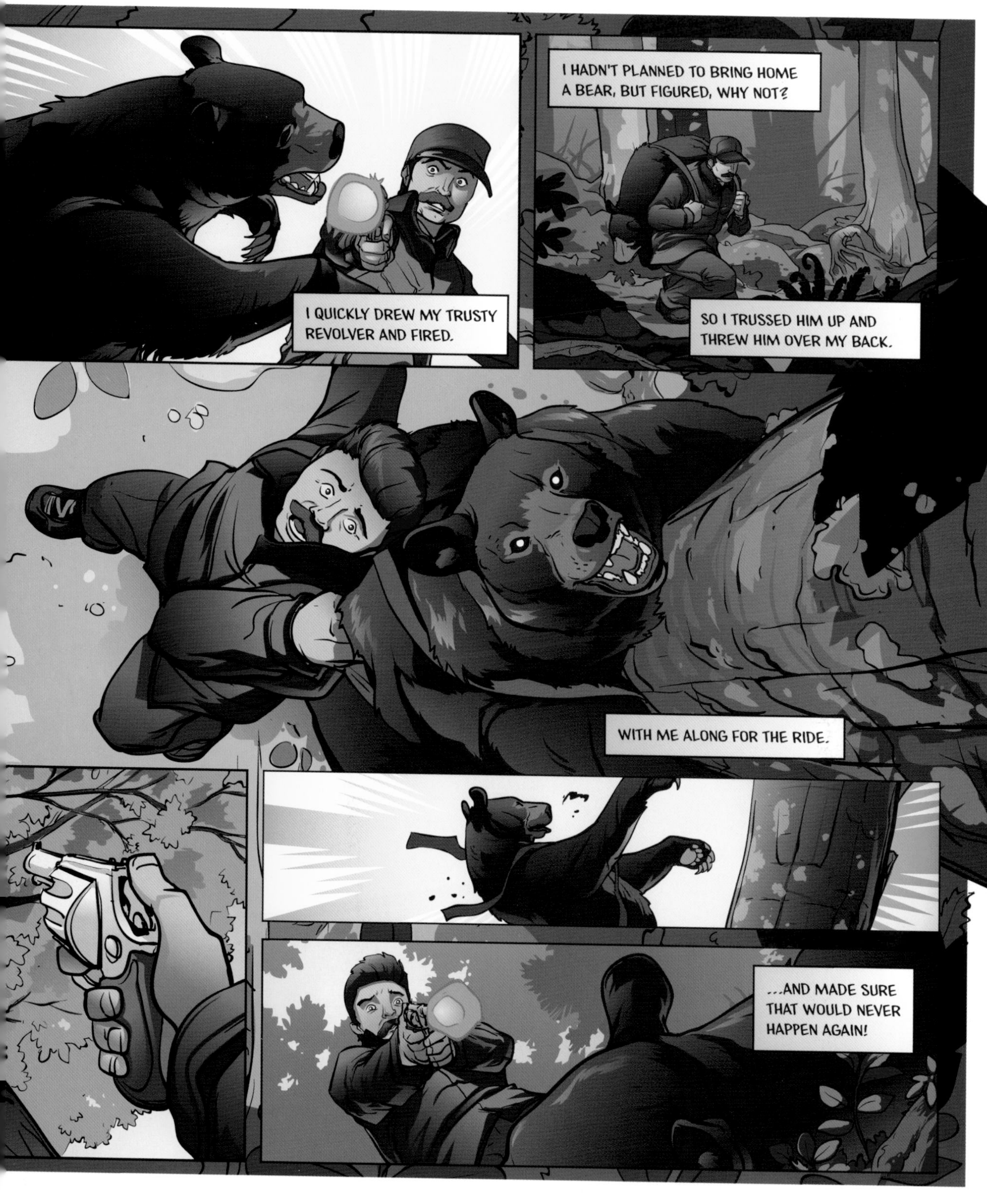
I QUICKLY DREW MY TRUSTY REVOLVER AND FIRED.
I HADN'T PLANNED TO BRING HOME A BEAR, BUT FIGURED, WHY NOT?
SO I TRUSSED HIM UP AND THREW HIM OVER MY BACK.
WITH ME ALONG FOR THE RIDE.
...AND MADE SURE THAT WOULD NEVER HAPPEN AGAIN!

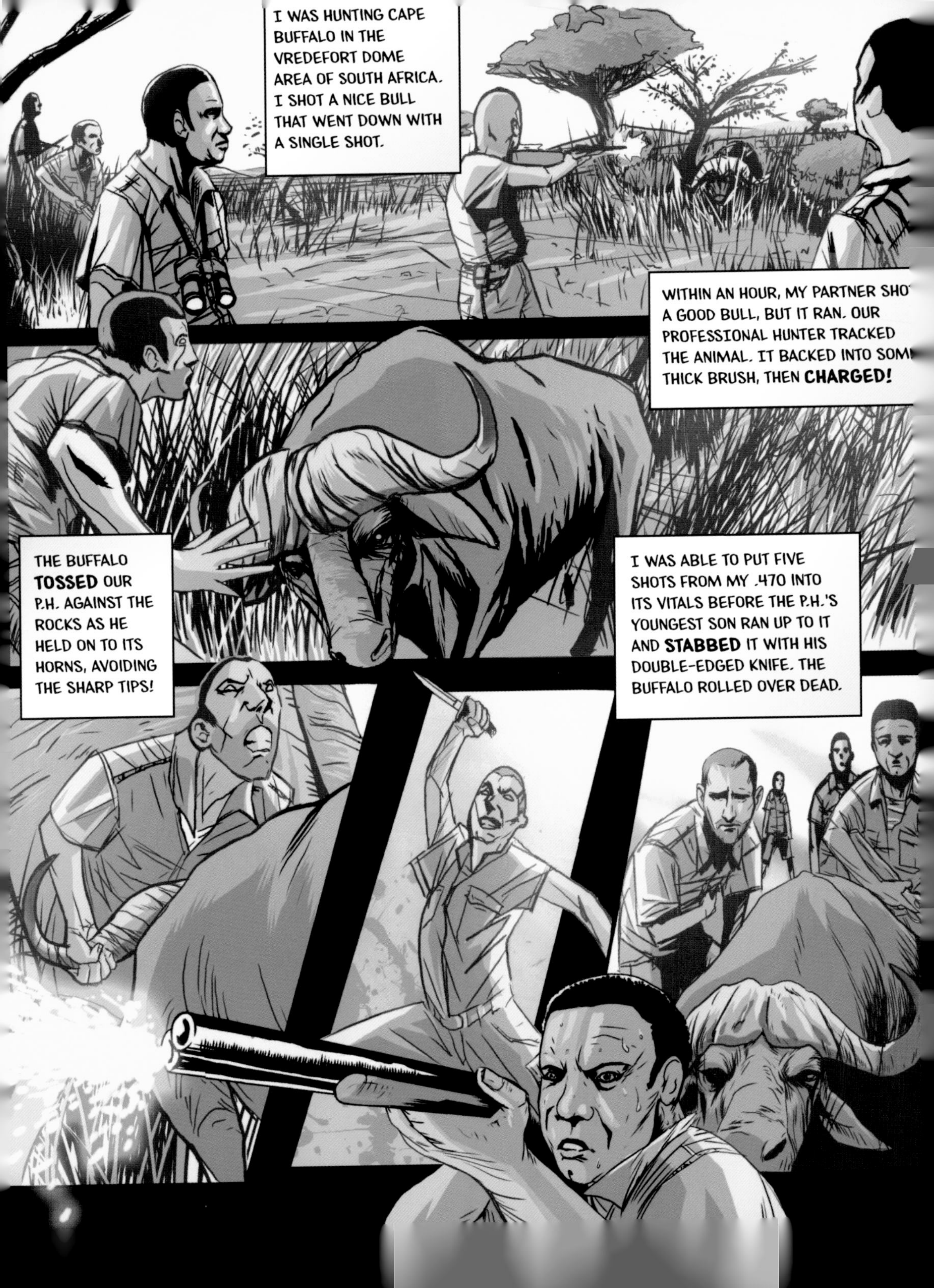
I WAS HUNTING CAPE BUFFALO IN THE VREDEFORT DOME AREA OF SOUTH AFRICA. I SHOT A NICE BULL THAT WENT DOWN WITH A SINGLE SHOT.
WITHIN AN HOUR, MY PARTNER SHOT A GOOD BULL, BUT IT RAN. OUR PROFESSIONAL HUNTER TRACKED THE ANIMAL. IT BACKED INTO SOM THICK BRUSH, THEN CHARGED!
THE BUFFALO TOSSED OUR P.H. AGAINST THE ROCKS AS HE HELD ON TO ITS HORNS, AVOIDING THE SHARP TIPS!
I WAS ABLE TO PUT FIVE SHOTS FROM MY .470 INTO ITS VITALS BEFORE THE P.H.'S YOUNGEST SON RAN UP TO IT AND STABBED IT WITH HIS DOUBLE-EDGED KNIFE. THE BUFFALO ROLLED OVER DEAD.

One Bad Bovine

The African or Cape buffalo is the largest bovine on the African continent, with a wide range of habitats, including forests, swamps, and savannah. Unlike the Asian water buffalo, it has not been domesticated, nor is it ancestral to modern domestic cattle. Though it is not a predator, it is still a dangerous and unpredictable animal, and is given nicknames like "Widowmaker" or "Black Death."

Cape buffalo can:
- Tip over cars, exerting four times the strength of an ox
- Grow a hide up to 2 inches thick on its neck to protect it in battles with other bulls
- Kill lions to prevent them from hunting buffalo
- Reach speeds of 50 mph in a sprint
- Remember human hunters who have attacked them, and return the favor—even years later

HORNED HAZARD Cape Buffalo are one of the "Big Five" dangerous game for hunters who travel to Africa (the other four being lions, elephants, rhinos, and leopards), and they're the only bovine on the list. They're easily able to camouflage themselves in tall grasses, and if wounded, will turn to attack their hunters or stalk and ambush them instead of the other way around.

To bring down a Cape buffalo quickly, a smart hunter uses well-made bullets of at least .357 caliber (and more gun is definitely better here), and make a well-placed shot to the vitals or the brain, which is a small target very well-protected by the animal's thick horns and dense skull.

KNOW THE NUMBERS:
Deer

130 Number of people killed by deer every year in the United States—mostly as a result of deer-on-vehicle collisions.

511 POUNDS Largest estimated live weight of a deer, a whitetail shot in November 1926 by Carl Lenander Jr. (its field-dressed weight was 402 pounds).

40 MILES PER HOUR Top speed of a running adult deer.

8 FEET Highest vertical leaping distance over an obstacle cleared by a deer (from a standing position).

319 ½ INCHES Largest recorded measurement of a whitetail deer's antlers, shot by Tony Lovstuen of Iowa, in 2003.

Dragged Like a Rag Doll // by Joe Binek, Burtrum, MN

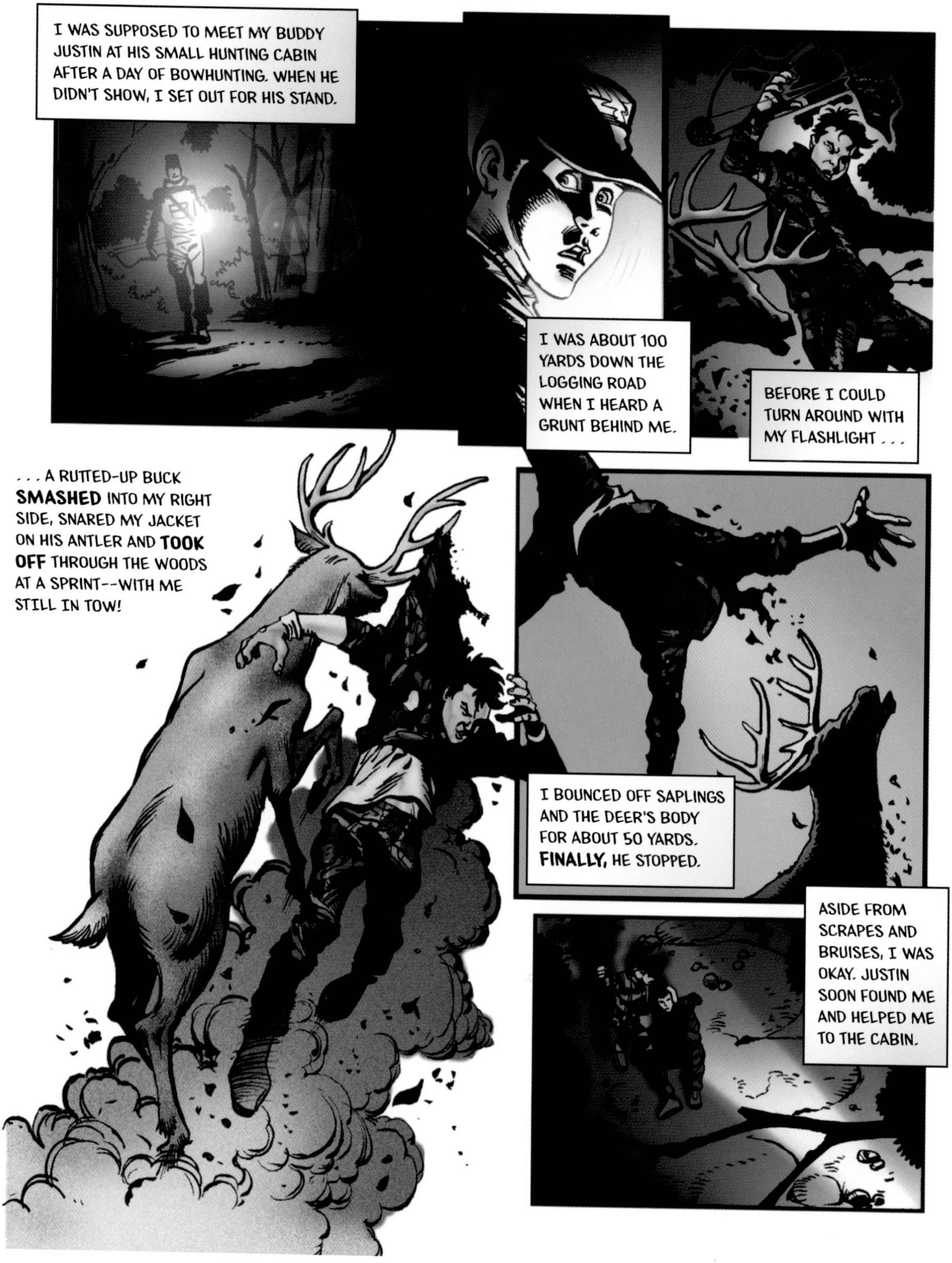

I WAS SUPPOSED TO MEET MY BUDDY JUSTIN AT HIS SMALL HUNTING CABIN AFTER A DAY OF BOWHUNTING. WHEN HE DIDN'T SHOW, I SET OUT FOR HIS STAND.
I WAS ABOUT 100 YARDS DOWN THE LOGGING ROAD WHEN I HEARD A GRUNT BEHIND ME.
BEFORE I COULD TURN AROUND WITH MY FLASHLIGHT . . .
. . . A RUTTED-UP BUCK SMASHED INTO MY RIGHT SIDE, SNARED MY JACKET ON HIS ANTLER AND TOOK OFF THROUGH THE WOODS AT A SPRINT--WITH ME STILL IN TOW!
I BOUNCED OFF SAPLINGS AND THE DEER'S BODY FOR ABOUT 50 YARDS. FINALLY, HE STOPPED.
ASIDE FROM SCRAPES AND BRUISES, I WAS OKAY. JUSTIN SOON FOUND ME AND HELPED ME TO THE CABIN.

Friend to the End // by Robbie Delliss, Michigamme, MI

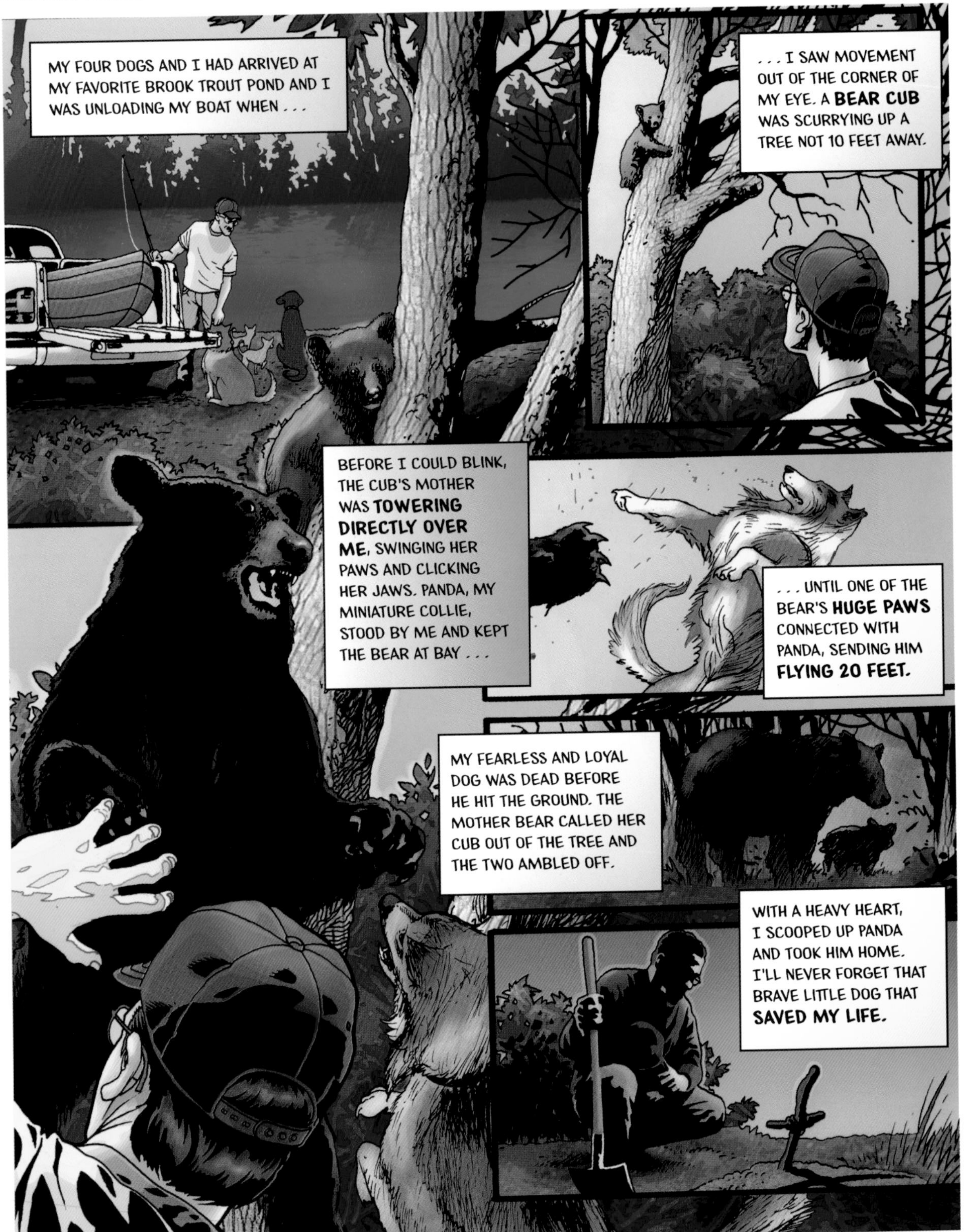
MY FOUR DOGS AND I HAD ARRIVED AT MY FAVORITE BROOK TROUT POND AND I WAS UNLOADING MY BOAT WHEN . . .
. . . I SAW MOVEMENT OUT OF THE CORNER OF MY EYE. A **BEAR CUB** WAS SCURRYING UP A TREE NOT 10 FEET AWAY.
BEFORE I COULD BLINK, THE CUB'S MOTHER WAS **TOWERING DIRECTLY OVER ME**, SWINGING HER PAWS AND CLICKING HER JAWS. PANDA, MY MINIATURE COLLIE, STOOD BY ME AND KEPT THE BEAR AT BAY . . .
. . . UNTIL ONE OF THE BEAR'S **HUGE PAWS** CONNECTED WITH PANDA, SENDING HIM **FLYING 20 FEET.**
MY FEARLESS AND LOYAL DOG WAS DEAD BEFORE HE HIT THE GROUND. THE MOTHER BEAR CALLED HER CUB OUT OF THE TREE AND THE TWO AMBLED OFF.
WITH A HEAVY HEART, I SCOOPED UP PANDA AND TOOK HIM HOME. I'LL NEVER FORGET THAT BRAVE LITTLE DOG THAT **SAVED MY LIFE.**

"He is your friend, your partner, your defender, your dog. You are his life, his love, his leader. He will be yours, faithful and true, to the last beat of his heart. You owe it to him to be worthy of such devotion."

—*Unknown*

Claws Encounter // by George Pendergrast, Coal City, WV

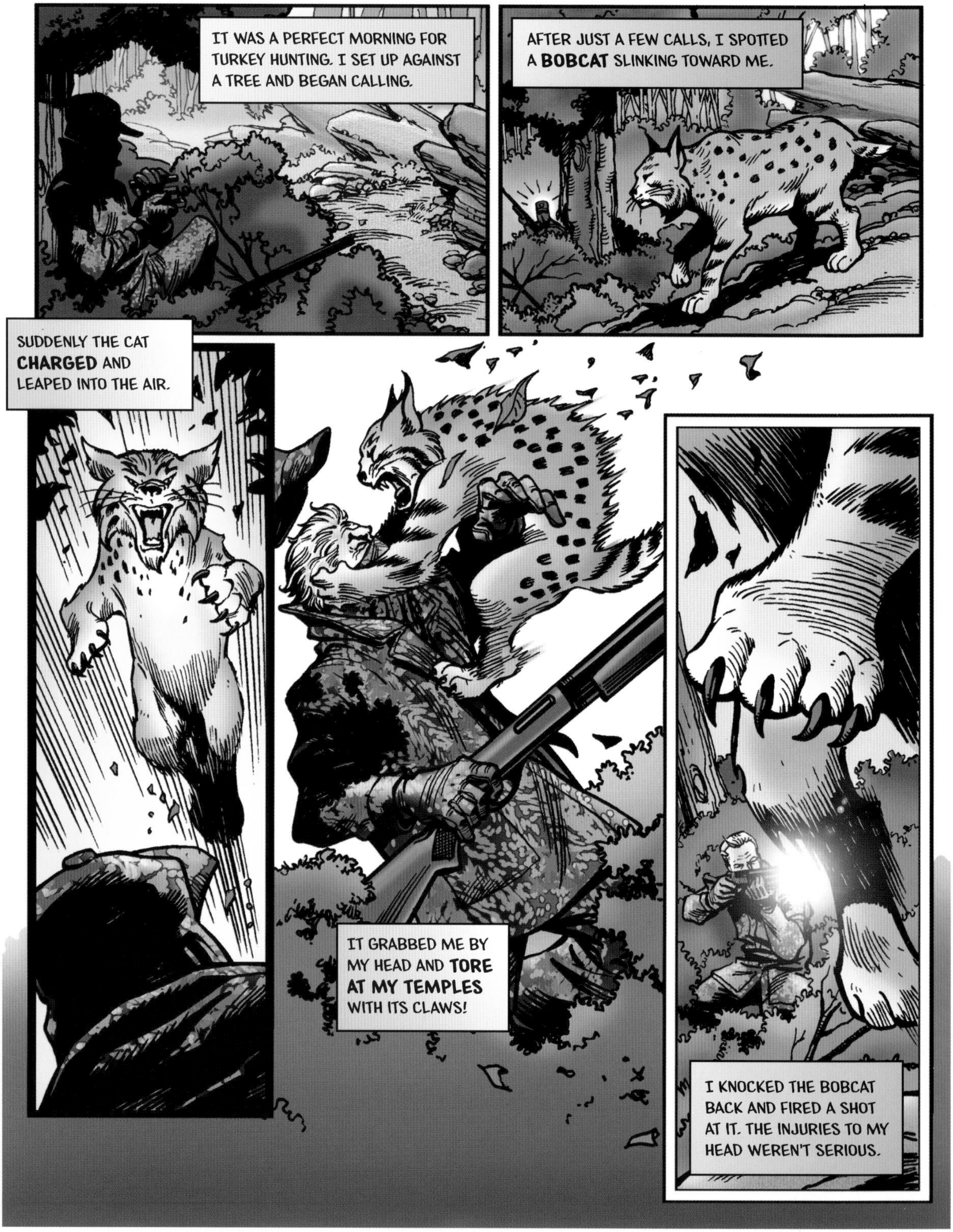
IT WAS A PERFECT MORNING FOR TURKEY HUNTING. I SET UP AGAINST A TREE AND BEGAN CALLING.
AFTER JUST A FEW CALLS, I SPOTTED A **BOBCAT** SLINKING TOWARD ME.
SUDDENLY THE CAT **CHARGED** AND LEAPED INTO THE AIR.
IT GRABBED ME BY MY HEAD AND **TORE AT MY TEMPLES** WITH ITS CLAWS!
I KNOCKED THE BOBCAT BACK AND FIRED A SHOT AT IT. THE INJURIES TO MY HEAD WEREN'T SERIOUS.

Goose Down // by Joshua Durphy, Eldred, PA

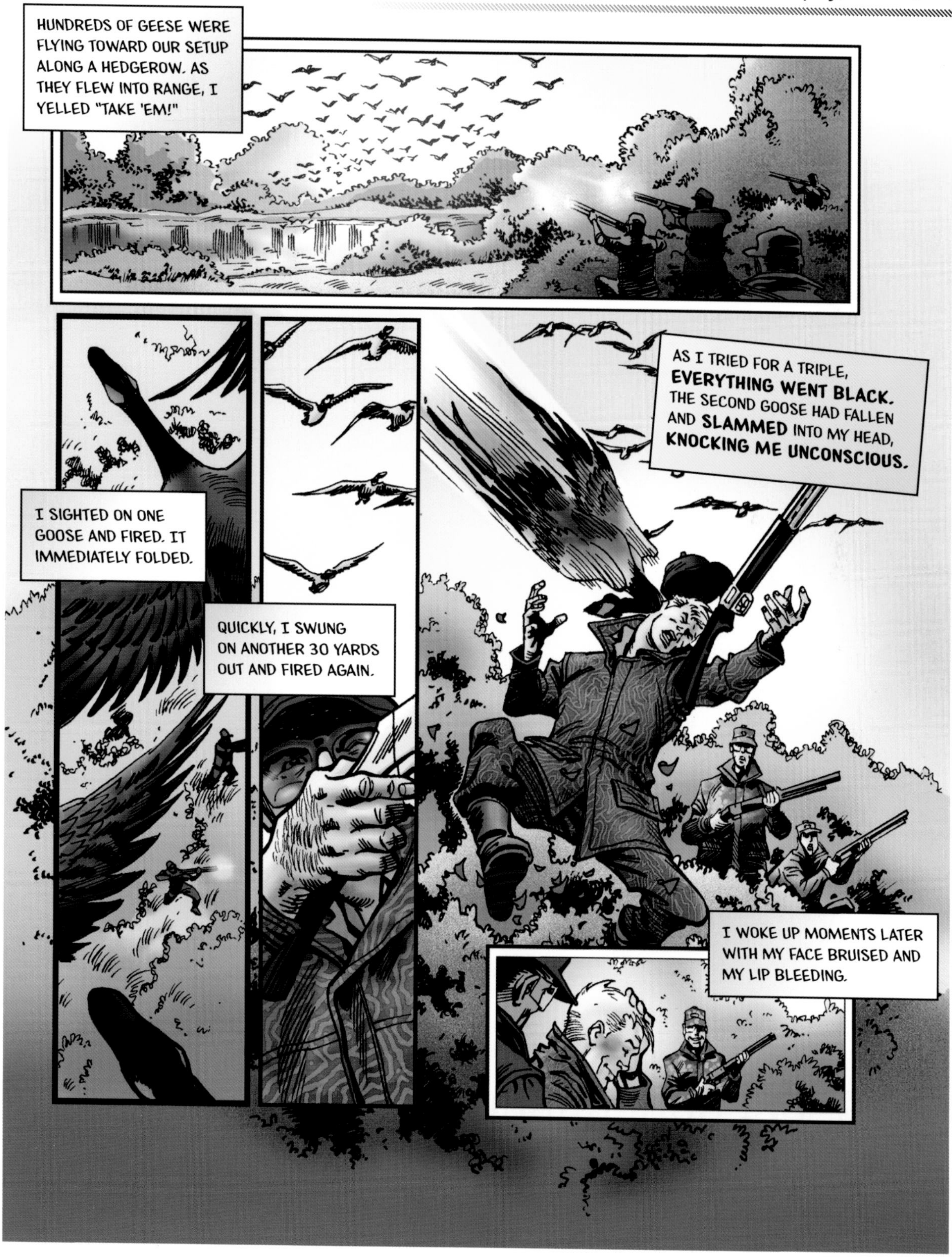
HUNDREDS OF GEESE WERE FLYING TOWARD OUR SETUP ALONG A HEDGEROW. AS THEY FLEW INTO RANGE, I YELLED "TAKE 'EM!"
I SIGHTED ON ONE GOOSE AND FIRED. IT IMMEDIATELY FOLDED.
QUICKLY, I SWUNG ON ANOTHER 30 YARDS OUT AND FIRED AGAIN.
AS I TRIED FOR A TRIPLE, EVERYTHING WENT BLACK. THE SECOND GOOSE HAD FALLEN AND SLAMMED INTO MY HEAD, KNOCKING ME UNCONSCIOUS.
I WOKE UP MOMENTS LATER WITH MY FACE BRUISED AND MY LIP BLEEDING.

Bearly Survived // by Andrea Baringer, Morrisville, VT

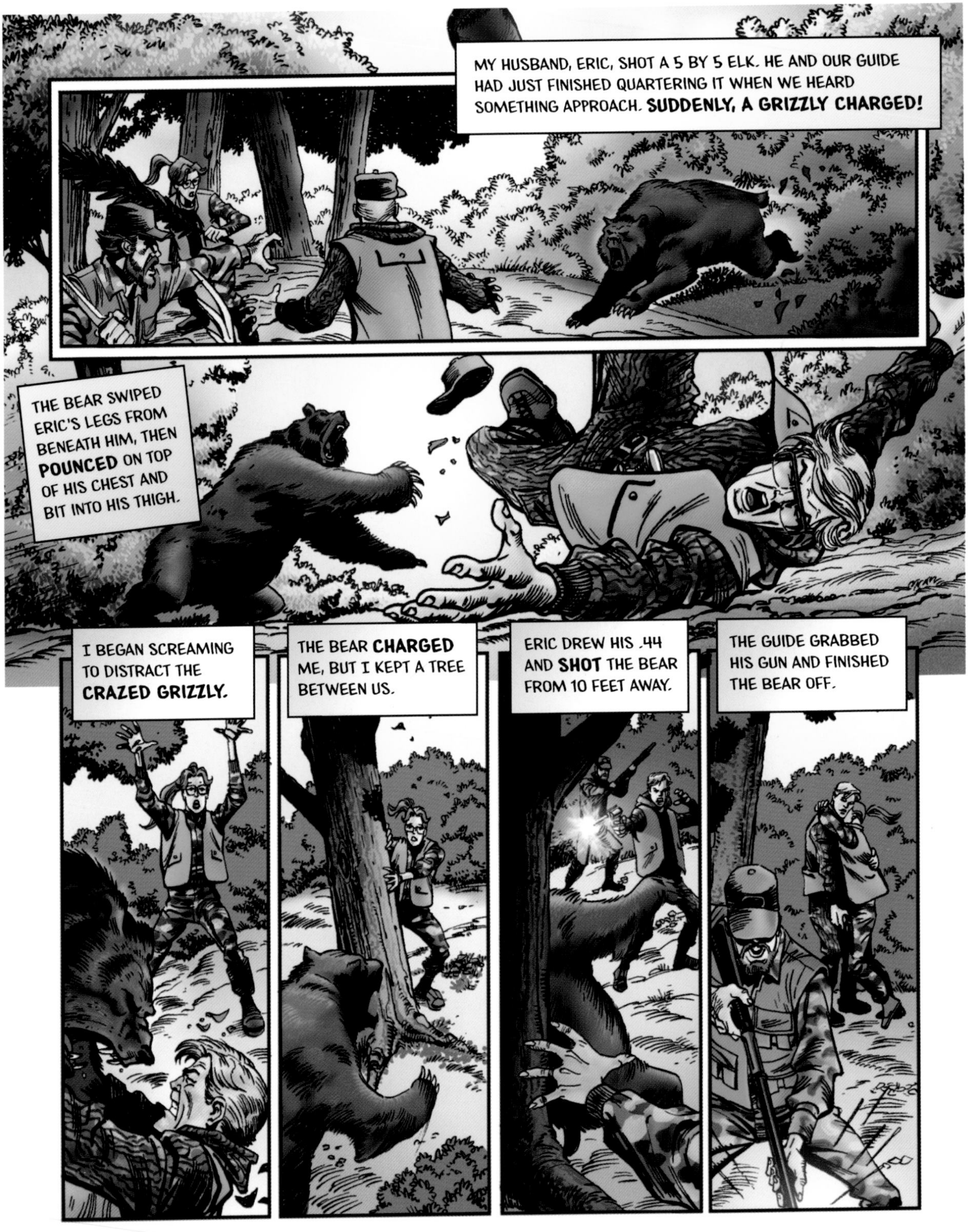

MY HUSBAND, ERIC, SHOT A 5 BY 5 ELK. HE AND OUR GUIDE HAD JUST FINISHED QUARTERING IT WHEN WE HEARD SOMETHING APPROACH. SUDDENLY, A GRIZZLY CHARGED!
THE BEAR SWIPED ERIC'S LEGS FROM BENEATH HIM, THEN POUNCED ON TOP OF HIS CHEST AND BIT INTO HIS THIGH.
I BEGAN SCREAMING TO DISTRACT THE CRAZED GRIZZLY.
THE BEAR CHARGED ME, BUT I KEPT A TREE BETWEEN US.
ERIC DREW HIS .44 AND SHOT THE BEAR FROM 10 FEET AWAY.
THE GUIDE GRABBED HIS GUN AND FINISHED THE BEAR OFF.

Furry Giants

Called the grizzly bear because of the gray or silvery "grizzled" tips of its fur, the brown bear is the most widely distributed bear species in the world, ranging mostly across North America and northern Eurasia. The size of a grizzly bear can vary just as much as its living environment, based on a multitude of factors including age, diet, season, and habitat. Despite its name, the brown bear's color is just as diverse.

Grizzly bears can:
- Grow claws up to 4 inches long
- Weigh up to 2,500 pounds
- Stand 10 feet tall on their hind legs
- Run up to 30 miles per hour

THAT AIN'T NO TEDDY Brown bears generally avoid humans, and seldom attack on sight, but can be unpredictable. While humans risk injury in an incident with a black bear, brown bear attacks are much more likely to be fatal if they occur. Grizzlies may attack if surprised or threatened, or if someone is between them and their cubs. If confronted by a grizzly, back away slowly without making eye contact and speak in a low, calm tone of voice. Turning and running is more likely to trigger an aggressive response. Bear pepper-spray repellent is generally more effective than firearms at stopping bears, although authorities recommend carrying a second deterrent such as a large-caliber gun. If attacked by a brown bear, lie face down on the ground or curl into a ball, and cover your head and neck with your hands to protect yourself.

Elk on the Brain // by Rick Fischer, Enterprise, OR

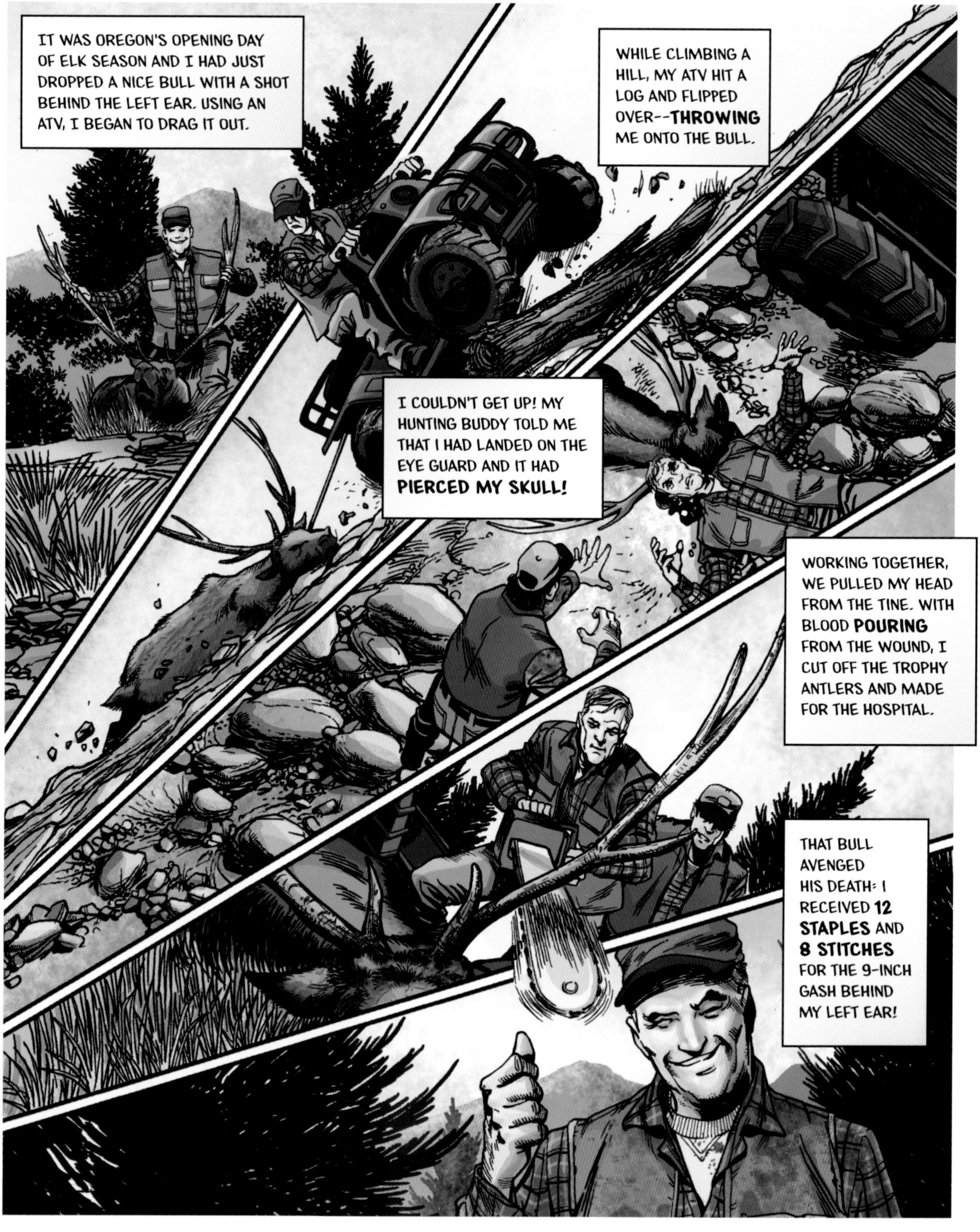
IT WAS OREGON'S OPENING DAY OF ELK SEASON AND I HAD JUST DROPPED A NICE BULL WITH A SHOT BEHIND THE LEFT EAR. USING AN ATV, I BEGAN TO DRAG IT OUT.
WHILE CLIMBING A HILL, MY ATV HIT A LOG AND FLIPPED OVER--**THROWING** ME ONTO THE BULL.
I COULDN'T GET UP! MY HUNTING BUDDY TOLD ME THAT I HAD LANDED ON THE EYE GUARD AND IT HAD **PIERCED MY SKULL!**
WORKING TOGETHER, WE PULLED MY HEAD FROM THE TINE. WITH BLOOD **POURING** FROM THE WOUND, I CUT OFF THE TROPHY ANTLERS AND MADE FOR THE HOSPITAL.
THAT BULL AVENGED HIS DEATH: I RECEIVED **12 STAPLES** AND **8 STITCHES** FOR THE 9-INCH GASH BEHIND MY LEFT EAR!

KNOW THE NUMBERS:
ATVs

500 POUNDS Average weight of a modern ATV.

80% Proportion of ATV riders who are male .

1 IN 5 ATV riders who wear helmets.

93,000 Estimated number of yearly ATV injuries treated in the ER.

400 Average number of ATV-related fatalities yearly in the United States.

30% Segment of ATV crashes that involves alcohol or drugs.

The Muck-and-Mire Buck // by Judd P. Stanberry, Jackson, NJ

[ON]E FALL EVENING, I WAS HUNTING WITH [MY] FRIEND MARCUS IN NEW JERSEY. [WE] HAD SHOT A NICE DEER AND WERE [DR]AGGING IT OUT OF THE WOODS.

WE CAME TO A MUDDY STREAM THAT WE HAD TO CROSS. I TOOK ONE STEP--AND **SANK** INTO MUD UP TO **MY CHEST!**

I BEGAN TO FREAK OUT AT THE FEELING THAT I WAS SINKING EVEN DEEPER. LUCKILY, MARCUS FOUND FIRM FOOTING AND **PULLED ME OUT!**

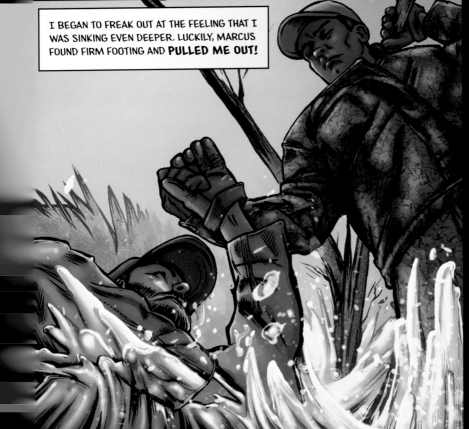

WE RETRIEVED THE DEER TOO AND MADE IT BACK TO MY TRUCK. I DROVE HOME IN MY [UNDERWEAR.]

Death Charge // by Earlis Rohret, Oxford, IA

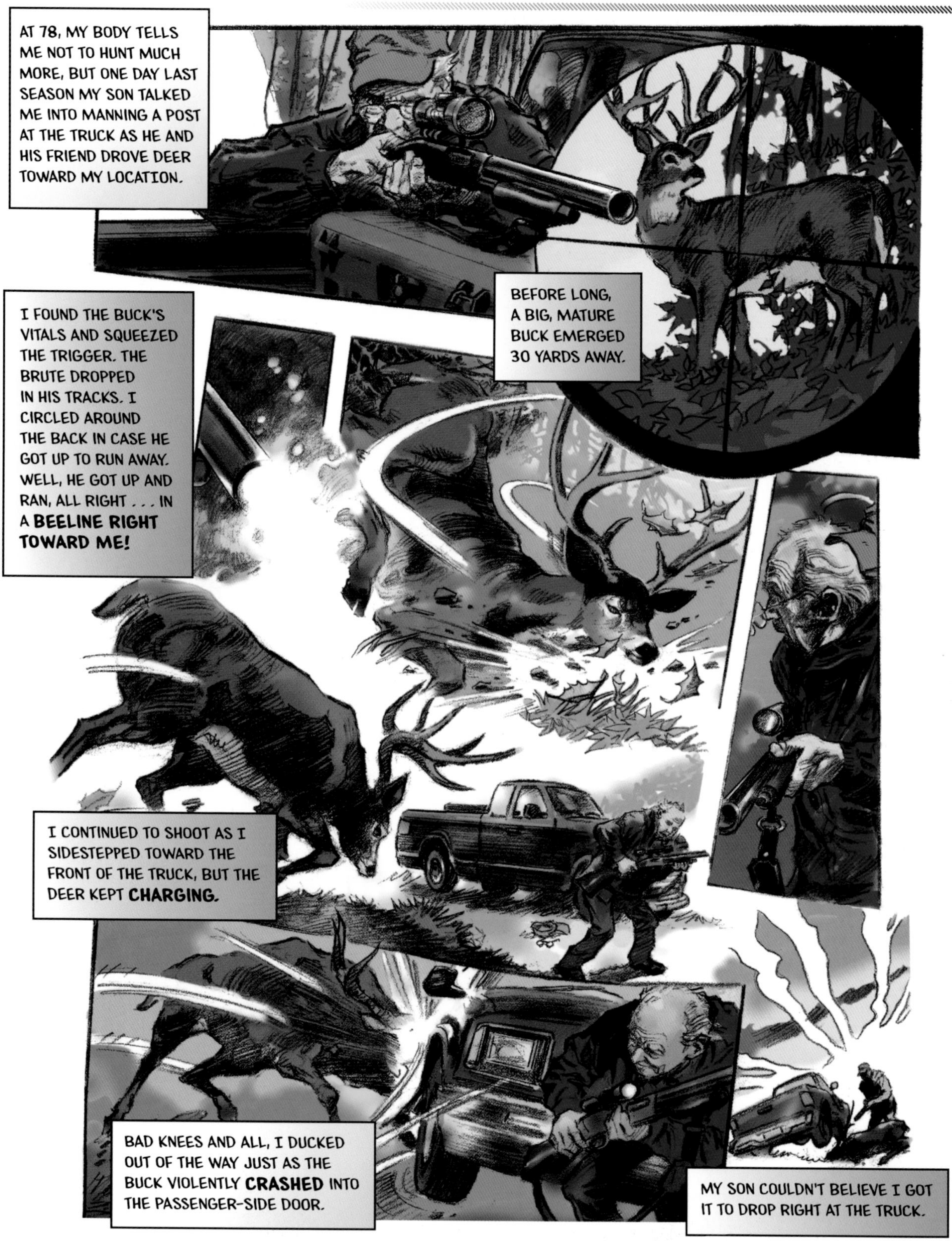
AT 78, MY BODY TELLS ME NOT TO HUNT MUCH MORE, BUT ONE DAY LAST SEASON MY SON TALKED ME INTO MANNING A POST AT THE TRUCK AS HE AND HIS FRIEND DROVE DEER TOWARD MY LOCATION.
BEFORE LONG, A BIG, MATURE BUCK EMERGED 30 YARDS AWAY.
I FOUND THE BUCK'S VITALS AND SQUEEZED THE TRIGGER. THE BRUTE DROPPED IN HIS TRACKS. I CIRCLED AROUND THE BACK IN CASE HE GOT UP TO RUN AWAY. WELL, HE GOT UP AND RAN, ALL RIGHT . . . IN A **BEELINE RIGHT TOWARD ME!**
I CONTINUED TO SHOOT AS I SIDESTEPPED TOWARD THE FRONT OF THE TRUCK, BUT THE DEER KEPT **CHARGING.**
BAD KNEES AND ALL, I DUCKED OUT OF THE WAY JUST AS THE BUCK VIOLENTLY **CRASHED** INTO THE PASSENGER-SIDE DOOR.
MY SON COULDN'T BELIEVE I GOT IT TO DROP RIGHT AT THE TRUCK.

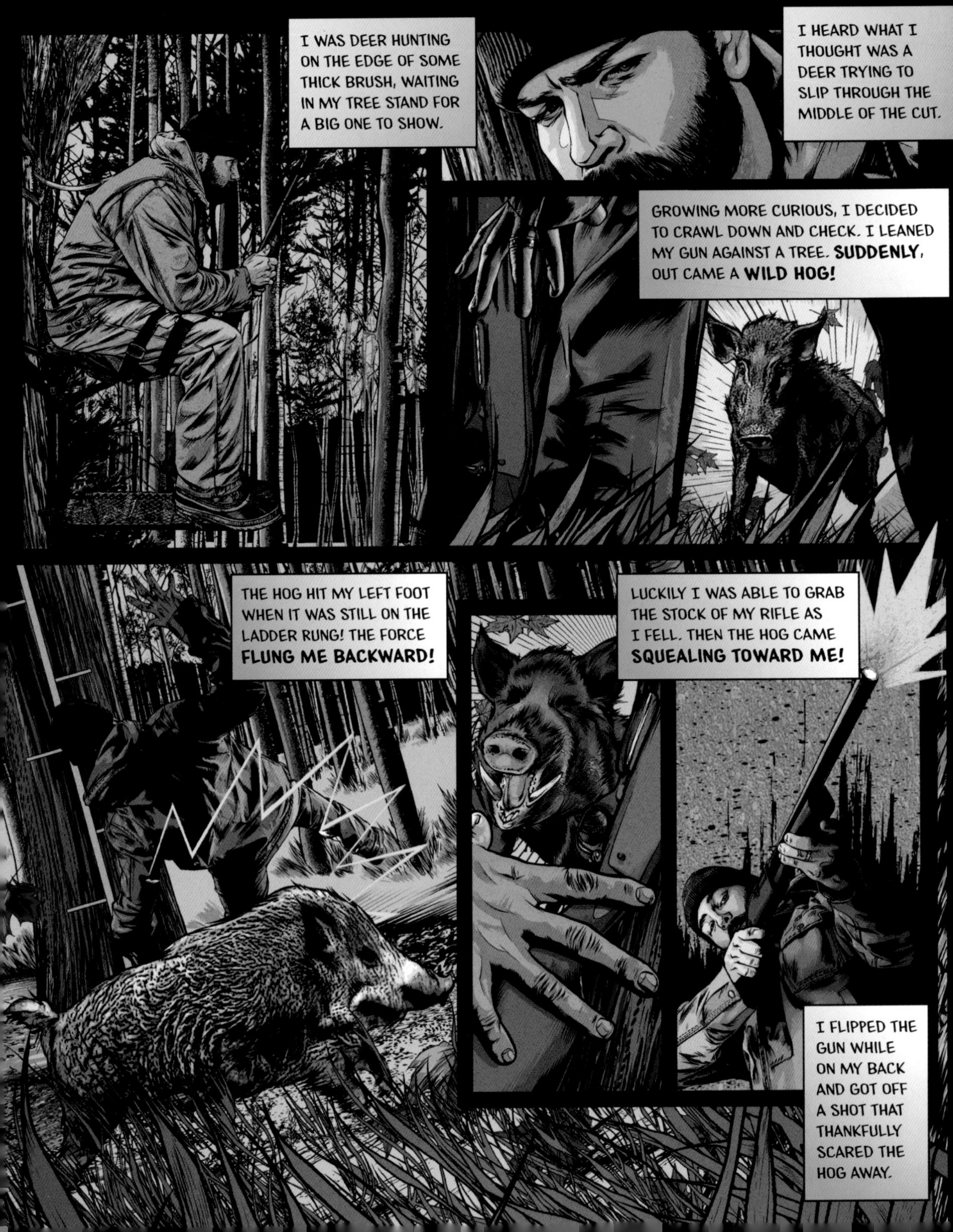
I WAS DEER HUNTING ON THE EDGE OF SOME THICK BRUSH, WAITING IN MY TREE STAND FOR A BIG ONE TO SHOW.
I HEARD WHAT I THOUGHT WAS A DEER TRYING TO SLIP THROUGH THE MIDDLE OF THE CUT.
GROWING MORE CURIOUS, I DECIDED TO CRAWL DOWN AND CHECK. I LEANED MY GUN AGAINST A TREE. **SUDDENLY**, OUT CAME A **WILD HOG!**
THE HOG HIT MY LEFT FOOT WHEN IT WAS STILL ON THE LADDER RUNG! THE FORCE **FLUNG ME BACKWARD!**
LUCKILY I WAS ABLE TO GRAB THE STOCK OF MY RIFLE AS I FELL. THEN THE HOG CAME **SQUEALING TOWARD ME!**
I FLIPPED THE GUN WHILE ON MY BACK AND GOT OFF A SHOT THAT THANKFULLY SCARED THE HOG AWAY.

"**Never wrestle with pigs. You both get dirty and the pig likes it.**"

—*George Bernard Shaw*

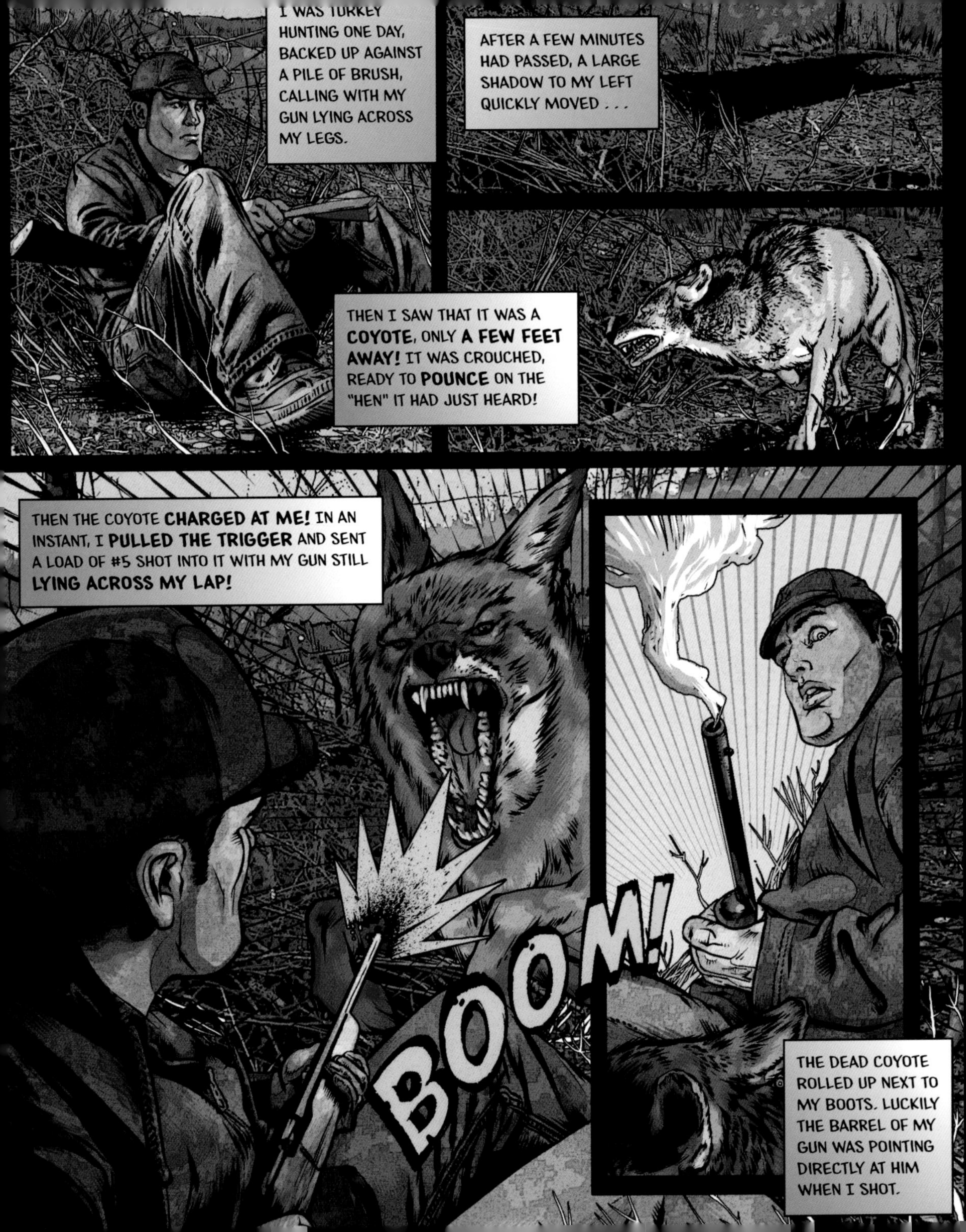
I WAS TURKEY HUNTING ONE DAY, BACKED UP AGAINST A PILE OF BRUSH, CALLING WITH MY GUN LYING ACROSS MY LEGS.
AFTER A FEW MINUTES HAD PASSED, A LARGE SHADOW TO MY LEFT QUICKLY MOVED . . .
THEN I SAW THAT IT WAS A COYOTE, ONLY A FEW FEET AWAY! IT WAS CROUCHED, READY TO POUNCE ON THE "HEN" IT HAD JUST HEARD!
THEN THE COYOTE CHARGED AT ME! IN AN INSTANT, I PULLED THE TRIGGER AND SENT A LOAD OF #5 SHOT INTO IT WITH MY GUN STILL LYING ACROSS MY LAP!
BOOM!
THE DEAD COYOTE ROLLED UP NEXT TO MY BOOTS. LUCKILY THE BARREL OF MY GUN WAS POINTING DIRECTLY AT HIM WHEN I SHOT.

Very Wily Indeed

Also known as the prairie wolf, brush wolf, or American jackal, the coyote ranges widely across Central and North America, in every habitat from Panama to Canada and Alaska. Though in a similar ecological niche as wolves and jackals, the coyote has proven more adaptable, and has even expanded its range to survive in urban areas.

Coyotes can:
- Run at speeds up to 43 mph
- Leap up to 13 feet horizontally
- Hear sounds at an even higher range than dogs (80 kHz vs 60 kHz)
- Pursue prey in extended hunts lasting up to 21 hours
- Bring down larger animals up to 15 times their weight

CUNNING CANINES Coyote attacks are rare, and don't often cause many serious injuries, but as coyote and human habitats continue to increasingly overlap, coyotes have slowly become less fearful and more aggressive. To date, several attacks have been recorded, with at least two known fatalities.

Just as with any other wild animal, don't feed coyotes, as it will only make them bolder, and increase risks to you and your immediate area. Consider carrying pepper spray if you are in an area known to be a coyote's habitat. If confronted, be aggressive and loud, and fend it off at range if you can, using thrown items like sticks and rocks. At close range, use the same items in hand. If you are bitten, visit your nearest available medical center immediately to test (and if necessary, be treated) for rabies.

When Grizzlies Attack // by Jared McAllister, Butte, MT

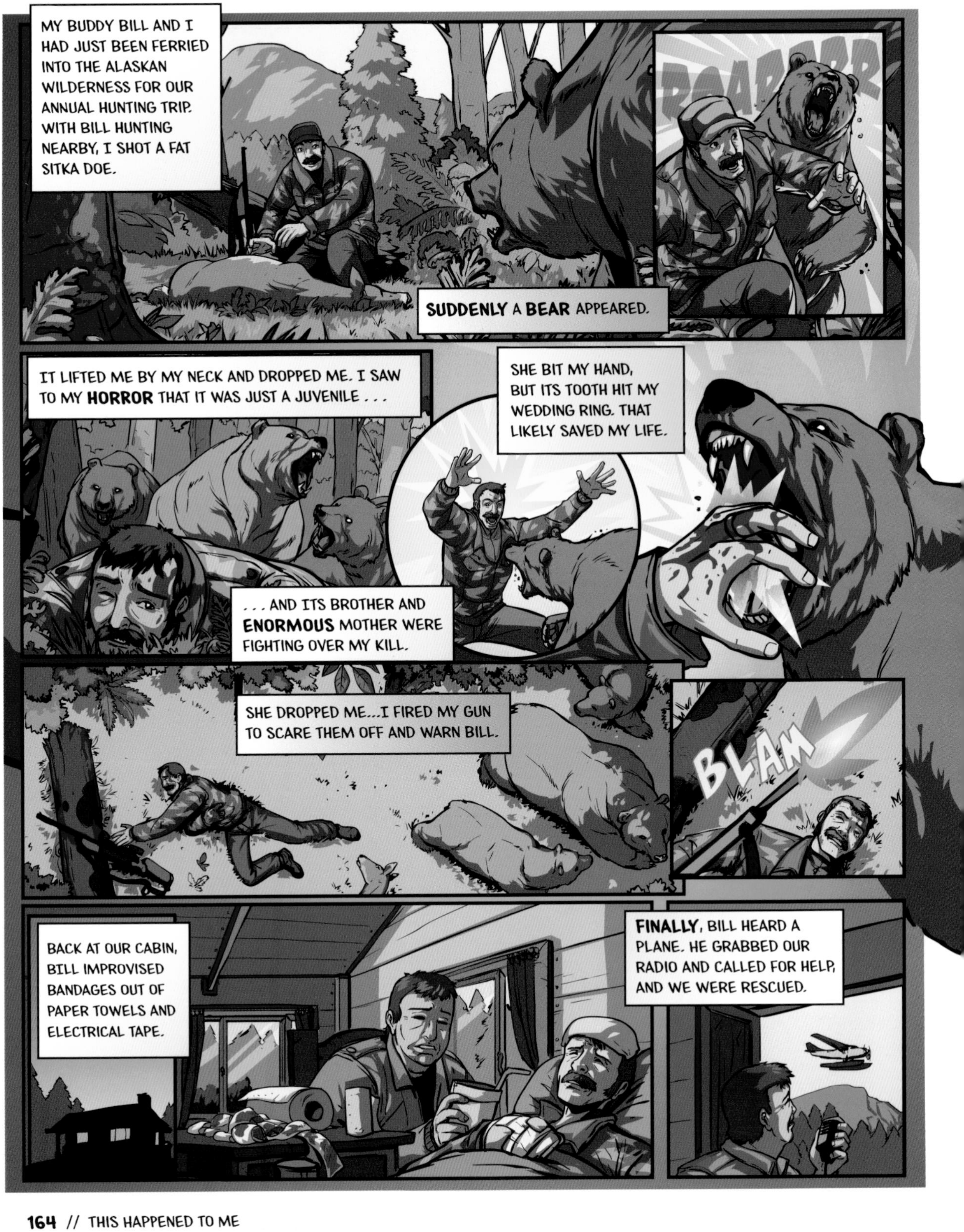

MY BUDDY BILL AND I HAD JUST BEEN FERRIED INTO THE ALASKAN WILDERNESS FOR OUR ANNUAL HUNTING TRIP. WITH BILL HUNTING NEARBY, I SHOT A FAT SITKA DOE.
SUDDENLY A BEAR APPEARED.
ROARRRR
IT LIFTED ME BY MY NECK AND DROPPED ME. I SAW TO MY HORROR THAT IT WAS JUST A JUVENILE . . .
. . . AND ITS BROTHER AND ENORMOUS MOTHER WERE FIGHTING OVER MY KILL.
SHE BIT MY HAND, BUT ITS TOOTH HIT MY WEDDING RING. THAT LIKELY SAVED MY LIFE.
SHE DROPPED ME...I FIRED MY GUN TO SCARE THEM OFF AND WARN BILL.
BLAM
BACK AT OUR CABIN, BILL IMPROVISED BANDAGES OUT OF PAPER TOWELS AND ELECTRICAL TAPE.
FINALLY, BILL HEARD A PLANE. HE GRABBED OUR RADIO AND CALLED FOR HELP, AND WE WERE RESCUED.

The Great Indiana Buck Slide // by Tim Auxier, Madison, IN

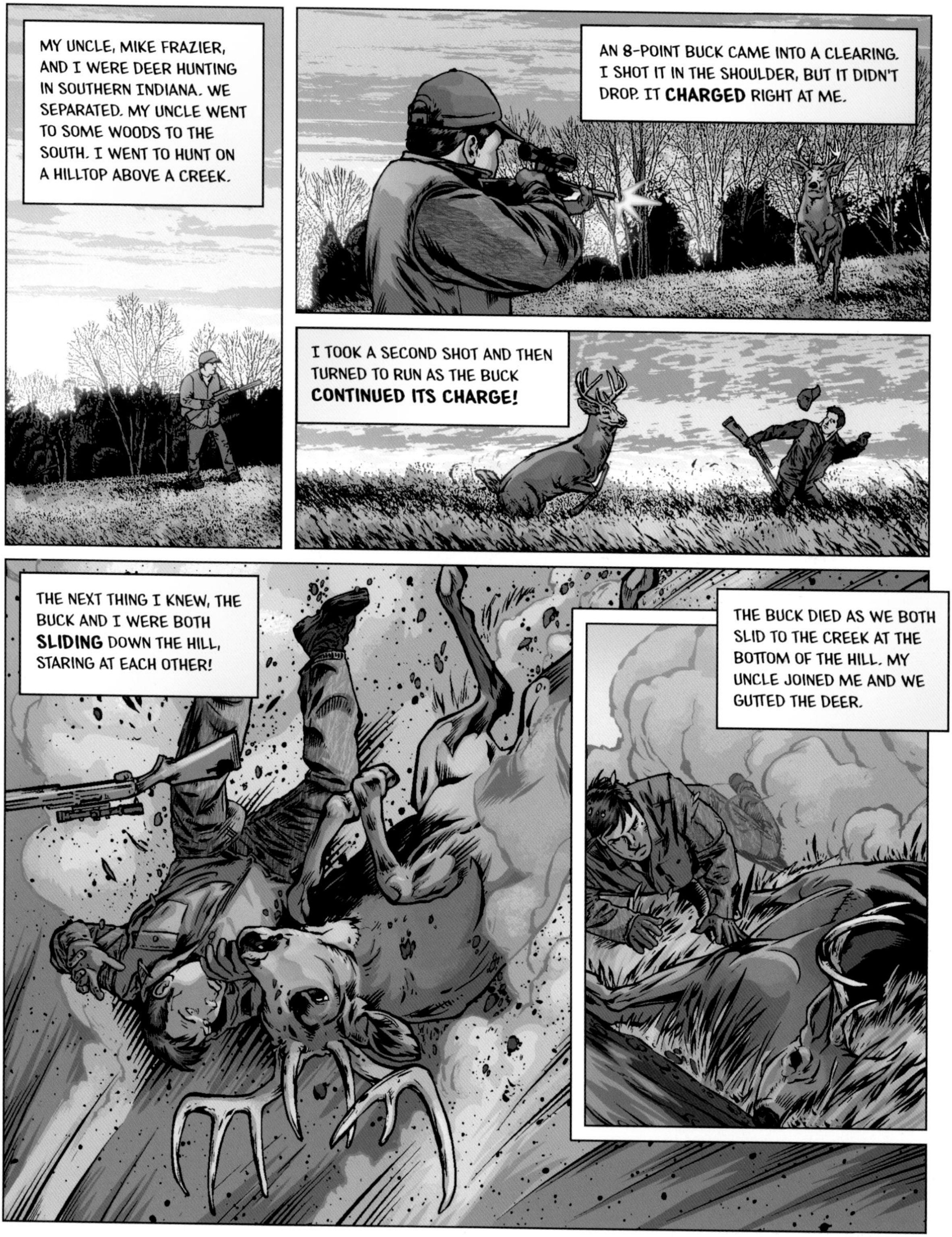

MY UNCLE, MIKE FRAZIER, AND I WERE DEER HUNTING IN SOUTHERN INDIANA. WE SEPARATED. MY UNCLE WENT TO SOME WOODS TO THE SOUTH. I WENT TO HUNT ON A HILLTOP ABOVE A CREEK.
AN 8-POINT BUCK CAME INTO A CLEARING. I SHOT IT IN THE SHOULDER, BUT IT DIDN'T DROP. IT **CHARGED** RIGHT AT ME.
I TOOK A SECOND SHOT AND THEN TURNED TO RUN AS THE BUCK **CONTINUED ITS CHARGE!**
THE NEXT THING I KNEW, THE BUCK AND I WERE BOTH **SLIDING** DOWN THE HILL, STARING AT EACH OTHER!
THE BUCK DIED AS WE BOTH SLID TO THE CREEK AT THE BOTTOM OF THE HILL. MY UNCLE JOINED ME AND WE GUTTED THE DEER.

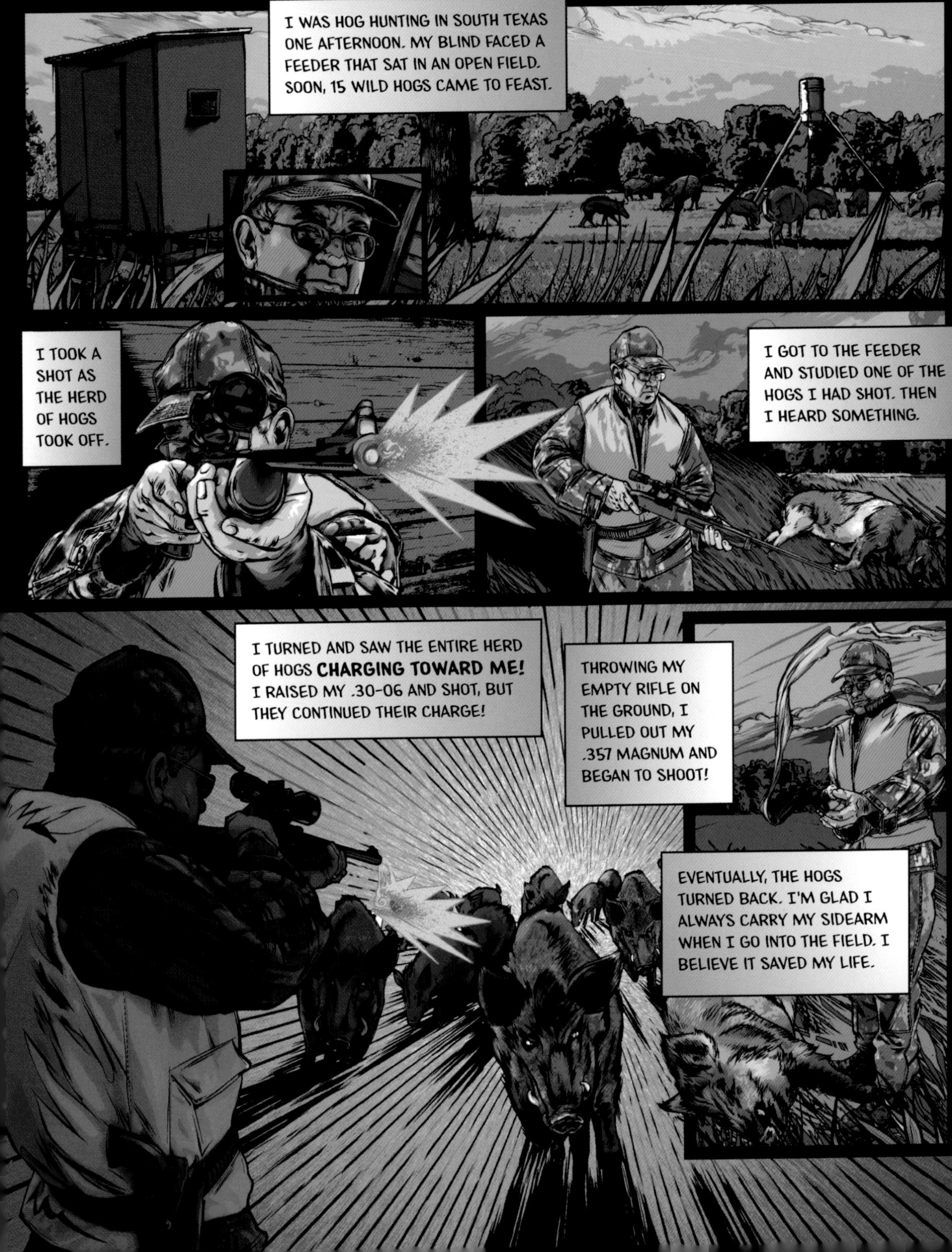
I WAS HOG HUNTING IN SOUTH TEXAS ONE AFTERNOON. MY BLIND FACED A FEEDER THAT SAT IN AN OPEN FIELD. SOON, 15 WILD HOGS CAME TO FEAST.
I TOOK A SHOT AS THE HERD OF HOGS TOOK OFF.
I GOT TO THE FEEDER AND STUDIED ONE OF THE HOGS I HAD SHOT. THEN I HEARD SOMETHING.
I TURNED AND SAW THE ENTIRE HERD OF HOGS **CHARGING TOWARD ME!** I RAISED MY .30-06 AND SHOT, BUT THEY CONTINUED THEIR CHARGE!
THROWING MY EMPTY RIFLE ON THE GROUND, I PULLED OUT MY .357 MAGNUM AND BEGAN TO SHOOT!
EVENTUALLY, THE HOGS TURNED BACK. I'M GLAD I ALWAYS CARRY MY SIDEARM WHEN I GO INTO THE FIELD. I BELIEVE IT SAVED MY LIFE.

KNOW THE NUMBERS:
Wild Pigs

1,100 POUNDS Weight of the largest feral pig on record, shot by Bill Coursey of Fayetteville, GA in 2007. (One domestic pig, Big Bill, weighed in at 2,500 lbs.)

7 INCHES Greatest recorded exposed length of wild pig tusks. (The total length, including root, was 12 inches.)

30 MPH Top running speed of a wild hog.

83 STITCHES Number of sutures needed to sew up the leg of a man injured by a boar attack near San Antonio, TX in 2008.

115 DB Volume of a pig's squeal. (An average jet airliner's engines are about 112 dB.)

Grab Your Gun

Based on early hand-held firearms, muzzleloaders are so named because wielders prepare these guns by loading propellant and ammunition through the muzzle, instead of inserting a prepared cartridge into the breech or feeding ammunition through a magazine. Older versions of the muzzleloader have seen extensive use throughout the centuries, across Europe and Asia, and later in the Americas, especially with historic models such as the famed Kentucky Long Rifle.

HISTORIC WEAPONRY Muzzleloaders were originally prepared by pouring powder down the barrel, followed by sets of wadding before (and sometimes also after) the bullet was inserted. The weapon was fired by a variety of methods developed over time, from matchlock to flintlock to percussion cap. Modern muzzleloader users have access to improvements such as waterproofing, smokeless powder, rifled barrels or ammunition with a sabot or jacket for smooth barrels, and primers set into an "in-line" design behind the powder charge for more efficient ignition.

Despite the availability of higher-tech modern breech-loaders and cartridge ammunition, there is still a sizeable number of muzzleloader enthusiasts, with multiple shooting associations devoted to the gun, and a variety of models available either fully assembled or as kits for shooters to build their own. Still, you might not want to use one as a club unless you absolutely have to.

Batter Up, Buck! // by Tom Harvey, Waterbury, VT

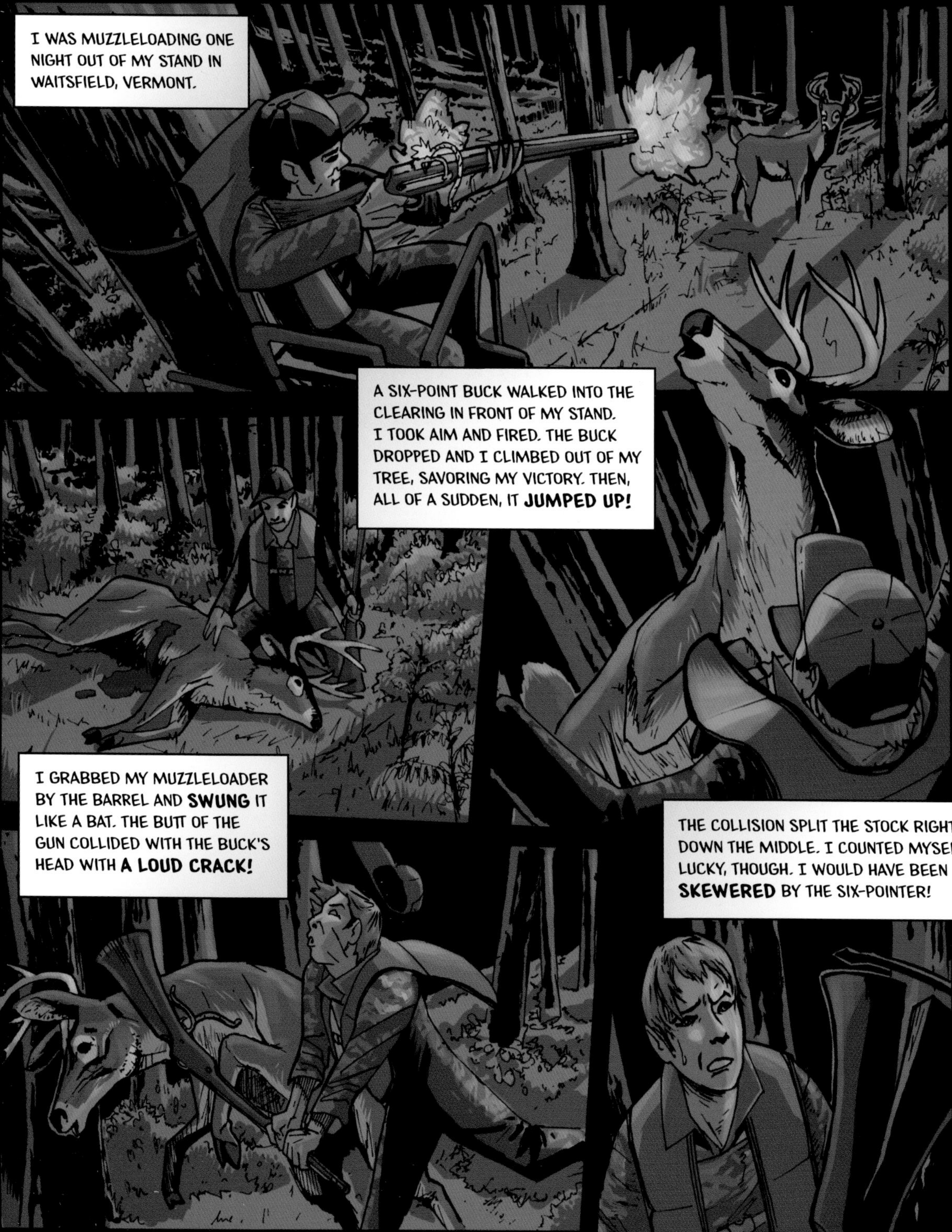
I WAS MUZZLELOADING ONE NIGHT OUT OF MY STAND IN WAITSFIELD, VERMONT.
A SIX-POINT BUCK WALKED INTO THE CLEARING IN FRONT OF MY STAND. I TOOK AIM AND FIRED. THE BUCK DROPPED AND I CLIMBED OUT OF MY TREE, SAVORING MY VICTORY. THEN, ALL OF A SUDDEN, IT **JUMPED UP!**
I GRABBED MY MUZZLELOADER BY THE BARREL AND **SWUNG** IT LIKE A BAT. THE BUTT OF THE GUN COLLIDED WITH THE BUCK'S HEAD WITH **A LOUD CRACK!**
THE COLLISION SPLIT THE STOCK RIGHT DOWN THE MIDDLE. I COUNTED MYSELF LUCKY, THOUGH. I WOULD HAVE BEEN **SKEWERED** BY THE SIX-POINTER!

"**They are sometimes dangerous to the hunter, and will not turn out for the hunter, but furiously rush upon him and trample him to death, unless he is lucky enough to avoid them by dodging round a tree.**"

—*Henry David Thoreau on moose*

Moose Point Blank // By Greg Vroman, Kenai, AK

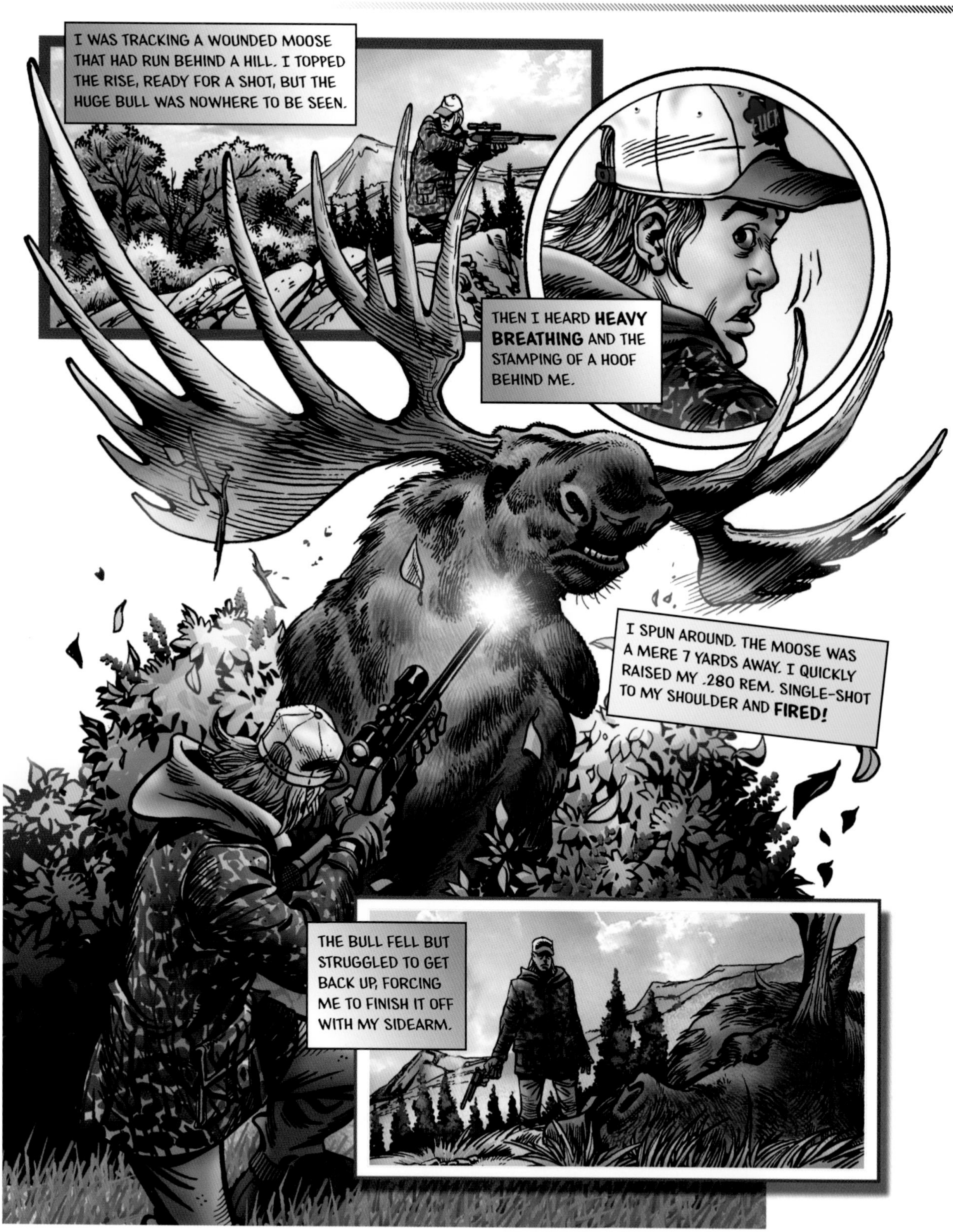

I WAS TRACKING A WOUNDED MOOSE THAT HAD RUN BEHIND A HILL. I TOPPED THE RISE, READY FOR A SHOT, BUT THE HUGE BULL WAS NOWHERE TO BE SEEN.
THEN I HEARD **HEAVY BREATHING** AND THE STAMPING OF A HOOF BEHIND ME.
I SPUN AROUND. THE MOOSE WAS A MERE 7 YARDS AWAY. I QUICKLY RAISED MY .280 REM. SINGLE-SHOT TO MY SHOULDER AND **FIRED!**
THE BULL FELL BUT STRUGGLED TO GET BACK UP, FORCING ME TO FINISH IT OFF WITH MY SIDEARM.

Gored in Georgia // by Thornton Hull, Locust Grove, GA

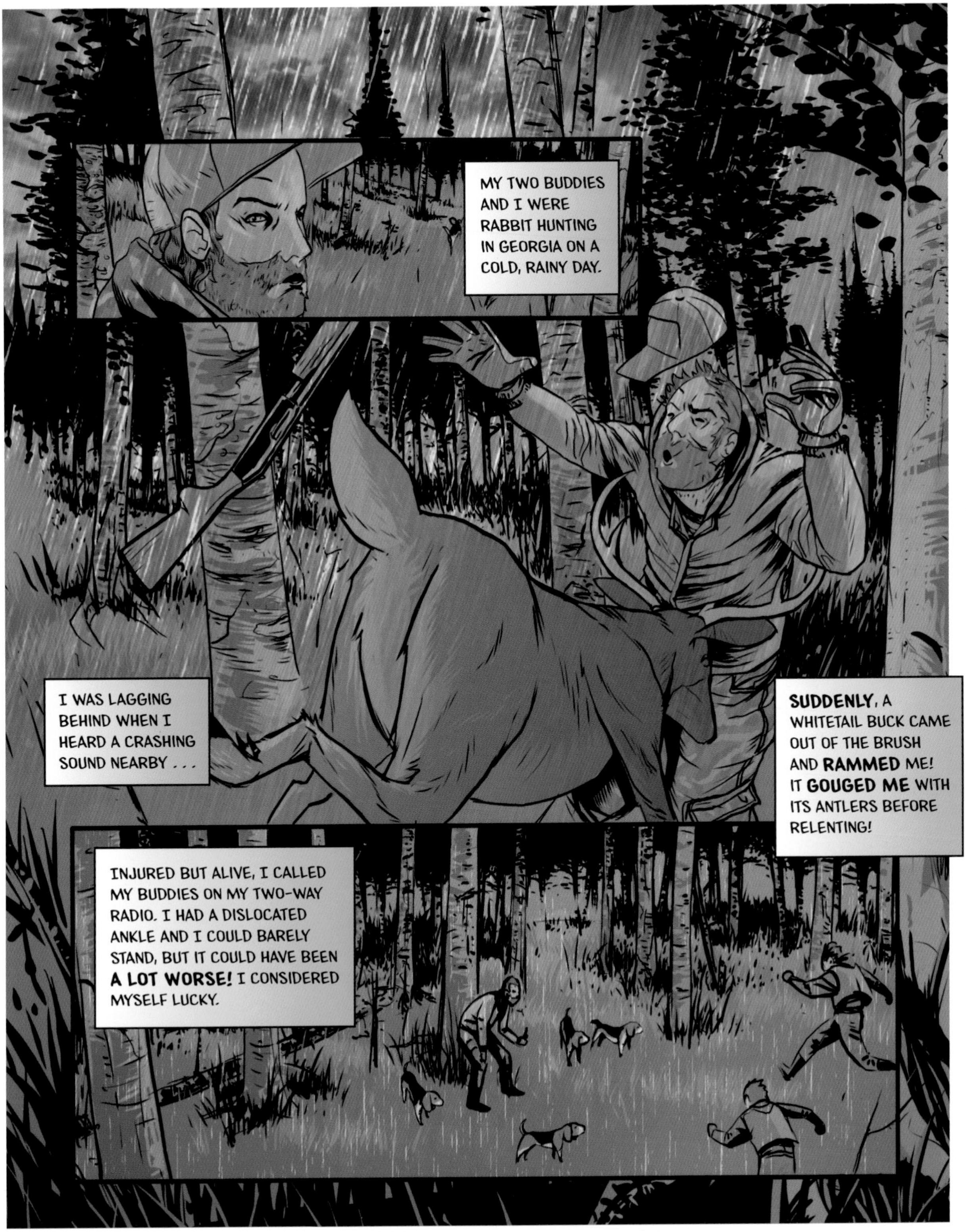

MY TWO BUDDIES AND I WERE RABBIT HUNTING IN GEORGIA ON A COLD, RAINY DAY.
I WAS LAGGING BEHIND WHEN I HEARD A CRASHING SOUND NEARBY . . .
SUDDENLY, A WHITETAIL BUCK CAME OUT OF THE BRUSH AND RAMMED ME! IT GOUGED ME WITH ITS ANTLERS BEFORE RELENTING!
INJURED BUT ALIVE, I CALLED MY BUDDIES ON MY TWO-WAY RADIO. I HAD A DISLOCATED ANKLE AND I COULD BARELY STAND, BUT IT COULD HAVE BEEN A LOT WORSE! I CONSIDERED MYSELF LUCKY.

Roughed Grouse Gone Wild // by Richard Braidwood, Alpena, MI

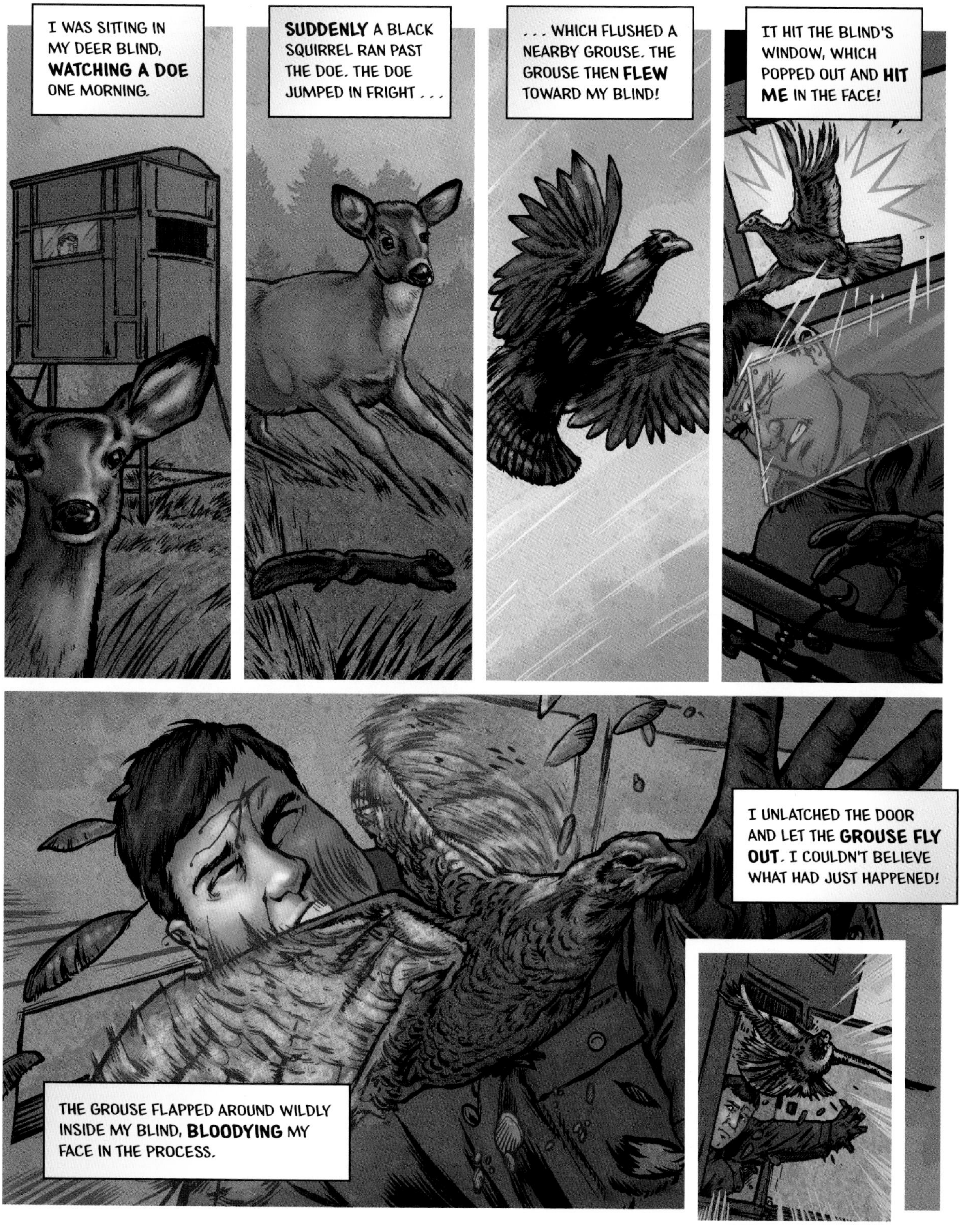
I WAS SITTING IN MY DEER BLIND, **WATCHING A DOE** ONE MORNING.
SUDDENLY A BLACK SQUIRREL RAN PAST THE DOE. THE DOE JUMPED IN FRIGHT . . .
. . . WHICH FLUSHED A NEARBY GROUSE. THE GROUSE THEN **FLEW** TOWARD MY BLIND!
IT HIT THE BLIND'S WINDOW, WHICH POPPED OUT AND **HIT ME** IN THE FACE!
THE GROUSE FLAPPED AROUND WILDLY INSIDE MY BLIND, **BLOODYING** MY FACE IN THE PROCESS.
I UNLATCHED THE DOOR AND LET THE **GROUSE FLY OUT**. I COULDN'T BELIEVE WHAT HAD JUST HAPPENED!

Standing My Ground // by Perry Blakeman, Marengo, WI

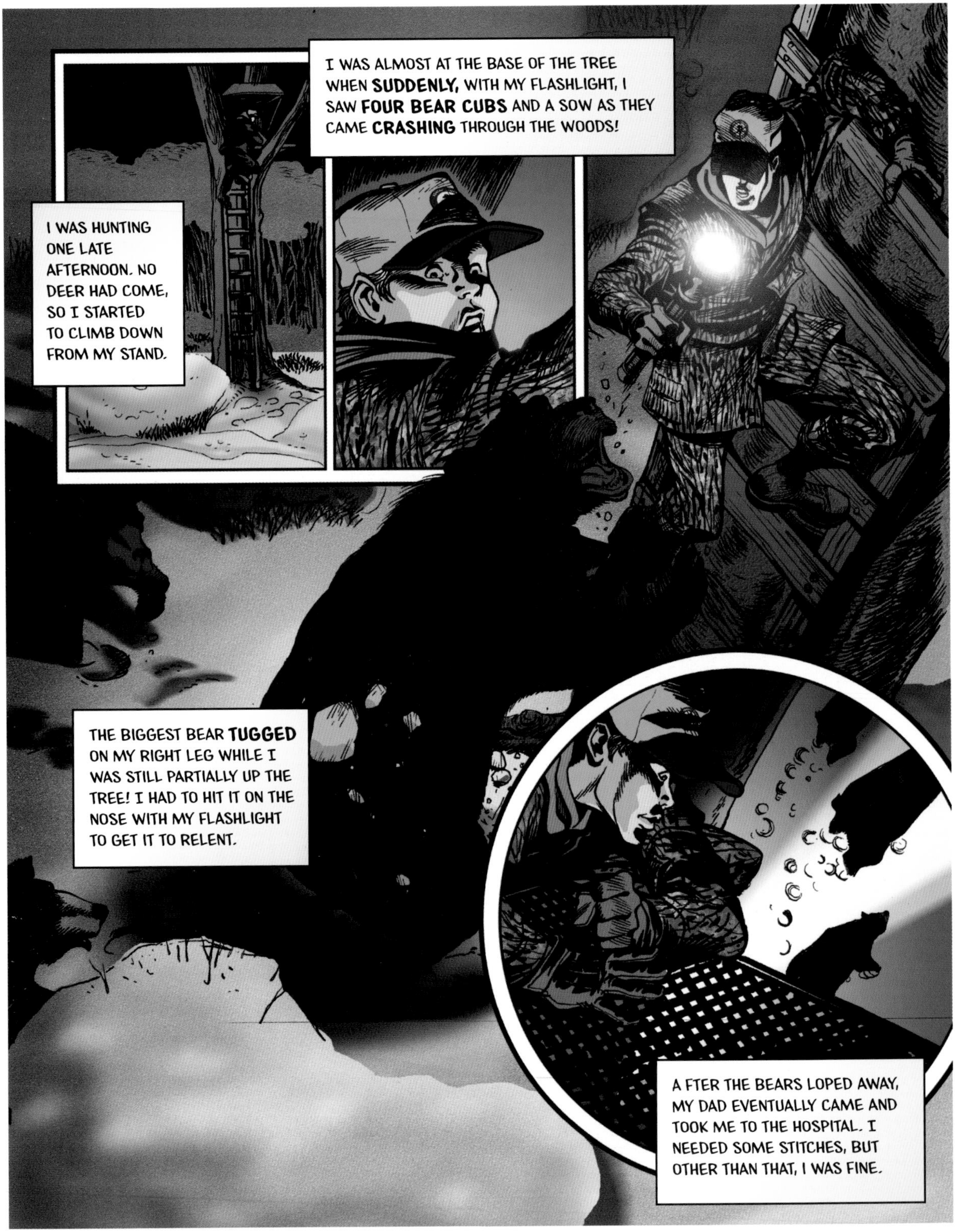
I WAS HUNTING ONE LATE AFTERNOON. NO DEER HAD COME, SO I STARTED TO CLIMB DOWN FROM MY STAND.
I WAS ALMOST AT THE BASE OF THE TREE WHEN SUDDENLY, WITH MY FLASHLIGHT, I SAW FOUR BEAR CUBS AND A SOW AS THEY CAME CRASHING THROUGH THE WOODS!
THE BIGGEST BEAR TUGGED ON MY RIGHT LEG WHILE I WAS STILL PARTIALLY UP THE TREE! I HAD TO HIT IT ON THE NOSE WITH MY FLASHLIGHT TO GET IT TO RELENT.
A FTER THE BEARS LOPED AWAY, MY DAD EVENTUALLY CAME AND TOOK ME TO THE HOSPITAL. I NEEDED SOME STITCHES, BUT OTHER THAN THAT, I WAS FINE.

The Bear Facts

With increasing human presence in their habitats, and more bears in human habitats, confrontations between the two omnivores are on the rise. If attacked by a grizzly, you're more likely to survive if you stay passive and cover vital areas; if it's a black bear, show a much more aggressive response to help save your skin.

Since both varieties of bear run through a range of fur colors from blond to pitch black, their names are a bit of a misnomer. A few other physical characteristics can help you tell the difference between black bears and grizzlies:

SIZE Grizzlies are almost always larger than black bears.

BACK Black bears have a smoothly shaped back; grizzly bears have a round, hump-like shape to their shoulders.

EARS Black bears' ears are larger and somewhat pointed, while brown bears have shorter, more rounded ears.

PAWS A black bear leaves slightly shorter paw prints with the claw marks closer set to the toes; grizzly paws leave longer prints with claws making imprints further from the toes.

In general, people traveling in the wilderness should avoid being too quiet to reduce the risk of stumbling upon a bear or getting between a mother and her cubs. If you're able to see bears, stay at least a quarter-mile away. If a bear acts agitated—growling, snapping its jaws, making bluff charges, or standing up—it is more likely to be afraid than aggressive. Avoid making eye contact, back away slowly, and speak calmly and softly. If a bear is approaching silently or in a determined manner, it's more likely to be acting in an aggressive or predatory fashion. Make yourself look larger and sound louder, wave objects or bang them together, and be prepared to fight. No matter what wild animal you may risk running across, carry pepper spray and do not hesitate to use it if one approaches you.

Trophy Takedown! // by Dan Williams, Casper, WY

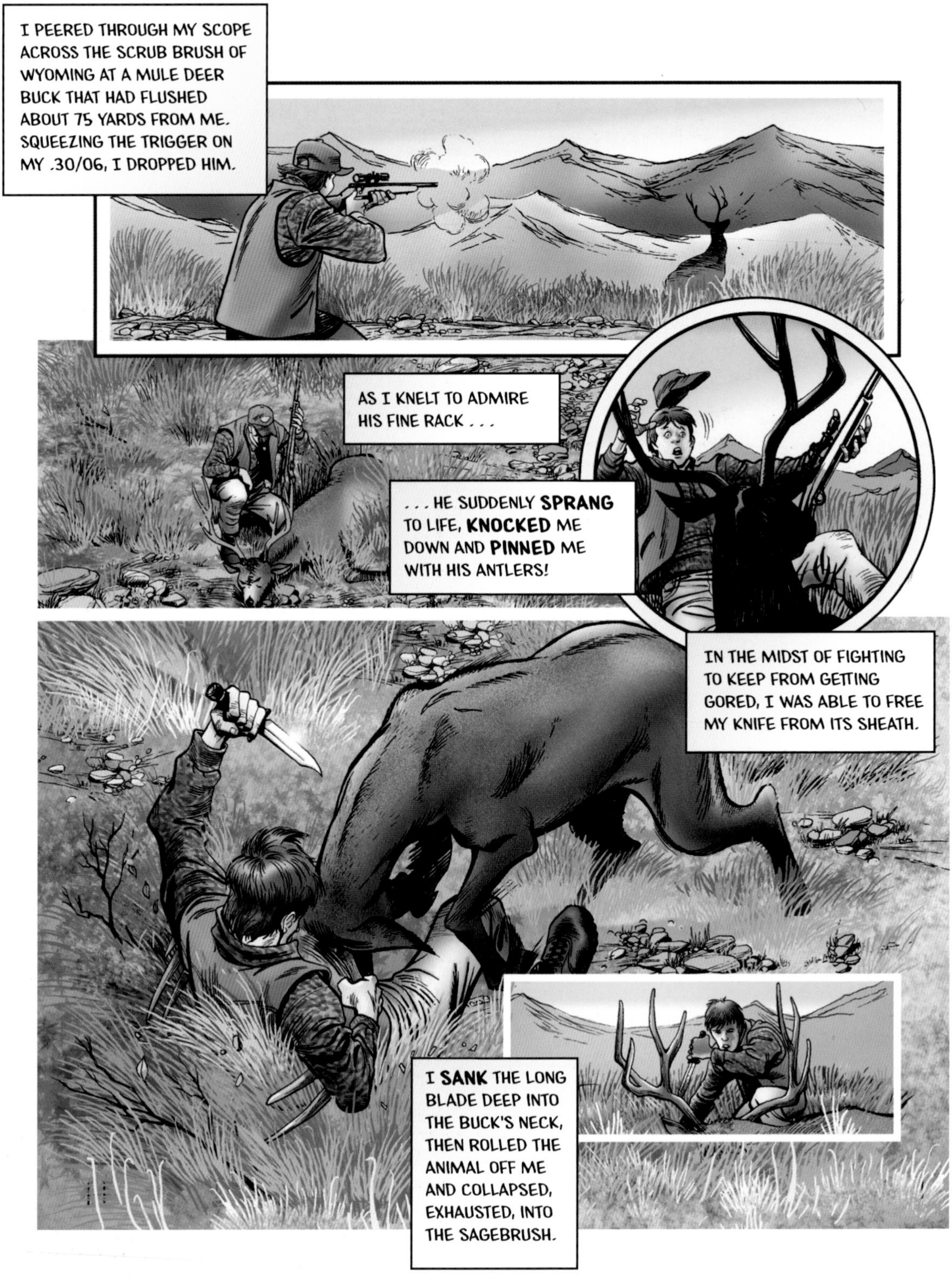

I PEERED THROUGH MY SCOPE ACROSS THE SCRUB BRUSH OF WYOMING AT A MULE DEER BUCK THAT HAD FLUSHED ABOUT 75 YARDS FROM ME. SQUEEZING THE TRIGGER ON MY .30/06, I DROPPED HIM.
AS I KNELT TO ADMIRE HIS FINE RACK . . .
. . . HE SUDDENLY **SPRANG** TO LIFE, **KNOCKED** ME DOWN AND **PINNED** ME WITH HIS ANTLERS!
IN THE MIDST OF FIGHTING TO KEEP FROM GETTING GORED, I WAS ABLE TO FREE MY KNIFE FROM ITS SHEATH.
I **SANK** THE LONG BLADE DEEP INTO THE BUCK'S NECK, THEN ROLLED THE ANIMAL OFF ME AND COLLAPSED, EXHAUSTED, INTO THE SAGEBRUSH.

Runaway Turkey Tag // by Norman Haase, Macomb, MI

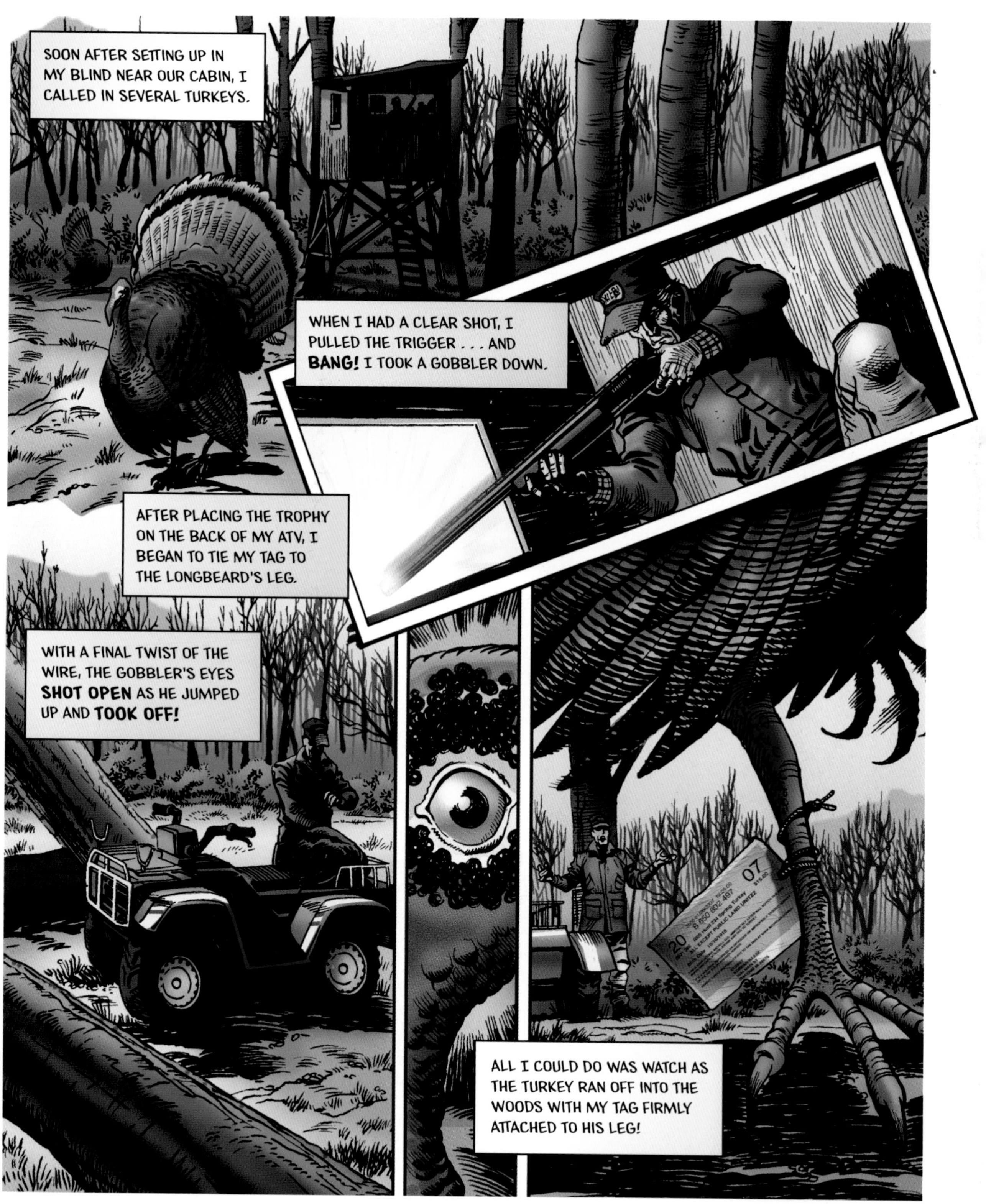
SOON AFTER SETTING UP IN MY BLIND NEAR OUR CABIN, I CALLED IN SEVERAL TURKEYS.
WHEN I HAD A CLEAR SHOT, I PULLED THE TRIGGER . . . AND BANG! I TOOK A GOBBLER DOWN.
AFTER PLACING THE TROPHY ON THE BACK OF MY ATV, I BEGAN TO TIE MY TAG TO THE LONGBEARD'S LEG.
WITH A FINAL TWIST OF THE WIRE, THE GOBBLER'S EYES SHOT OPEN AS HE JUMPED UP AND TOOK OFF!
ALL I COULD DO WAS WATCH AS THE TURKEY RAN OFF INTO THE WOODS WITH MY TAG FIRMLY ATTACHED TO HIS LEG!

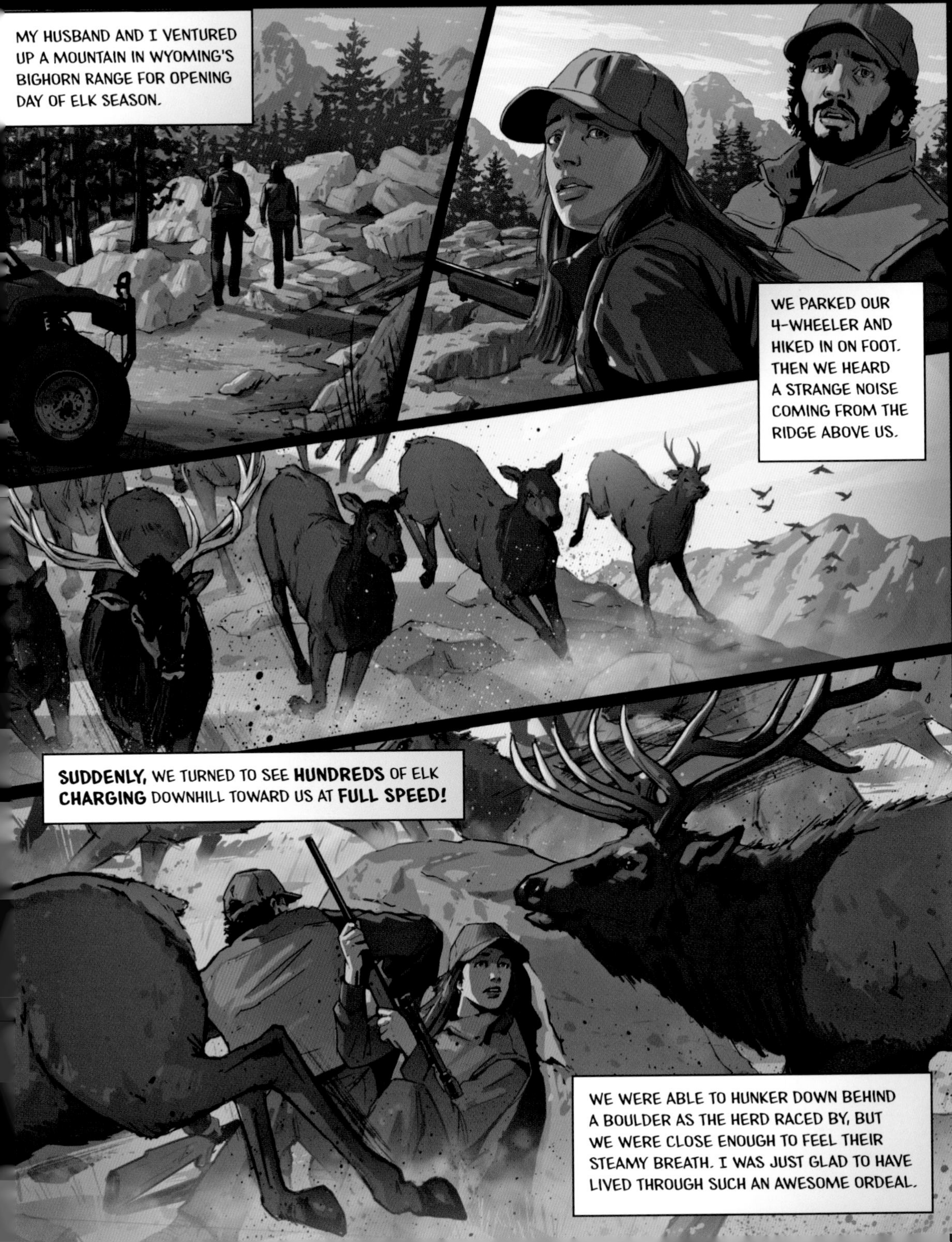
MY HUSBAND AND I VENTURED UP A MOUNTAIN IN WYOMING'S BIGHORN RANGE FOR OPENING DAY OF ELK SEASON.
WE PARKED OUR 4-WHEELER AND HIKED IN ON FOOT. THEN WE HEARD A STRANGE NOISE COMING FROM THE RIDGE ABOVE US.
SUDDENLY, WE TURNED TO SEE HUNDREDS OF ELK CHARGING DOWNHILL TOWARD US AT FULL SPEED!
WE WERE ABLE TO HUNKER DOWN BEHIND A BOULDER AS THE HERD RACED BY, BUT WE WERE CLOSE ENOUGH TO FEEL THEIR STEAMY BREATH. I WAS JUST GLAD TO HAVE LIVED THROUGH SUCH AN AWESOME ORDEAL.

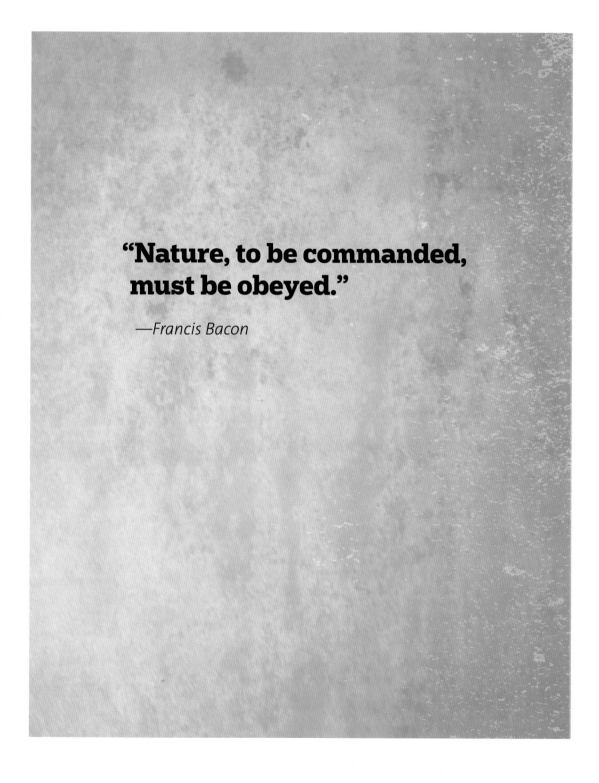

"**Nature, to be commanded, must be obeyed.**"

—*Francis Bacon*

Trailing Trouble // by Harold L. Jones, Keystone Heights, FL

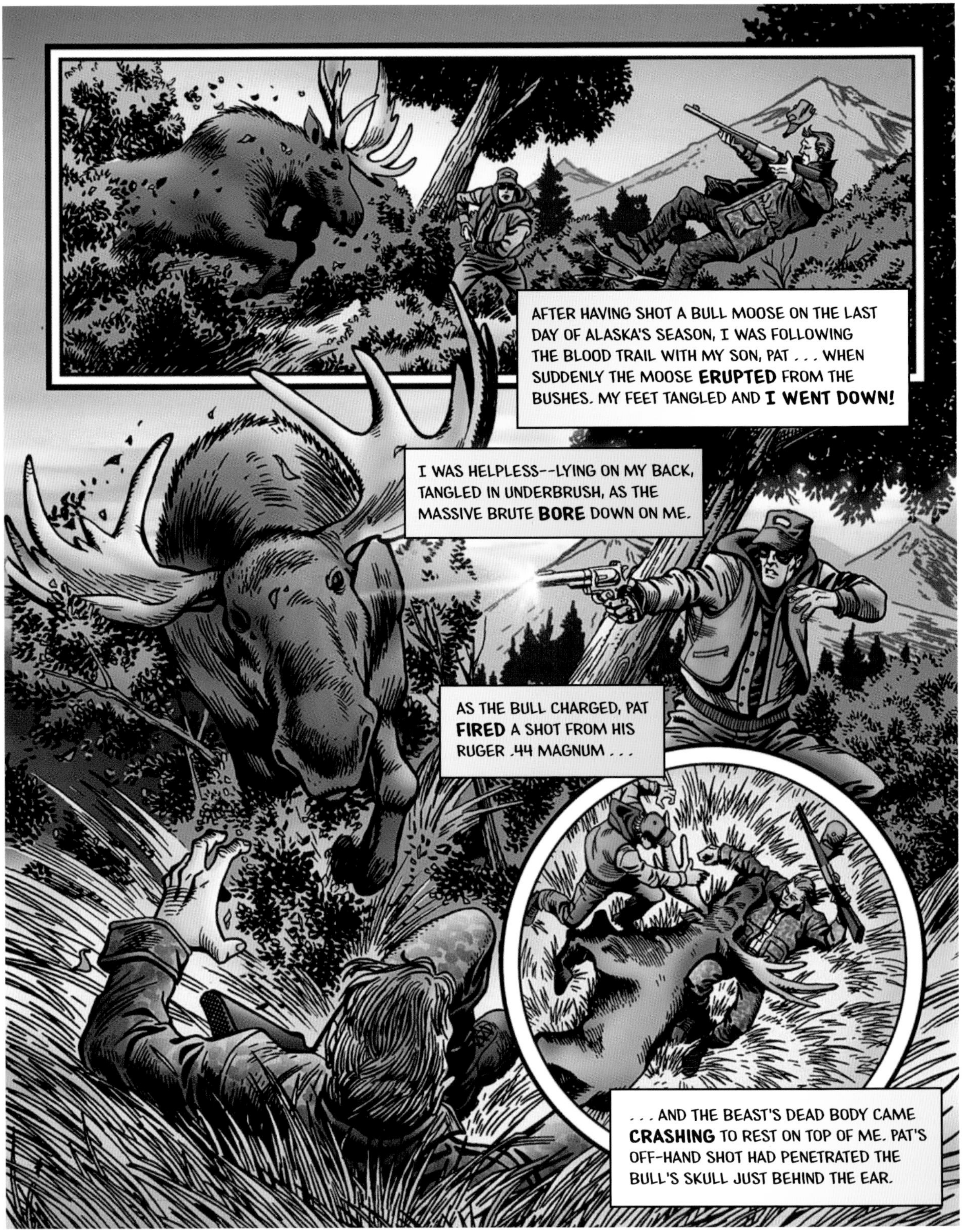

AFTER HAVING SHOT A BULL MOOSE ON THE LAST DAY OF ALASKA'S SEASON, I WAS FOLLOWING THE BLOOD TRAIL WITH MY SON, PAT . . . WHEN SUDDENLY THE MOOSE **ERUPTED** FROM THE BUSHES. MY FEET TANGLED AND **I WENT DOWN!**
I WAS HELPLESS--LYING ON MY BACK, TANGLED IN UNDERBRUSH, AS THE MASSIVE BRUTE **BORE** DOWN ON ME.
AS THE BULL CHARGED, PAT **FIRED** A SHOT FROM HIS RUGER .44 MAGNUM . . .
. . . AND THE BEAST'S DEAD BODY CAME **CRASHING** TO REST ON TOP OF ME. PAT'S OFF-HAND SHOT HAD PENETRATED THE BULL'S SKULL JUST BEHIND THE EAR.

Moose (and no Squirrel)

The largest member of the deer family, the moose inhabits evergreen and deciduous forests across the northern hemisphere. Although they are generally slow and peaceful, if they're startled, or competing for mates in fall, moose can become surprisingly fast and aggressive creatures.

Moose can:
- Eat 10,000 calories of plant matter a day to maintain their weight
- Weigh up to 1,500 pounds
- Grow to stand over 6 feet high at the shoulder
- Bear a rack of antlers nearly 7 feet wide

ANGRY ANTLERS Unless you're properly geared and on the hunt for moose, your best bet is simply to keep your distance. While not normally aggressive, moose can be territorial, and are also more likely to respond aggressively during mating season or spring when new mothers are protecting their calves. If charged by a moose, run away as quickly as possible to avoid being trampled or kicked; moose will generally only run a modest distance. If you do happen to be knocked down, move into a fetal position and cover your head and neck, and do your best to remain still, as fighting back will encourage a moose to continue kicking or stomping at the perceived threat.

Hit-and-Run Buck // by Pete Goudreau, Baraga, MI

EARLY ONE MORNING DURING RIFLE SEASON, I WAS HEADED OUT TO MY DEER BLIND DOWN A VERY OVERGROWN OLD HIGHWAY IN THE U.P.

AS I WAS TOOLING ALONG, A LARGE DOE **BOUNDED** FROM THE THICK TREES. I **SWERVED** JUST IN TIME TO AVOID HER.

I DROVE ON WITH MY HEART IN MY THROAT, THINKING ABOUT WHAT COULD HAVE HAPPENED. I FELT PRETTY GOOD ABOUT MY REACTION TIME, CONSIDERING THE HOUR OF THE DAY.

SUDDENLY, A LITTLE FARTHER DOWN THE ROAD, A SMALL BUCK CAME **CRASHING** THROUGH THE TREES AND **SMASHED** INTO MY RIBCAGE.

I WAS **KNOCKED** CLEAR OF MY ATV. THE BUCK LAY BACK IN THE ROAD.

THE DEER CLIMBED TO HIS FEET AND FOLLOWED THE DOE. IT WAS THE ONLY BUCK I SAW ALL SEASON.

Up on the Rooftop... // by Gary F. McKay, Berryville, VA

CHRISTMAS EVE MORNING, 2005, I WAS ON MY WAY TO MY HUNTING SPOT IN THE BLUE RIDGE MOUNTAINS. AS I CREPT UP THE GRAVEL DRIVE I SAW TWO DOES AND A SMALL BUCK HOP A FENCE ONTO THE ROAD. I LAUGHED WHEN THE BUCK SLIPPED ON THE ICY GROUND AND DID A FULL SOMERSAULT BEFORE GAINING HIS FOOTING.

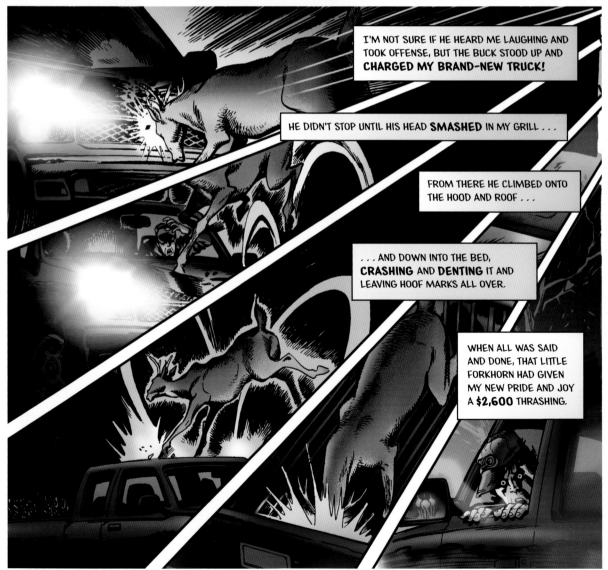

I'M NOT SURE IF HE HEARD ME LAUGHING AND TOOK OFFENSE, BUT THE BUCK STOOD UP AND **CHARGED MY BRAND-NEW TRUCK!**

HE DIDN'T STOP UNTIL HIS HEAD **SMASHED** IN MY GRILL . . .

FROM THERE HE CLIMBED ONTO THE HOOD AND ROOF . . .

. . . AND DOWN INTO THE BED, **CRASHING** AND **DENTING** IT AND LEAVING HOOF MARKS ALL OVER.

WHEN ALL WAS SAID AND DONE, THAT LITTLE FORKHORN HAD GIVEN MY NEW PRIDE AND JOY A **$2,600** THRASHING.

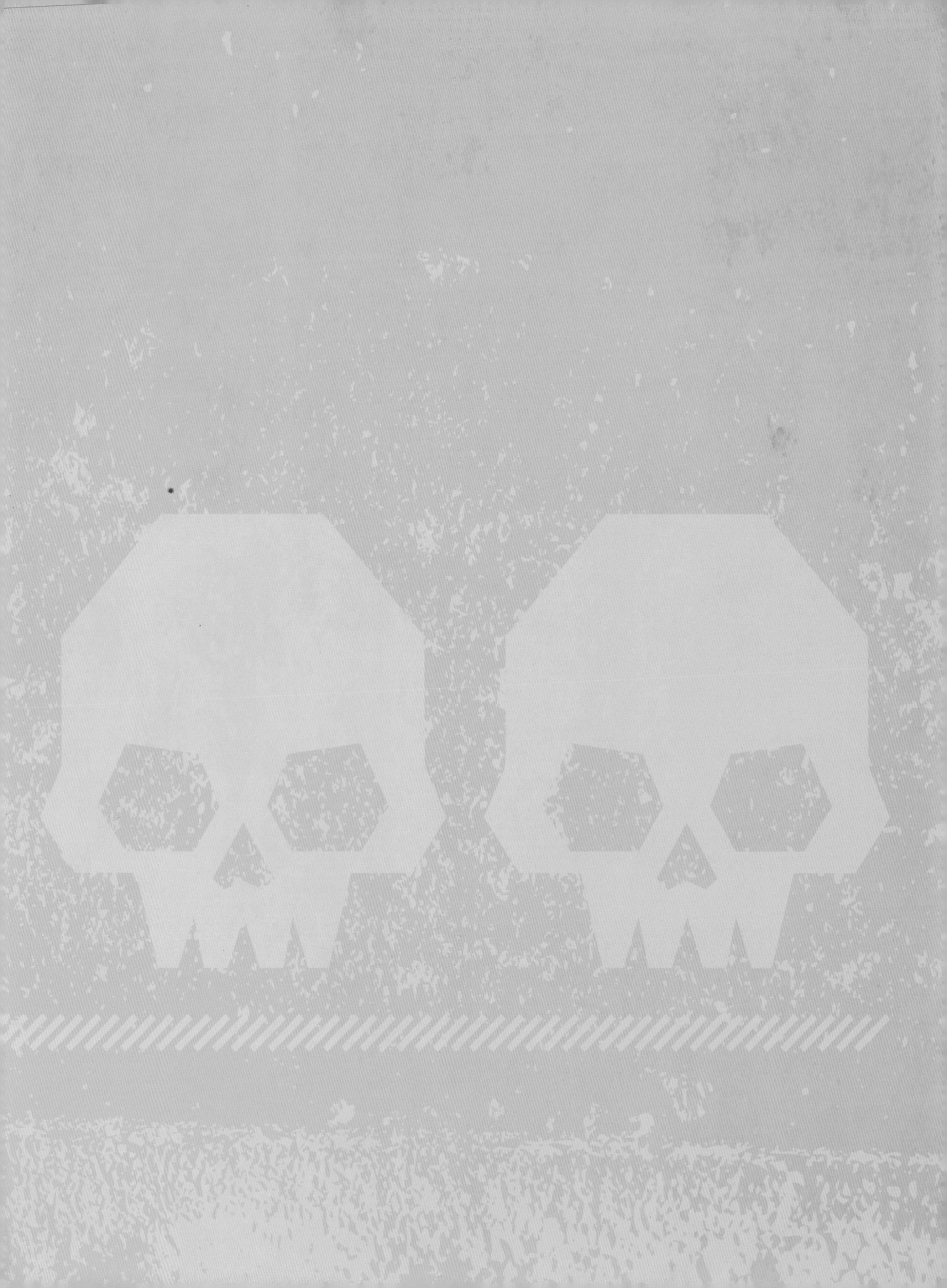

About *Outdoor Life*

Since it was founded in 1898, *Outdoor Life* magazine has provided survival tips, wilderness guides, gear reports, and other essential information for hands-on outdoor enthusiasts. Each issue delivers the best advice in sportsmanship as well as thrilling true-life tales, detailed gear reviews, insider hunting, shooting, and fishing hints, and much more to nearly 1 million readers. Its survival-themed Web site also covers disaster preparedness and the skills you need to thrived anywhere from the backcountry to the urban jungles.

About the Editor

Andrew McKean is the Editor of *Outdoor Life* magazine and a lifelong outdoorsman. Raised on a Missouri farm, he grew up hunting deer, turkeys, predators, and upland birds. A former newspaper and magazine editor, McKean is the author of *Hunting the West*. He served a stint as editor of *Rocky Mountain Fishing & Hunting News* before joining *Outdoor Life* as its Western Columnist. He later joined the magazine staff as Hunting Editor and Optics Editor, titles he still holds. He is a Hunter Education instructor and Scout leader. In his career with the Montana Department of Fish, Wildlife & Parks, he took national honors from the Association for Conservation Information for magazine writing. He has hunted around the world with a rifle, shotgun, and bow for big game, birds, predators, and small game. McKean lives on a ranch in Glasgow, Montana with his family.

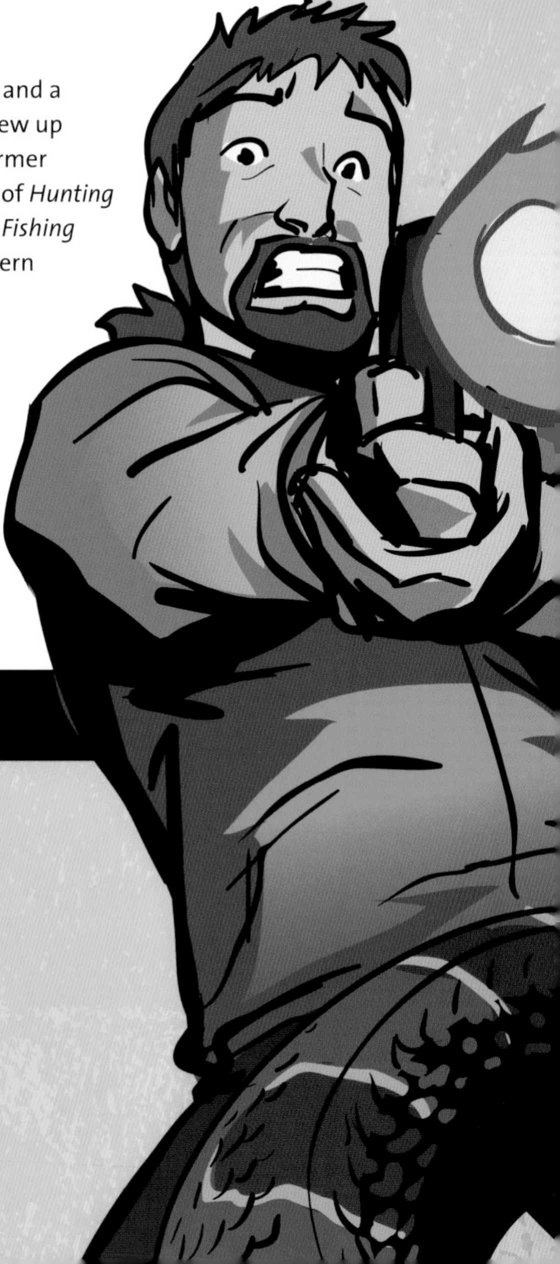

How to Submit Your Real-Life Story

Have you had a terrifying, thilling, or hilarious adventure in the great outdoors? Would you like to share it with the world, illustrated by one of our amazing artists? *Outdoor Life* magazine pays cash for every true story that's published in the magazine . . . and there's one published every month! Send your story to:

Outdoor Life
THTM
2 Park Avenue
New York, NY 10016

Or email to OLLetters@bonniercorp.com, with the subject line THTM. Please include a contact number so we can verify just how big that grizzly really was!

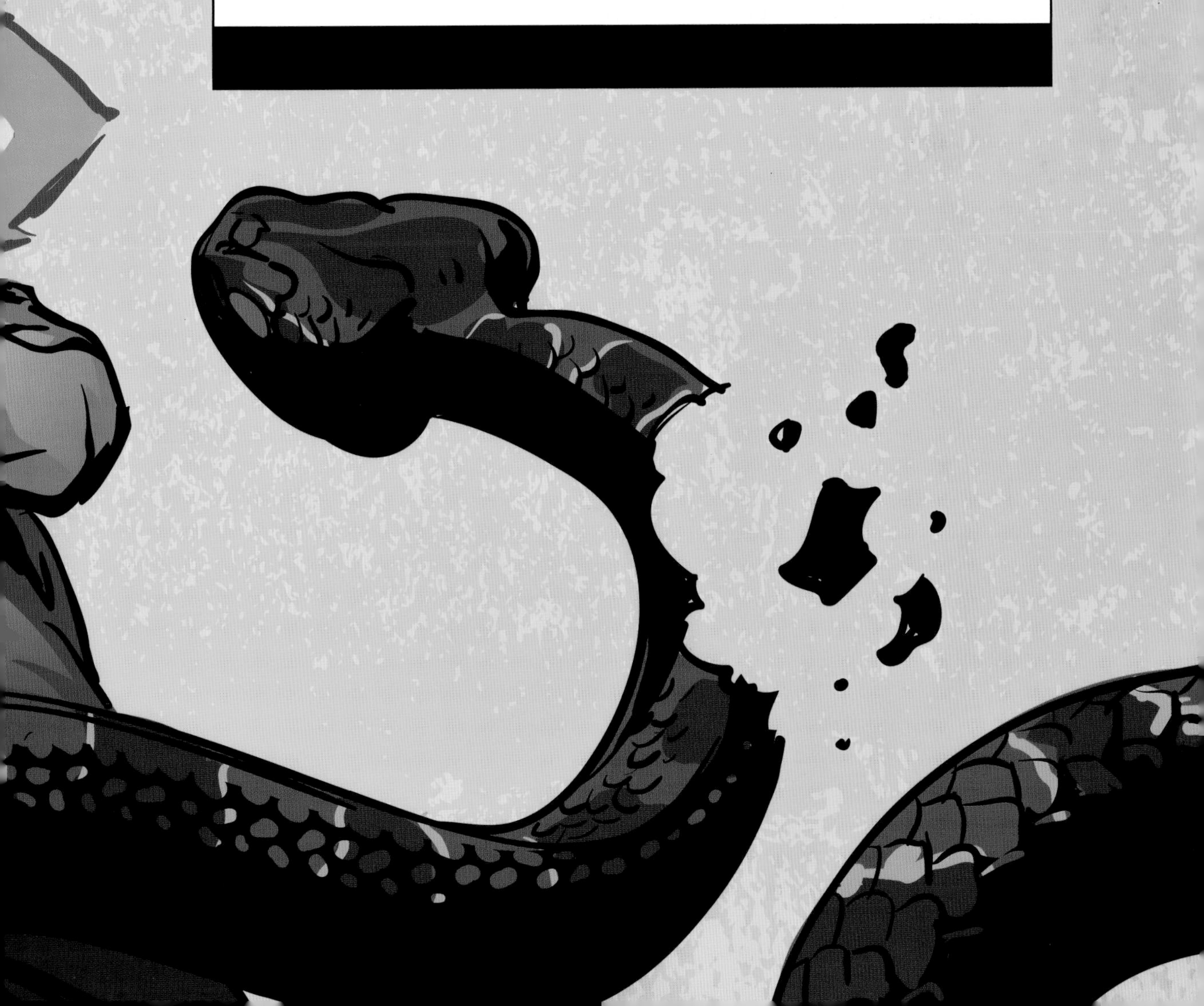

About the Artists

Juan Calle has worked for Disney Interactive Studios, Red Ocean Entertainment, and INMOTION Studios, and has illustrated a number of books, including the *Outdoor Life Ultimate Survival Manual*. He lives in Colombia, where he runs an animation studio.

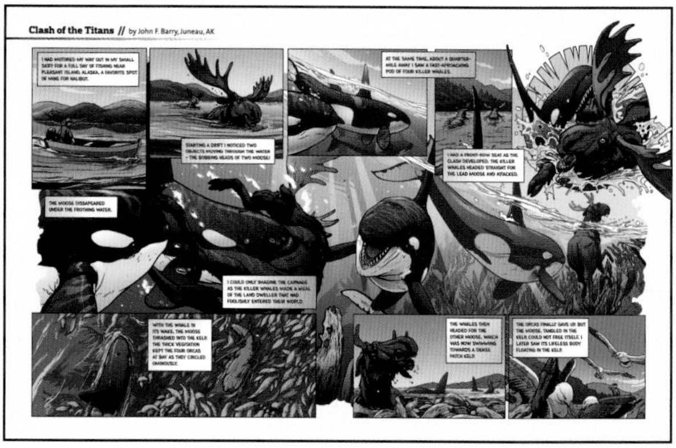
Clash of the Titans // by John F. Barry, Juneau, AK

Gene Colan Born in 1926, Colan was part of the Silver Age of comics. He was best known for his work with Marvel, where his signature titles included *Daredevil, Howard the Duck,* and *The Tomb of Dracula*. He was inducted into the Will Eisner Hall of Fame in 2005.

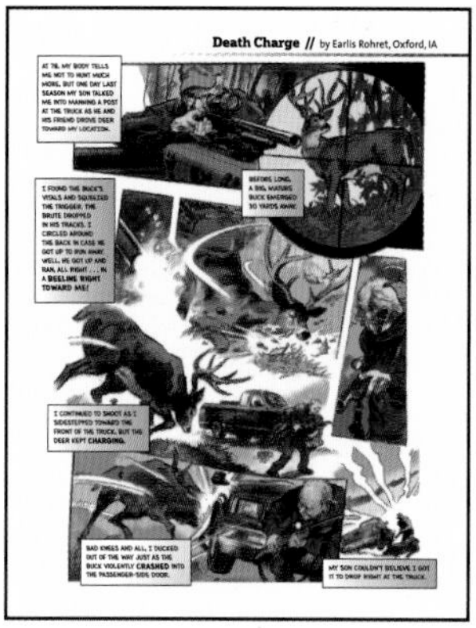
Death Charge // by Earlis Rohret, Oxford, IA

Jack Forbes is a New York–based artist and underground cartoonist, whose work spans fan art, gaming images, and a wide range of popular-culture inspired pieces. He is current working on several graphic novel projects.

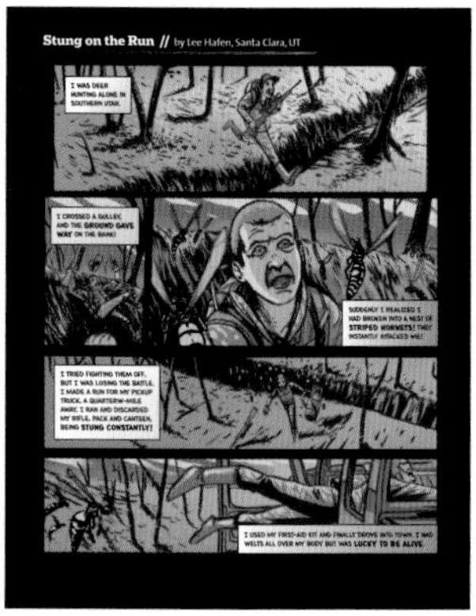
Stung on the Run // by Lee Halen, Santa Clara, UT

Ron Frenz is best known for his work with Marvel, particularly his seminal 1980s illustration on *The Amazing Spider-Man* series. Frenz's other work includes such titles as *The Mighty Thor, Star Wars, Marvel Saga,* and *Superman*.

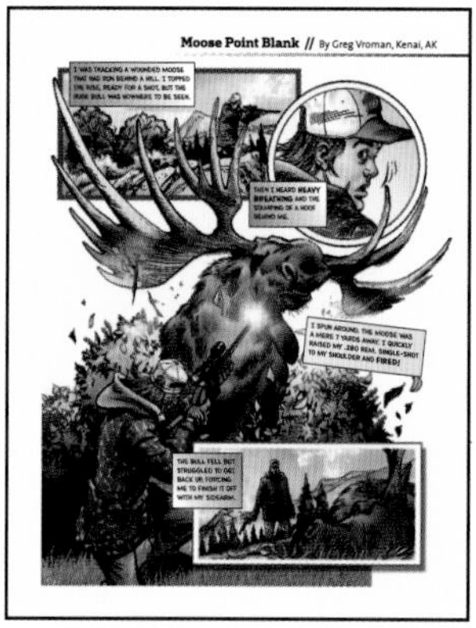
Moose Point Blank // By Greg Vroman, Kenai, AK

Charlie Griak is a freelance illustrator and animator who works in a range of traditional and digital media for clients including *National Geographic* magazine, Microsoft, St. Martin's Press, Coors, *ESPN* and many more. He is the creator of an award-winning animated film, *Fever.*

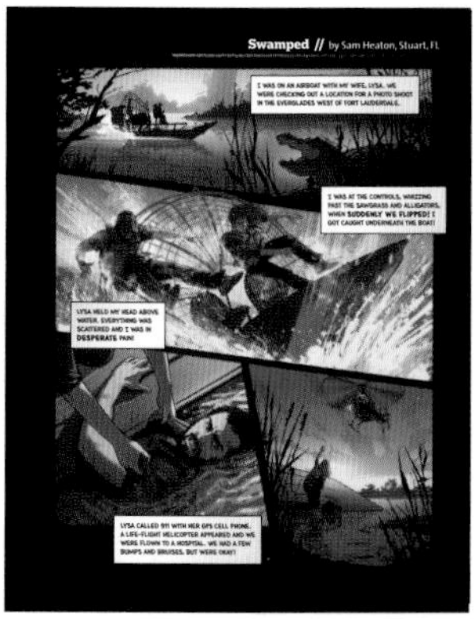
Swamped // by Sam Heaton, Stuart, FL

Tony Harris made his first splash in 1994 with the appearance of DC Comics' *Starman*. He has since drawn for *Batman, Superman, The Hulk, Spider-Man, The Fantastic Four, Iron Man, X-Men, Green Lantern, Planet of the Apes,* and many more. He has been nominated for five Eisner Comic Industry Awards (the "Oscar" of the comics world.)

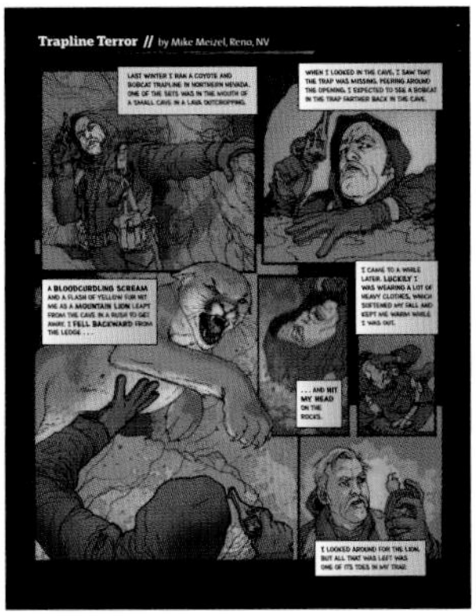
Trapline Terror // by Mike Meszel, Reno, NV

Dan Panosian is a Los Angeles–based graphic designer who specializes in comic books, advertising, and storyboards. His work has appeared in Marvel comics, among many others, and in a wide range of other graphic novels.

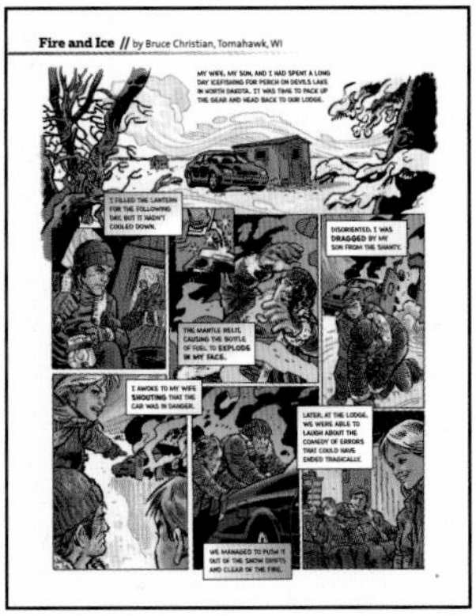
Fire and Ice // by Bruce Christian, Tomahawk, WI

Tony Shasteen is an illustrator whose many clients include DC Comics. He has worked on graphic novels including USA Network's *Burn Notice* and *The Talisman* by Stephen King and Peter Straub. Notable other work has been featured in the *Shadowrun* series and by White Wolf and Realms of Fantasy gaming systems.

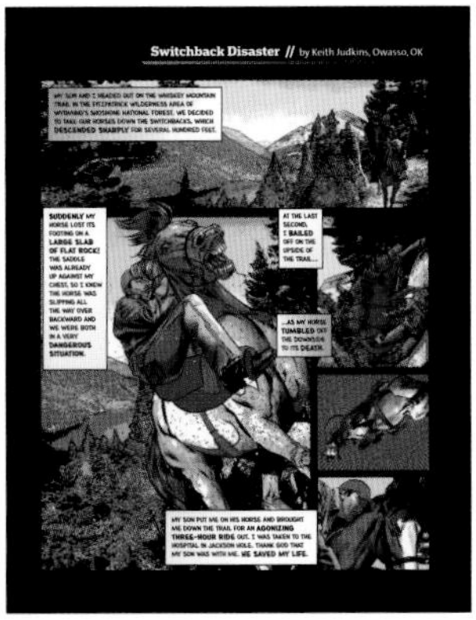
Switchback Disaster // by Keith Judkins, Owasso, OK

Ken Laager got his start painting cover art for a wide range of major publishers. The longest-standing "This Happened to Me" illustrator, he created memorable comic strips and covers for some 25 years, beginning in 1981. He is currently a freelance artist and illustrator.

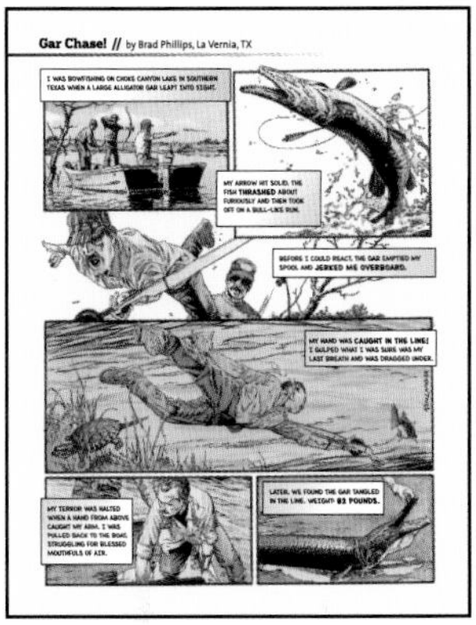
Gar Chase! // by Brad Phillips, La Vernia, TX

Paul Ryan has worked extensively for both Marvel and DC comics, on a number of superhero titles including *Iron Man, The Avengers, Fantastic Four, Superman*, and many other iconic figures. He notably woked with Stan Lee on pencilling the syndicated strip for *The Amazing Spider-Man*.

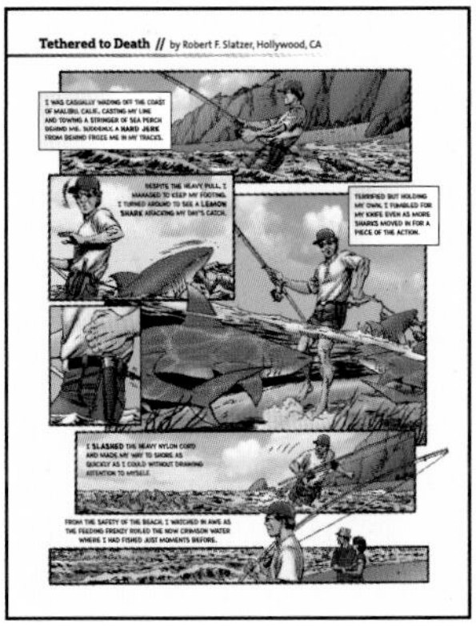
Tethered to Death // by Robert F. Slatzer, Hollywood, CA

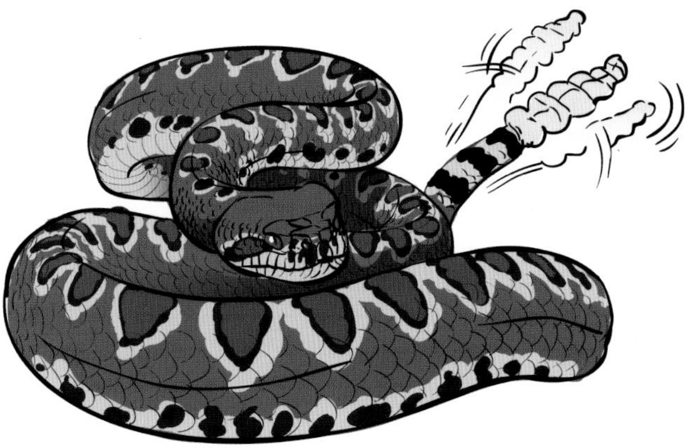

Art was created by:

JUAN CALLE: cover, 16, 32, 38, 46, 58, 74, 102, 112, 144, 164, 191.

GENE COLAN: 159

JACK FORBES: 76, 83, 117, 146, 169, 172

RON FRENZ: 18, 24–25, 34–35, 40–41, 50, 53, 60, 62–64, 68, 70–72, 77–78, 81, 87–90, 94, 96, 97, 104, 109, 111, 114, 120, 129, 132, 134, 136, 138–139, 149, 152-154, 156, 171, 174, 176–177, 180, 183

CHARLIE GRIAK: 30, 127, 178

TONY HARRIS: 44, 46, 92, 122–123, 125, 150, 182

KEN LAAGER: 130

DAN PANOSIAN: 22

PAUL RYAN: 128

TONY SHASTEEN: 21, 29, 36, 43, 52, 66, 82, 84, 107, 110, 116, 118, 158, 160, 162, 165, 166, 173

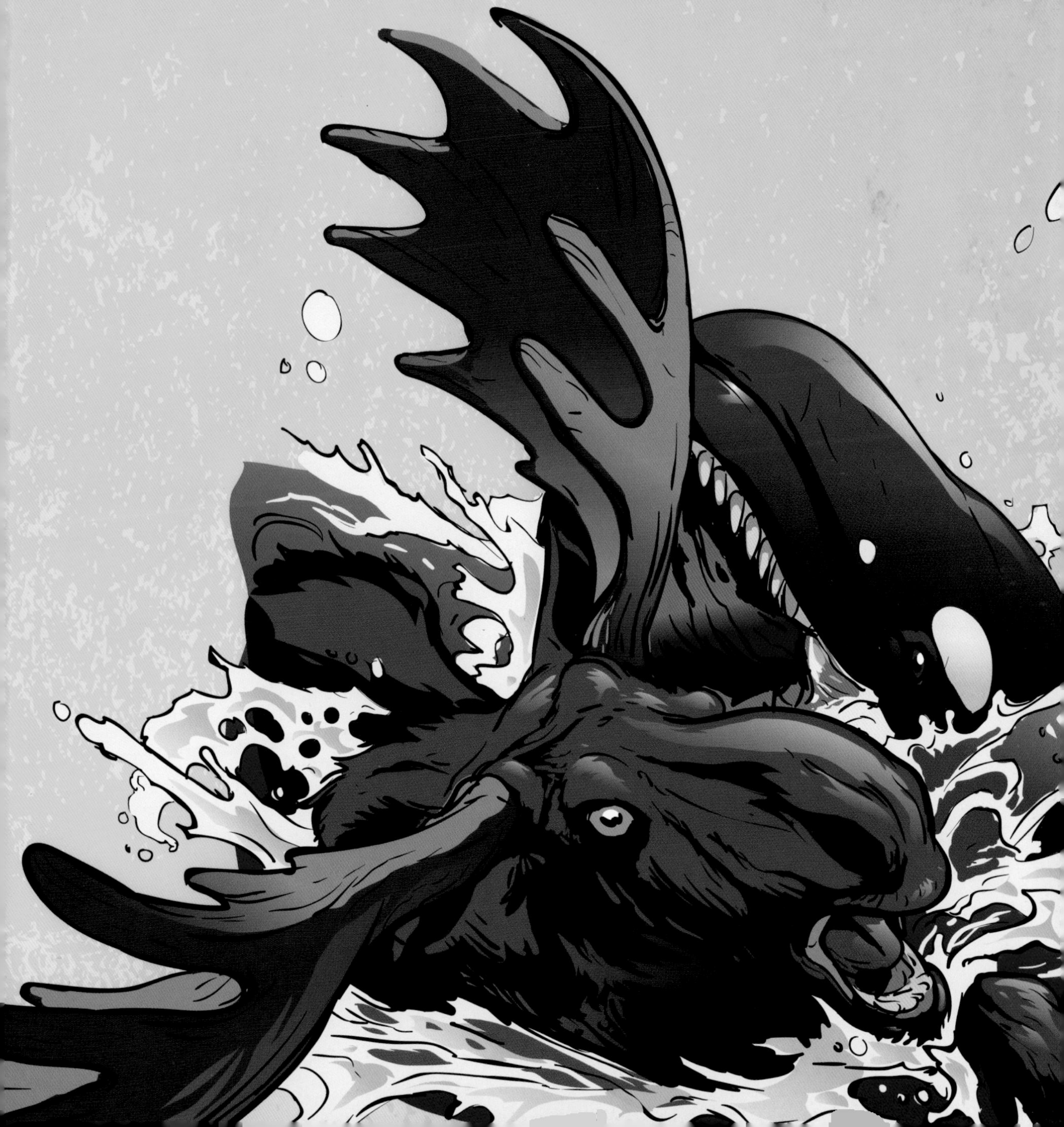

weldon**owen**

President, CEO Terry Newell
VP, Publisher Roger Shaw
Executive Editor Mariah Bear
Project Editor Bridget Fitzgerald
Editorial Assistant Ian Cannon
Creative Director Kelly Booth
Art Director William Mack
Illustration Coordinator Conor Buckley
Production Director Chris Hemesath
Production Manager Michelle Duggan

Additional design asistance from Meghan Peterson, Jenna Rosenthal, and Daniel Triassi. Editorial help was provided by Katharine Moore and Katie Schlossberg.

Additional text written by Ian Cannon.

© 2013 Weldon Owen Inc.

415 Jackson Street
San Francisco, CA 94111
www.wopublishing.com

OutdoorLife and Weldon Owen are divisions of

BONNIER

Library of Congress Control Number on file with the publisher.

ISBN 13: 978-1-61628-588-3
ISBN 10: 1-61628-588-5

10 9 8 7 6 5 4 3 2 1
2013 2014 2015 2016

Printed in China by 1010 Printing International

OUTDOORLIFE

Executive Vice President Eric Zinczenko
Editorial Director Anthony Licata
Editor Andrew McKean
Senior Editor John Taranto
Managing Editor Jean McKenna
Senior Deputy Editor John B. Snow
Deputy Editor Gerry Bethge
Assistant Editor Alex Robinson
Design Director Sean Johnston
Photography Director John Toolan
Deputy Art Director Pete Sucheski
Associate Art Directors Kim Gray, James A. Walsh
Production Manager Judith Weber
Digital Director Nate Matthews
Online Content Editor Alex Robinson
Online Producer Kurt Shulitz
Assistant Online Editor Martin Leung

2 Park Avenue
New York, NY 10016
www.outdoorlife.com